The Sound of Leadership

The Sound of LEADERSHIP

Presidential Communication in the Modern Age

Roderick P. Hart

The University of Chicago Press
Chicago and London

Roderick P. Hart is the F. A. Liddell Professor of
Communication at the University of Texas, Austin. He is the
author of *Public Communication, The Political Pulpit,* and
Verbal Style and the Presidency. He is a three-time recipient
of the Speech Communication Association's Golden
Anniversary Monograph Award.

The University of Chicago Press, Chicago 60637
The University of Chicago Press, Ltd., London
© 1987 by The University of Chicago
All rights reserved. Published 1987
Printed in the United States of America

96 95 94 93 92 91 90 89   5 4 3 2

Library of Congress Cataloging-in-Publication Data

Hart, Roderick P.
    The sound of leadership.

    Includes index.
    1. Political oratory—United States. 2. Presidents—
United States—Language. I. Title.
PN4193.P6H37   1987   815'01'093523512   87-5863
ISBN 0-226-31812-5
ISBN 0-226-31813-3 (pbk.)

To
the children of Ora Major
For their love and laughter, but mostly for their love

Contents

Illustrations

Tables

Acknowledgments

Writing a book is hard. No one should attempt it alone. Fortunately, I have not been alone when writing this book. Any strengths to be found here result from the counsel and the kindness of others. I, alas, am alone responsible for any weaknesses, and so I rush to thank, and to absolve, each of the following:

My departmental colleagues at the University of Texas at Austin, each of whom, without exception, is treasurable, and each of whom, without exception, I treasure.

The David Ross Foundation, the Kaltenborn Foundation, and the University Research Institute, each of which supported my work on this project.

Associates such as Carroll Arnold, Rick Cherwitz, Wayne Danielson, Bob Doolittle, Kathleen Jamieson, Max McCombs, and David Swanson whose scholarly advice has been especially acute and whose personal support has been especially welcome.

Colleagues like Jim Andrews, Art Bochner, Karlyn Campbell, Bob Friedman, Jill McMillan, Vickie O'Donnell, and Tom Scheidel, who invited me to their campuses and, for better or worse, permitted me to try out these ideas on their students.

Scholarly "cousins" like Bruce Buchanan, Murray Edelman, David Paletz, and Michael Robinson whose own work in this area has been both inspiring and helpful.

Research assistants like Charla Ann Baker, Karen Carter, Dan French, Tom Lessl, Janine Rudnick, Craig Roberts, Jim Smith, and Ken Zagacki, who performed many ignoble tasks in noble ways.

David Frame, Jo Hansen, Deanna Matthews, Charlotte Richards, and G. Morgan Watkins whose technical assistance was both timely and professional.

Peggy, Chris, and Kate—for all things—but especially for their support of my musical interests.

And E. D. R., who inspires idolatry even as she decries it.

Introduction

Between April 16, 1945, and December 31, 1985, American presidents spoke in public on 9,969 occasions. That fact has special meaning for me because for the last eight years I have spent a good deal of time reading and cataloging these speeches. The presidents' addresses ranged from the brave to the self-serving and from the sublime to the silly. Presidents delivered these speeches dressed in morning coats or wearing ten-gallon hats and chaps. The speeches were delivered from the platforms of trains and warehouses, from the decks of paddle wheelers and aircraft carriers, and from the stages of palaces and high school gymnasiums. The speeches were heard by small gaggles of listeners in village greens and by a nation-full of unseen auditors via television. The presidents' speeches provoked tears and anger, warmth and hopefulness, confusion and dismay. Some of them generated all of these sentiments simultaneously. When a president of the United States gives a speech he is more an artisan than an artist—precious few of these ten thousand texts were remembered by listeners even a day after their delivery. But what was often recalled was the speech event itself—the crowds and the color and the dramaturgy and the physical presence of the chief executive. The president's thoughts and phrases quickly passed through the mind, but the *fact* of his having spoken often lingered on.

The Sound of Leadership is a comprehensive, factual interpretation of modern presidential communications. The book emphasizes a dimension of the executive branch of government—communication—which has become undeniably important but has heretofore been largely overlooked or, if not overlooked, misunderstood or underestimated. The book argues that a new American presidency has grown up in our midst without our knowing it. The book describes what this new presidency looks like and what it has done to leadership and to citizenship. And the book argues that what it has done to both is manifestly unfortunate for the American people.

Although many observers have drawn attention to the communication revolution taking place in the White House, facts about this revolution have been hard to come by. Some of these facts are curious. Why, for example, did no president speak in Massachusetts during one ten-year period? Why are home viewers two-and-one-half times more likely to see a president speak on the nightly news than to hear him speak? Why did Lyndon Johnson speak ninety times in Texas during his presidency? Why did Jimmy Carter partic- ipate in four times the number of ceremonies in which Harry Truman par- ticipated? Why were more than half of Jerry Ford's campaign rallies closed to the public? Why did Lyndon Johnson travel extensively in Republican states *after* his reelection? Why did Ronald Reagan rarely give speeches to federal employees? The answers to these and many other questions are pro- vided here, but the archetypal question considered is the following: Why did Gerald Ford deliver a public speech once every six hours during 1976, and why was his behavior characteristic of that of modern presidents? The answer to this two-part question is neither simple nor easily anticipated, but it may shed light on the most important feature of contemporary political leadership.

This book is really not based so much on *what* the presidents said as on why they said what they said when and where they said it. The research supporting the claims made here has dealt with speech acts, not with mes- sages per se. That is, the specific content of a president's speech was treated here as being slightly less important than the president's even more basic social/political decision to speak in the first place—in a particular locality, about a particular topic, to a particular group of citizens, at a particular time. Unlike my previous work, *Verbal Style and the Presidency,* which dealt with the microscopic features of presidential language,[1] this volume treats ma- crorhetorical trends. My data base here bears more resemblance to the pages of a daily appointment calendar than to transcripts of tape-recorded conver- sations. It tells only who said what to whom, when, and where. But, as we shall see, careful inspection of such a large and comprehensive data base can tell us much about *why* who spoke to whom, then, and there.

Some of the facts commented upon in this book may seem trivial at first—who used "closed" political rallies, who spoke repeatedly about eco- nomic matters, who visited Ohio often—and not at all suited to the complex, increasingly scientific enterprise known as modern politics. To ask who said what to whom seems too primitive a question to ask in an era that has produced psychographic testing of voters, double-blinded attitude sampling, and computerized simulations of political campaigns. My rejoinder is that it is precisely because of the complexities of modern politics that it has become necessary to ask simple, even primitive, questions of that process—if not for our edification, then at least for our protection as political consumers. Pres- idents, after all, do everything they can to make voters attend to what they have said rather than to the circumstances surrounding their saying it. To be

ignorant of such circumstances is, then, to be doubly victimized by the per-
suasions directed to us as voters. Or so goes my argument here.

The essential logic of this book is as follows: by choosing to utter words
to another, a speaker makes at least these decisions—to speak to A and not
to B; to speak now and not then or never; to speak here and not there; to
speak about this matter and not about all other matters; to speak for this
period of time, not longer or shorter. These rhetorical decisions by a speaker
contain "information" for us as observers if we are wise enough and patient
enough to track these decisions. And such tracking is especially important
today because the speech of a modern president is speech capable of multiple
and simultaneous actions. There is not only a politics to the speech of a
president but also a history and a literature. And there is more: a psychology
and a sociology as well as an economics and even a geography. The "social
action" accomplished daily by the president and his speech is therefore not
unlike the actions of playwright Wallace Shawn's characters in *My Dinner
with André*. Shawn's characters, as one critic observes, "don't talk to avoid
action, they behave as if talk *were* action. It's as if they believed that just
articulating their hidden thoughts were enough to make something happen,
as if language were itself magic."[2] Presidents, too, are magicians, at least in
part.

This book describes how presidential speaking has been used during
the last forty years. The book treats speechmaking as an essential presidential
tool and explains how that tool has been used in the Truman through Reagan
administrations. These eight presidencies were selected for special study here
because they were the first presidencies to have at their disposal the most
revolutionary aid to presidential speech ever invented—the modern mass
media industry. In a sense, these eight presidencies were the first truly "modern" presidencies, and all future presidencies will be measured by their me-
dia-centered standards, standards ranging from high to low, often low.

When doing the research for this book, we tagged each of the presidential speeches appearing in the *Public Papers of the Presidents* with an identifying number and then entered it by date into a computer data bank so that
various statistical patterns could be examined. In addition, each speech was
coded with the following information: (1) president, (2) year in office, (3) general location of the speech (e.g., domestic, international, etc.), (4) regional
location (Northeast, Midwest, etc.), and (5) state. The general and specific
topic (e.g., science and agriculture, economics, international conflict) were
also recorded as was the audience being addressed (e.g., government employees, invited guests, etc.). Attention was paid to the timing of the speech
during the president's administration, to its timing during the political year
(e.g., fall vs. summer), and to its timing on the day of delivery (the only speech
given? one of several?). The social setting of the speech was cataloged, with
discriminations being made between ceremonies, briefings, political rallies,

etc.; moreover, the political setting was noted, with distinctions being made, for example, between speeches delivered in small, partisan states and those in large, nonpartisan states. Finally, a range of collateral measurements was examined for each speech, with its date of delivery linked to presidential popularity, national unemployment, party control of Congress, legislative success rates, and amount of mass media coverage. Although these various measurements were somewhat crude, the *complex* of data was highly suggestive of how the presidents used public speaking to advance their political goals.[3]

As we shall see, these uses have been prodigious. Modern presidents now view their opportunities to speak to the American people as their greatest political assets. In Chapter One we will see how and why presidential speechmaking has increased between the 1940s and the 1980s and what such increases mean for governance. Chapter Two explains why speech, of all things, has been used to transform presidential leadership (or, at least, to transform images of presidential leadership) and to provide a modern chief executive with an unprecedented kind of political momentum. The curious yet constant linkage between speech and power is examined in Chapter Three. Here, we will witness how leaders like Lyndon Johnson and Richard Nixon used their public appearances as political bludgeons or, during their more charitable moments, as political bouquets. Chapter Four describes the fascinating relationship between the president and the mass media, details the "rule book" employed by the press when covering the president, and shows how the chief executive uses his speaking schedule to counteract, if not control, the treatment he receives from the media.

The modern presidential election becomes the focus of Chapter Five. We shall see that elections call forth highly institutionalized speeches from presidents and that such speech acts become the ultimate political tokens during a reelection campaign. Chapter Six draws together the various themes of the book and poses several questions which ought to vex all citizens: What happens when a president spends so much time thinking about speaking and so little time thinking about thinking? Can governance of the nation be entrusted to an individual who treats his constituents as an audience and his political platform as a script? How have the demands of citizenship changed in the Communications Era and who, ultimately, is the keeper of political wisdom in such an era?

To ask broad-gauged, communication-based questions like these requires one to operate on the somewhat radical assumption that the *public* character of the American presidency is worthy of careful inspection. Such an assumption has not always been radical. In earlier times, it was assumed that public matters were alone important when studying presidential matters. But books on the presidency have clearly taken a turn for the private, if not for the better. Now, it is assumed that only a presidential cabinet officer, or a presidential spouse, or a presidential butler knows where to find the secret keys for the secret locks that will liberate public understanding of life in the White House. My book, in contrast, examines only the public record. I assume here that some of the most interesting things about the presidency are hidden where people are least likely to look for them—in the open. I assume that the most essential fact about the Bay of Pigs was that John Kennedy found a way to explain the situation successfully to the American people and that the most important of the thousand known facts about the Watergate affair was that Richard Nixon could find no such explanation. No matter what John Dean or Bob Haldeman or John Erlichman might have written subsequently about Watergate, and no matter what impertinences were later found among the Watergate tapes, Richard Nixon left public office because Rhetoric left him first. Even the impending impeachment proceedings, it might be argued, could have been "toughed out" by Richard Nixon for months, if not for years, *if he could have found an argument* that would have satisfied *him* that he could have satisfied others. The public record shows that he never found such an argument. And so he stopped presiding soon after he stopped speaking.

But just because our data here are public data does not license us to be dull-witted when examining them. To study public behavior requires a special kind of discernment.[4] That is, we must begin by assuming (1) that public things are not always what they seem to be; (2) that people who make public products (like presidential speeches) do so for obvious as well as nonobvious reasons and for reasons both immediate and removed; (3) that how one behaves in public may bear only faint resemblance to how one behaves in private *and that that difference makes no difference at all in many cases* (certainly in many presidential cases); and (4) that the act of "becoming public" is essentially an act of persuasion, an acknowledgment that private life is not fulfilling enough—socially or psychologically—and that others, witnesses, are necessary for self-satisfaction or for social progress. This latter fact is true for all public performers—artists, actors, athletes—and it is no less true for presidents. Naturally, one cannot be naive when examining public matters, but one also must resist being cowed by those "introversionists" in the press who believe that all reliable knowledge is secret knowledge. Walking around after a president, noting merely whom he tips his hat to, whom he regales and whom he does not, is humble work. But it is not work without profit, especially if one watches patiently, and with cleverness.

Naturally, this volume examines only one aspect of the modern presidency. As such, it cannot tell us all we need to know about who governs us and how. But because its focus is communication and because contemporary presidents spend so much time persuading us to think and feel as they do, this volume can act as a fairly detailed map for that unsettling yet undeniably important terrain known as modern politics. Presidents constantly beseech us to accompany them on their several valiant quests. *The Sound of Leadership* may become a guidebook for those tempted to embark on such journeys.

ONE

Speech and Effort: The New American Presidency

THIS BOOK IS ABOUT HUMAN SPEECH AND THE PRESIDENTS WHO USE IT. To contemporary Americans, a discussion of presidential speaking may seem a colossal redundancy since, to them, presidents and their speeches are indistinguishable in the way that a ballplayer cannot be conceived of apart from the tools of the trade—a bat, a glove, a rosin bag. If asked to draw a freehand sketch of their president, most modern Americans would begin with a podium. They would do so because the evening news they watch is largely designed to let them overhear their president, because *Time* magazine's photo essays about life at the White House depict at least as many microphones as presidents, and because their own fondest memories of their presidents are of moments oratorical—John Kennedy warning the Russians about certain missiles in Cuba; Lyndon Johnson imploring his fellow Southerners to grant voting rights to all Americans; Gerald Ford embracing his former congressional mates, promising that the nation would survive Watergate. Americans would also remember other moments equally rhetorical: Lyndon Johnson admitting in March of 1968 that his cajolery had finally proven no match for the criticisms of his younger fellow Americans, Richard Nixon denouncing the excesses committed by the press and the Democrats in the name of Watergatism, Jimmy Carter probing the nation's sundry crises of the conscience as energy prices soared and as energy resources dwindled, Ronald Reagan at an obscure cemetery in West Germany. These presidential moments etched their ways into consciousness in part because public speech is a powerful etching tool and in part because the nation's mass media love rhetorical moments above all other moments and, in re-presenting them to us, make these moments doubly rhetorical.

Life was not always thus at the White House. The political scientist James Ceaser and his colleagues correctly remind us that America's earliest presidents rarely spoke in public, a habit springing in part from a constitutional (as opposed to a monarchial) mentality and in part because public opinion was not "on line" as it seems to be today.[1] In contemporary times, presidential speech constitutes both the stuff of an administration as well as a means of making commentary about that administration. Presidents are no longer content to let the press write the reviews, and so presidential speech increasingly turns back upon itself, with today's remarks being used to denounce the press's denunciations of yesterday's remarks. Presidents are now extraordinarily active players in the game of public opinion, and all of their public statements—even the most casual—are strategically designed to position the president for the next one in an endless series of moves and countermoves.

It is significant that computer and game metaphors can be drawn upon when describing the life of a modern president, for both suggest that they are now clearly subordinated to a matrix of countervailing forces—the press, opposition parties, special interest groups, and the like. This is to say much more than merely that politics is political. It is to say that *speech*—the most human, the most personal, the most physical, the most risking, the most loving, the most hating, the most public, the most cognitive, the most emotionally expressive thing a person can do—is now ruled by a set of iron laws which stand apart from the human speaker when that speaker also happens to be the president of the United States. It is to say that virtually every activity in the modern White House is designed to shape or reshape something that the president has said or will say. Bradley D. Nash and his colleagues[2] have noted that White House staffs have grown inexorably over the years, and they might well have added that much of the day-to-day business of these ever-expanding staffs is demonstrably rhetorical business—gathering speech materials, countering press reactions, rehearsing image-conscious presidents, drafting TelePrompTer cues, relocating family photos in the presidential background, assisting the media in "contextualizing" presidential gaffes, doing advance work for the Grand Rapids appearance, leaking texts to appropriate persons in the media. Activities like these require an army of aides; the White House has had them, and it increasingly has more of them.

It has been argued before, and will be again in this book, that such an excessive concentration on matters rhetorical may bode ill for leadership, if not for the Democracy itself. The Founding Fathers were concerned not to erect an executive branch that could become overwrought by constant appeals to the national rabble. Indeed, the Constitution mandates not a single oratorical duty for an American president. While concerned with intergovernmental coordination, the Constitution did not specify that the chief executive should deliver a State of the Union address in a three-piece suit replete with lapel flag or WIN button, as Richard Nixon and Gerald Ford did. Although sensitive to the pressures of foreign relations, the authors of the Constitution did not feel it incumbent on the president to declare himself a Berliner for a day or to celebrate his roots in Ballyporeen, as John Kennedy and Ronald Reagan did. The Founding Fathers also chose not to specify that succeeding presidents should gently encourage the nation's citizens during times of travail, or punctuate national holidays with a message of good cheer, or personally solicit votes in every hamlet in southwestern Montana. But these and many more duties were performed by Franklin Roosevelt, Dwight Eisenhower, and Harry Truman. The Founding Fathers did not envision (nor would they have countenanced) John Kennedy's live press conferences, Jimmy Carter's town meetings, or Richard Nixon's serial apologia.

In defense of their activities, modern presidents would no doubt claim that the Founding Fathers were ignorant about governance in the modern age—especially in the modern, mediated age—and that the commonweal can only be insured these days by a speech-ready president savvy about persuasive opportunities, sensitive to audience shares, knowledgeable about applause lines, skilled in unemotional repartee, and distrustful of any reporter, Political Action Caucus, or piece of legislation threatening his standing in the Gallup polls. Today's presidents might even argue that the Founding Fathers themselves had set up an inherently rhetorical brand of government in which the proponent of a bill in Congress or a miscreant in court or an incumbent on election day succeeds only if he or she can realign the thinking of legislators, jurors, and voters by talking to them. The tenets of democracy, the presidents would claim, began with freedom of speech because that is the only modality by which a people can govern itself.

Several observers, however, have called for greater freedom *from* speech, at least from the speech of presidents. Dwight Eisenhower, a piker by modern rhetorical standards, was termed a "part-time President" by critics of his time because of his forays into the hinterlands.[3] As we shall see in this chapter, John Kennedy spoke much more often than Eisenhower, and he too came under criticism, with one publication observing that during his first ten months on the job Kennedy spent only nine full weekends in Washington, D.C.[4] Claiming that "overexposure" had become a "presidential policy," the editors of *America* similarly observed that Lyndon Johnson was doing too much, talking too much, and traveling too much. But they also noted that "Mr. Johnson believes that the people like to see and hear their President," and predicted, correctly, that Johnson would continue his speechmaking.[5] On the eve of the Reagan inauguration, *Time* magazine's Hugh Sidey urged the new president to "relax, stay home and meditate," observing that "presidents like to hear themselves prattle on" but that the Carter presidency fell on hard times because of Mr. Carter's penchant to talk so frequently in public.[6] "Language ultimately was cheapened and meaning diminished," observed Sidey, and he added, "Presidential restraint of tongue might restore some credibility to talk and heighten the impact when the right moments come for the Chief Executive of the nation to sound off for the people."[7] There is more than a bit of legerdemain in Sidey's lament, however, for without the president's cooperation in providing the rhetorical stimuli, writers like Mr. Sidey would be hard-pressed to offer the color commentary needed in a weekly column published in a popular newsmagazine. Presidents will stop speaking, no doubt, when reporters stop listening.

When Presidents Speak

In this chapter, we shall trace the evolution of the modern rhetorical establishment which is the presidency of the United States. We shall see how often presidents speak, where, why, and when they do so, and what it means that they speak so often. In focusing this closely on presidential speech we will be focusing on an act—the act of speaking—which is so ubiquitous that attention is rarely paid to it. Yet it would be virtually impossible for a contemporary American to imagine what a president could do if he (she?) could not speak. If a paraplegic George Wallace had, by some fate, succeeded a Ronald Reagan who had gone blind, the American people would have somehow muddled through their president watching. Such physical handicaps, they might have sensed, would not interfere with the president's essential business of articulating the nation's aims and intents. Public reactions like these could be contemplated, even if the events seem implausible. But surely it is a political law (perhaps the only thing in politics that is law-like) that no mute could ever be elected president of the United States. It is a subsection of that law that a president who had lost his capacity to speak would, perforce, resign his job or be forced to resign it. "How could he assure us when our ambassadors are held hostage?" members of Congress might reason. "How could he entertain us at the State Fair?" citizens would query. "How could he position himself for reelection?" party members would ask. And the press, especially the press, would be set adrift, bereft of purpose, when confronted with a president who could reason, decide, and act, but who could not utter words.

It is neither accidental nor trivial that speech will be examined in such depth in this book. Speech is, after all, the most native human possession. Scientists, for example, recently withdrew human status from Neanderthal "man" when it was discovered that the bone structure of his upper throat was ill-suited to producing what we now recognize as spoken discourse.[8] Ashley Montagu, famed student of human society, claims that when we declare the human being to be the only logical or rational animal, we are, in effect, saying no more than that man is the only discursive animal.[9] In day-to-day life, people constantly affirm the wisdom of Montagu's observation. When angry, they instinctively reward their mates with "the silent treatment," thereby denying them, for the time being, the privileges that come with being human. The greatest delight of young parenthood comes when recognizable sounds from their offspring are first heard. The most damning designation to be made of so-called primitive societies is that such societies resolved their disputes by armed conflict rather than by public discussion. Society's last act of charity to a criminal condemned by the state to die is to ask if he or she has anything to say. When lovers misunderstand each other they talk it out. When one's neighbors speak expectantly to inanimate objects they are declared mentally unstable. When a defendant in court is highly inarticulate that person is especially likely to be found guilty (or so says recent research).[10] When asked to name their greatest fear, people designate speechmaking as more terrifying than snakes, the dark, rape, or even death itself. Speech attends our greatest joys and sorrows in life (wedding receptions, funeral visitations) because such joys and sorrows bring out our essential humanity.

Speech attends politics, too. Politics is oftentimes little more than an endless exchange of public conversations between those who control scarce resources and those who wish to control them. Presidents especially depend on speech, even though they do not speak as ordinary people do. Presidents, for example, speak in public more often than persons in virtually any other occupation. When performing their job, presidents do not use their hands to make a watch, their legs to run a race, or their arms to lift a bale of hay. Presidents exert influence over their environment only by speaking, and it is largely through speech that their environment responds to them. Their aides report what seem to be current attitudes in Moscow; their television sets report how the people are reacting to farm prices; their colleagues in the House warn them what the political future holds. What is most remarkable about the Watergate tapes is not the opportunistic strategizing found there, nor the expletives needing deletion, but simply the amount of *time* Richard Nixon spent talking to his advisors about how Watergate might be explained away. Indeed, until his legs carried him to an awaiting helicopter on August 9, 1974, Watergate was, for Richard Nixon, little more than an endless series of symbolic exchanges—parrying with the press, explaining to the nation, berating his aides, beseeching his friends. He left office because of rhetorical crimes he had committed: not telling the right audiences what he knew as soon as he knew it. When he walked to the helicopter that day, Richard Nixon could not even savor the physiological memories retained by the Watergate burglars themselves—the smell of mimeographing fluid, palpitating heartbeats, the sounds of keys jingling, light suddenly piercing the darkness. Deprived of physicalness, Mr. Nixon could only remember words said unwisely or words not said at all.

Unlike you or me, a president must speak on a great variety of topics, only some of which have meaning for him personally. Moreover, presidents cannot choose their interlocutors as freely as you or I can; their appointment calendars remind them each day that they produce speech for hire. Unlike us, presidents speak *in public* virtually all of the time because of the reporters who surround them, even when coming out of church or going to a family softball game. The president's liver, his drug-addicted nephew, his sexual appetites—all these are topics for the speech of the press and the counter-speech of the president. It is also true that presidents speak frequently with persons they cannot see or hear, with persons whose reaction they cannot assess. Confronted with speech via television, presidents must live in a world of positing—they must imagine how they look and sound to people whose own looks and sounds cannot be witnessed. Because a president so often addresses topics about which there is no consensus (i.e., he must address *political* matters), he is denied the possibility of universal acceptance by his auditors, a possibility that, while modest, attends virtually any citizen's discussions about crabgrass or the weather.

When most ordinary Americans speak, they speak in behalf of themselves or, at most, in behalf of their friends, families, and work associates. Presidents, in contrast, represent the viewpoints of abstract entities—their party, the administration, government itself, the Western Alliance. Thus denied the me-ness of human speech, thus encumbered with role requirements and an institutional persona, thus responding in part to a dialogue begun by their forebears in office, presidents usually speak cautiously. Presidents lose their tempers in public no more often than they cry in public, thereby attesting to the rigidities under which their speech labors daily.

Linguist Charles Hockett has observed that one of the most distinctive aspects of human speech is what he calls "rapid fading," the tendency of the speech signal to deteriorate even as it is produced.[11] It is this transitoriness people depend on when gossiping and emoting. When gossiping and emoting, we do not expect our listeners to remember our words verbatim, nor do we expect them to somehow preserve the speech signal so that others, later, can share our experiencing. We therefore prize our discreet friends above all others. Presidents, of course, have few friends (one need only witness the predictable series of postadministration exposés authored by White House chiefs-of-staff and presidential valets alike); they must presume that virtually all of their oral words will be captured instantly and for all times by the electronic equipment constantly pointed at them by members of the press. Presidential speech is speech for the record, speech that cannot fade, speech whose echo will never cease. Because this is so, presidents must insure that words spoken on Tuesday dovetail with those spoken on Monday and cannot be undone by events still to transpire on Wednesday. It is not surprising then that so many presidential speeches stop well short of being brave declarations, or that the remarks made by presidents in press conferences seem more like a series of set pieces than direct replies to the questions asked them by reporters. One need only witness Ronald Reagan's abysmal (uncharacteristically abysmal) performance in such exchanges to learn that a president would rather run the risk of being inarticulate than of being unwisely spontaneous.

This is not to say that the pleasures of spoken exchange are completely denied the chief executive. Throughout this book, we will see presidents devise novel ways for coping with the pressures of their job, and we will see that they often depend on public talk—despite its peculiarities—to help them solve the problems they face. As mentioned previously, the Founding Fathers would be disconcerted to discover how often and in what ways modern presidents speak. But the Founding Fathers did not have to live in a politically saturated, information dense, and electronically mediated society in which presidential words mean little and all at the same time. The Founding Fathers did not live in a world in which the immediacy, sociability, and essential privacy of spoken interchange must be foresworn by a president intent on governing well. Presidents speak as they do because we and our scribes insist that they do. The Founding Fathers were not acquainted with people like us, our scribes, and the presidents who perform for us.

On Stage in the White House

The Founding Fathers would be dismayed to see a theatrical subtitle being used to describe life at 1600 Pennsylvania Avenue. But the metaphor is an apt one, judging by life as lived at that residence during the last forty years. Beginning in 1945 and continuing through 1985, presidents spoke in public twenty times per month, approximately one speech per working day. Dwight Eisenhower spoke least often (averaging ten speeches per month) and Gerald Ford most frequently (forty-three per month). Indeed, taking 1976 as an example, Jerry Ford can be seen as a rhetorical iron man. Presuming that he was on the job for an average of twelve hours each day (weekends included), and knowing that he delivered 682 speeches in 1976, we are left with the remarkable total of one presidential speech being delivered *every six hours* during his last year in office. Admittedly, 1976 was an election year, and Gerald Ford, as an unelected incumbent, faced unusual pressures. But Ford's behavior that year was not exceedingly far off the (modern) presidential mark.

Table 1.1 lists the speech totals for each of the last eight American presidents, and figure 1.1 displays these data graphically. Several items are worth noting: (1) presidential first-years have become more and more rhetorical over time, suggesting that speechmaking has become increasingly accepted as a presidential life-style; (2) many presidents increase their speaking substantially during their second year in office, suggesting that such personal appearances are judged to be rewarding (politically, psychologically, culturally); and (3) there have been marked changes during the last forty

Table 1.1 *Frequency of Speechmaking within and across Presidencies*

Year in Office*	Truman	Eisenhower	Kennedy	Johnson	Nixon	Ford	Carter	Reagan	All Presidents
First	57	96	189	35	249	157	282	211	1276
Second	83	138	298	471	225	392	323	344	2274
Third	69	88	284	236	165	682	272	384	2180
Fourth	385	92	…	296	155	5	436	421	1790
Fifth	144	92	…	267	133	…	…	277	913
Sixth	164	87	…	309	108	…	…	…	668
Seventh	155	147	…	22	…	…	…	…	302
Eighth	347	176	…	…	…	…	…	…	523
Ninth	3	9	…	…	…	…	…	…	12
Total speeches	1407	925	771	1636	1035	1236	1322	1637	9969
Months in office	93	96	35	61	68	29	48	60	490
Monthly speech average	15.1	9.6	22.0	26.8	15.2	42.6	27.5	27.3	20.3

*Refers in each case to *calendar* year.

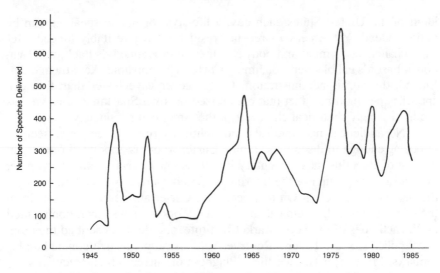

Figure 1.1. Yearly totals of presidential speechmaking (1945–1985).

years in the frequency with which presidents speak in public. Three major plateaus are revealed in these data, with Truman and Eisenhower speaking comparatively infrequently, Kennedy through Nixon speaking roughly twice as often as their immediate predecessors, and Ford through Reagan substantially surpassing even that total. Figure 1.1 reveals, quite naturally, the peaks and valleys in speechmaking one would expect to find in election years and nonelection years. But figure 1.1 also shows that both election and nonelection years have witnessed more and more presidential speech over time.

Between 1945 and 1985, only one month (October of 1955) found the president of the United States speech-less, a feat occasioned by Dwight Eisenhower's coronary. Not a single month in the Kennedy, Johnson, Ford, and Carter administrations contained fewer than five speeches, even though each of these presidents suffered a variety of ailments from time to time. And it is important that we reckon with the physical toll exacted by public speaking, especially when produced in such prodigious quantity by a middle-aged (or older) chief executive. Public speaking is normally done standing up, a fact that places roughly 200 pounds of pressure on the legs and feet. Adrenalin courses through the body; the sweat glands become activated; the larynx, the trachea, the glottis, the pharynx, and even the nasal cavity are exercised; chemical secretions in the stomach change dramatically; blood pressure increases, as does electrical activity in the brain; normal patterns of breathing are altered. All such physical processes, of course, are quite natural responses to intensified psychosocial activities, but there is equally little doubt that with a steady regimen of such strains placed upon the president of the United States each day, a life-style of public speaking can be taxing indeed. Yet America's recent presidents have veritably lunged after such challenges of mind and body. Neither John Kennedy's back, nor Lyndon Johnson's gallbladder, nor Jimmy Carter's hemorrhoids kept them quiet. Indeed, during his administration, Carter never gave fewer than fourteen speeches per month, a fact that epitomized his own Spartan zeal as well as the increasingly rhetorical character of the American presidency.

No audience, no topic, and no political circumstances ever seemed imposing enough to discourage Jimmy Carter from his appointed rounds. In August of 1978 (his most sedentary month as chief executive), for example, even an arcane group like the International Labor Press Association received the best he had to offer. On that occasion, Carter answered questions from the editor of the Oil, Chemical and Atomic Workers newspaper, commented on the activities of the Food Market Institute, and deftly described the monetary policies of the Federal Reserve Administration. When concluding his remarks, Mr. Carter typified the willingness of current chief executives not only to accept but also to encourage a full schedule of spoken exchanges: "This is a rare occasion when I have a chance to sit down with a group because of the pressures on me of time, but your opinions are very valuable to me . . . Your readers are my constituents, and I want to serve them well. And I think you can help me to do it. I thank you for coming and letting me meet with you."[12] Despite his heartfelt remarks, Mr. Carter misspoke—the occasion was hardly rare: he encouraged in like manner some 322 other audiences that year.

Presidents are not only speaking more often, they are speaking to a greater variety of audiences as well. During his first two years in office, Ronald Reagan presented remarks in over two-thirds of the states, even though his reelection bid was more than two years off. During his slightly more than two years in office, Gerald Ford visited all but four of the states. Lyndon Johnson traveled to thirty-three different states in 1965 alone. While it took only thirty-one speeches in October of 1956 to secure Dwight Eisenhower's reelection, it took eighty-nine to turn the trick for Lyndon Johnson in October of 1964. Gerald Ford and Jimmy Carter who spoke, respectively, 107 and 105 times in the Octobers of their reelection years, did so to no avail, even though each visited as many states during their campaign as Harry Truman had on his famed caboose ride across the plains in 1948.

As shall be noted later, the steady rise in presidential speechmaking cannot be explained merely by calculating the respective political odds against reelection. Even during nonelection years, presidents are speaking more often these days. Harry Truman's busiest nonelection month was October 1951, during which he gave twenty-three addresses to such groups as the American Dental Association, the National Guard Association, and the American Hungarian Foundation. During his busiest nonelection month

(September 1975), Jerry Ford gave fifty-two such speeches, and, unlike Mr. Truman, Ford traveled outside of Washington, D.C., to do so: a Republican fund-raiser in Portland, the annual meeting of the National Baptist Association in St. Louis, a Southern Methodist University convocation in Dallas, and the National Association of Life Underwriters in Anaheim. The contrast between Truman and Ford is stark, especially when we consider three facts: (1) September of 1975 was the month during which Mr. Ford was almost shot to death in San Francisco; (2) these speeches occurred on four separate trips; and (3) despite his extensive traveling that month, Ford also gave more speeches *in Washington, D.C.,* than Harry Truman did during his busiest month in office. Presidents' speaking schedules have no doubt been made more manageable by the comforts of air travel, but such conveniences cannot alone explain why we hear from our chief executive so much more often in the 1980s than we did in the 1940s and 1950s.

Although we shall examine such matters in greater detail later, it is also true that modern chief executives are expected to address a bewildering variety of topics. Lyndon Johnson was an especially opportunistic rhetor who, in one three-week period in February of 1964, presided over the annual Prayer Breakfast, did a guest appearance at the Weizmann Institute of Science, talked to key officials at the Internal Revenue Service, celebrated the bicentennial of St. Louis, Missouri, broke ground for the Florida Cross-state Barge Canal, presented an upbeat address on U.S.-Mexican relations (and gave ten other speeches in addition). The breadth of such discussions no doubt seems altogether unremarkable to latter twentieth-century Americans. We have come to expect our presidents to speak knowingly about such diverse matters and about a great many others as well. We find it quite natural, now, that a chief executive would be thoroughly familiar with tax law, scientific breakthroughs, American history, and the ways of the Lord. Plucky professionals that they are, our presidents are not about to disappoint us. They will gladly speak about any topic that can be spoken about; they will do so with whatever frequency suggested and in whatever location deemed appropriate; if their families would permit it, they would probably speak more often than they do. The rhetorical appetite of presidents cannot be sated.

The rising amount of speech during the last four decades may signal many things—personality differences in the minds of people wishing to serve as president, alterations in White House scheduling occasioned by domestic and international pressures, increasing recognition that oratory equals publicity equals political success in Congress. During the Truman and Eisenhower administrations, speechmaking was highly utilitarian, a resource called upon when minds needed changing and votes needed soliciting. Indeed, table 1.1 clearly demonstrates that Harry Truman spoke extensively only during his reelection bid in 1948 and during his ill-fated stumping in behalf of Adlai

Table 1.2   *Presidential Speaking vs. Party Control of Congress*
                (1945–1982)

Party	% Years Controlling Congress (N = 38)	% Speeches When Controlling Congress (N = 4395)
Democratic	89.5	94.4
Republican	10.5*	5.6

*1953–1954.

Stevenson (and in behalf of his own administration's reputation) in 1952. Table 1.2 shows a similar instinct within Eisenhower, with congressional opposition calling forth greater rhetorical effort on his part. When his party controlled the Congress (during 1953–1954), Ike reached only 50% of his "rhetorical potential," thereby revealing what used to be political truisms: (1) it is necessary to speak only when speech is necessary, and (2) that applause is best that is provided without prompting.

Today, presidents speak no matter which party controls Congress; also, speech is no longer summoned exclusively by the electoral genie. It is now the daily affair of an individual wishing to be all things to all of the American people. Thus, it is not surprising that Ronald Reagan addressed most of the White House reporters by their first names during press conferences, thereby becoming a political god more immanent than transcendent. Such behavior no longer surprises, nor did Jimmy Carter surprise when he attended innumerable "town meetings" in badly ventilated gymnasiums, was subjected to questions about his grammar school grades, his views on premarital sex, or his brother's alcoholism, or that these questions were posed by shopkeepers and gardeners. Because their president is now with them so often in so many local contexts, the American people have come to think of him as a kind of national housepet.

These quantitative jumps in speechmaking presage changes in rhetorical tone. Propinquity often encourages informality; in the United States it encourages melodrama as well. For example, between 1945 and 1985, the state of South Dakota provided the occasion for only six presidential speeches, one of which was an address at the Mount Rushmore National Monument by Dwight Eisenhower. The introduction to his speech is restrained and formal, a fitting tone for one who was rarely a guest in America's homes. His introduction is institutional and impersonal, and he wastes little time in getting down to business:

> I have been signally honored in the invitation from this organization to come to this beautiful spot today. I have been privileged to come with the two dis-

tinguished United States Senators from this state, Senator Mundt and Senator Case, and with them Congressman Berry and Congressman Lovre.

We are further complimented today by the presence here of a group of young Republicans now serving you and all of us in Congress. So all in all it makes it an occasion that will live long in my memory.

Now one of the many responsibilities I acquired last year was that of becoming leader of the Republican Party. I am very proud—and I may add that I am kept intensely aware—of this special responsibility.

Most Americans would agree with me that it is not appropriate for the President of the United States to indulge incessantly in partisan political activities—every day on every possible occasion. Many of the most critical problems before our country are in no sense partisan issues. They involve all Americans; and in meeting them the President must strive to serve all our citizens. For these problems threaten freedom itself. They summon and demand unadulterated patriotism.[13]

Richard Nixon also spoke in South Dakota—sixteen years and a relationship-sensitive generation later. When he dedicated a library at General Beadle State College in Madison, Mr. Nixon was warm where Eisenhower had been cold, specific where Eisenhower had been vague, and dilatory where Eisenhower had been succinct:

I feel at home here because I, too, grew up in a small town. I attended a small college about the size of this one; and when I was in law school, at a much larger university, one of the ways that I helped work my way through that law school was to work in the law school library.

So I feel very much at home here before a great, new library, on the campus of a small college which is growing larger, and in a small town in the heartland of America.

I would like to relate what I have said a little more, perhaps, closely to this state. I suppose the best thing I could say would be that I was born in South Dakota. I was not. I was born in California. I could also say, possibly, that Mrs. Nixon was born in South Dakota. She was not. She was born in Nevada.

But I can go very close to that, because my wife's mother and father, Mr. and Mrs. Thomas William Ryan, were married and lived in their early years, before they moved to Nevada, in Lee, South Dakota. So we have a South Dakota background.[14]

There is more here than simply Richard Nixon's personalism. When he spoke, Mr. Nixon spoke as one well versed in the role requirements imposed upon the New Presidency. Mr. Nixon knew that listeners in South

Dakota felt close to him (psychologically, if not emotionally) because he had visited them in their homes so often on television. Mr. Nixon knew that frequency of contact breeds familiarity which, in turn, breeds contempt if one is not fully "relational." Mr. Nixon knew that the excessive exposure enjoyed by a modern president has its costs and that each specific, personal speech given in North Dakota causes the citizens of South Dakota to expect the same when their turn comes in the presidential audience. Perhaps the most fundamental point made by these contrasting examples is that Richard Nixon fully understood the existence of a type of paragovernmental structure in the United States (the Department of Image Maintenance) which Dwight Eisenhower would neither have understood nor condoned.

Rhetoric as Governance

One of the key conclusions of my investigations is this: public speech no longer attends the processes of governance—it *is* governance. The presidency has been transferred from a formal, print-oriented world into an electronic environment specializing in the spoken word and rewarding casual, interpersonally adept politicians. No matter which set of data is considered, the differences between the Early Modern presidents (Truman and Eisenhower) and their successors are sharp indeed. Consider, for example, this assortment of facts:

1. Whereas only 13.1% of Harry Truman's nonelection year speeches were delivered outside Washington, D.C., that proportion was doubled by John Kennedy and Jimmy Carter, tripled by Richard Nixon, and quadrupled by Gerald Ford.
2. Jimmy Carter, Ronald Reagan, and Richard Nixon gave the same percentage of international speeches during election years as they did during nonelection years.
3. Whereas Gerald Ford spoke proportionally more often in ceremonial settings during nonelection years (46.5% vs. 30% for election years), the actual *number* of election-year ceremonies in which he participated increased considerably ($N = 188$ vs. 252).
4. While almost half of the speeches delivered by the Early Modern presidents occurred during the fall (no doubt connected with electoral activities), their successors' speeches were fairly evenly distributed across the various seasons of the year.
5. Although he was in office only one-third of the time enjoyed by Harry Truman, Jerry Ford participated in more organizational meetings ($N = 144$ vs. 125) than did Truman.[15]

Clearly, presidents no longer use speech merely to get elected. Instead, they increasingly balance their workday on the fulcrum of public discourse, discourse both weighty and silly, and many Americans have come to believe that governance occurs only when their presidents talk to them. What used to be a natural "seam" between election and nonelection years no longer exists. Depending upon one's perspective, the reelection campaign never begins or it never ends. Presidents are out and among us constantly. The slow, steady drip of their words is a kind of torture to which they and we have become addicted. Although the mass media often cynically decry this incessant flow of words, these appearances never go unnoticed by the press. In some senses, it makes little difference *how* the press reacts to the specific address being covered, whether they find it edifying or vacuous.[16] The very fact that media coverage is lavished upon such performances reinforces the notions that all real governance occurs in public and that no president can lead the American people if he cannot speak artfully or, if not artfully, at least willingly and frequently.

The increasing "rhetoricalization" of the presidency is evidenced in any number of ways. Figure 1.2 demonstrates one way; it shows the steadily growing similarity between election-year topics and those discussed in odd-

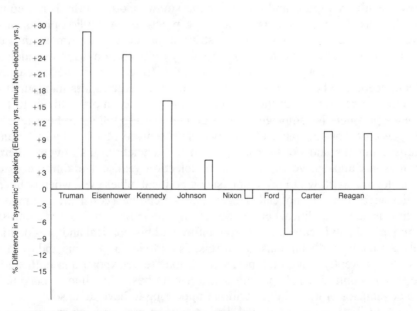

Figure 1.2. Comparative emphasis on "systemic" speaking in election vs. nonelection years (vs. "humanistic" speaking).

Table 1.3   *Harry Truman vs. Gerald Ford: Ceremonies vs. Rallies*

	Election-Year Ceremonies (Monthly Average)	Nonelection-Year Rallies (Monthly Average)
Truman	2.35 (48 months)	0.13 (45 months)
Ford	14.80 (17 months)	2.51 (12 months)
Ratio (Truman/Ford)	1/6.3	1/19.3

numbered years. Truman, Eisenhower, and, to a lesser extent, John Kennedy, brought their election-year addresses back to the established, concrete realities of American politics, while the Johnson through Reagan administrations did not distinguish so dramatically between what was discussable when. For these latter presidents, issues like economic fluctuations, agricultural subsidies, labor-management problems, and the federal bureaucracy were not just election-year priorities. Another, equally valid, way of interpreting these data is to observe that "humanistic" topics like food stamps, education, political ethics, and democratic values are discussed with growing frequency during congressional and federal elections. Our most recent presidents do not evidence the political schizophrenia Harry Truman and Dwight Eisenhower evidenced (guns and butter for the stump, God and the Boy Scouts for the East Room), perhaps because the pressures of public opinion now even themselves out across an administration, or because the American people are no longer content to be governed by off-again, on-again presidents, or perhaps because a growing consistency of rhetorical formatting has caused electioneering to be less interruptive of the workload and less manipulative in appearance. Whatever the reason, it is now much more difficult to tell when a president is campaigning. It is equally hard to tell when he is not.

A corroborating piece of evidence is presented in table 1.3 which compares Truman's and Ford's participation in "asynchronous" events (ceremonies in campaign years, rallies in nonelection years). The differences in behavior are stark, with Ford emphasizing political rallies even when political rallies were nominally not called for, but also spending a considerable amount of time in tacitly apolitical ceremonies during campaign seasons. (In contrast, Truman's old-style campaign sharply bifurcated his political and presidential selves.) Jerry Ford's administration reveals a mixing of persons and events, his bet apparently being that incremental, long-term exposure in both traditional and nontraditional speech settings would best allow him to maximize the advantages of incumbency without appearing to have done so.

Equally, Ford spent a good deal of time in precampaign campaigning. In September of 1975, for example, he addressed the members of the Republican National Committee, hinting broadly at the furious political schedule he would follow in the year ahead. He said: "I can assure you that in the months ahead, a major part of my effort in travel will be to work with you in your respective states. Now, that includes not only party organization but it includes the financial aspects of the party in each of the states."[17] What Mr. Ford did not say then was that he also intended to exploit every nondescript rhetorical opportunity that would come his way in the days ahead. Had he been more candid, he would have explained that he would use the forthcoming Bicentennial celebrations to cover himself in reelectable glory. Had his listeners in September of 1975 been particularly discerning, they could have guessed at that strategy, for later in his speech he appropriated the ceremonial language he would use so frequently in the upcoming months. He pointed out that the aim of the "first century was to establish a government . . . that was strong and viable. The second century was to develop . . . as an industrial country . . . strong and capable of meeting the challenge from other industrial countries." And then, seizing the opportunity, he grandly dedicated the third century to "freedom for the individual."[18]

Mr. Ford's political use of ceremonies was not unique to him, a matter we shall examine in more depth in Chapter Three. But it is important to note here that the Later Modern presidents (essentially, Presidents Kennedy to Nixon) and the Recent Modern presidents (Ford to Reagan) found themselves in ceremonial surroundings twice as often proportionally, *but four times as often absolutely,* as the Early Modern presidents.[19] These ceremonies increased in Washington, D.C., as well as in the states; they increased both domestically and internationally. The more recent presidents have invested the most pedestrian settings with ceremonial grandeur (e.g., the winning of a football championship); they memorialized every war hero, college building, and historical occurrence available; and they have added speechmaking to events that might not otherwise have been thought of as ceremonial (e.g., airport arrivals and departures) as well as to ceremonial events previously devoid of rhetorical flourishes (e.g., the signing of legislation).

For these and other reasons, the multispeech day has become common. In the *election* years between 1945 and 1957, 628 speeches were given on such multispeech days; in the *nonelection* years occurring between 1970 and 1982, however, almost as many speeches (520 in all) were delivered by U.S. presidents on such days. (During this latter period, the chief executives also gave almost 1,200 speeches on multispeech days during election years.) In other words, the sheer *density* of presidential speechmaking has gone up sharply; presidents now work harder at their speaking, and they do so in both electoral and nonelectoral contexts.

Gerald Ford is again a good example of the communicative effort demanded of an American president. On September 4, 1975, he traveled to the Northwest. Although he did not begin speaking until noon, he managed to give six fairly lengthy addresses that day. He began with a Republican fund-raiser in Seattle, then spoke at a party luncheon, after which he went across town to a White House Conference on domestic and economic affairs. He next flew to Portland, made brief remarks to reporters, followed that up with another fund-raiser, and then met with throngs of young people at a Bicentennial Rally for Youth which began at 8:25 in the evening. In the first five minutes of this latter speech, Mr. Ford discussed the relative merits of the Salvation Army, the Declaration of Independence, the Pacific Northwest, the electric light bulb, and his Sunday School teacher.[20] It is difficult to discern how the Republic was served by Mr. Ford's whirlwind tour of that September 4 or by the many forgettable remarks he made that day. But he did the same thing eight days later (in Texas) and worked even harder at his speechmaking in 1976.

Our three most recent presidents have spoken as often internationally during election years as the middle-most presidents did during nonelection years. Moreover, they campaigned just as hard in the domestic United States as the Early Modern presidents but spoke in these locations three times as often during nonelection years. In other words, the rhetorical ante has been upped across the board for the recent presidents—relative to all audiences, with regard to all topics and speech settings—and a great deal of what now passes for decision making in the United States occurs on an airplane transporting an exhausted president.[21] If rhetoric really is governance, then a great deal of rhetoric must translate into a great deal of governance. If this is so, then wisdom and eloquence must be increasingly united by these very busy chief executives, and their speech texts must bear the scrutiny of the most perspicacious critic. Alas, despite their efforts, America's recent presidents have generated no such impressions of leadership in the minds of the citi-

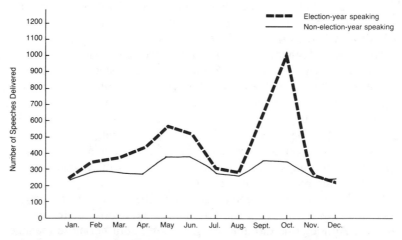

Figure 1.3. Monthly totals of presidential speechmaking (1945–1982).

Table 1.4   *Topical Focus of Democratic vs. Republican Speeches*

Topic	% Democratic Speeches (N = 5136)	% Republican Speeches (N = 4833)
Science	8.6	6.1
Economics	6.7	9.8
Governance	12.5	11.1
Human services	9.4	6.2
Human values	12.2	12.6
International cooperation	17.1	21.5
International conflict	5.6	6.8
Multiple	22.3	19.1
Other	5.7	6.7

zenry. The opinion polls offer little solace to overworked presidents. Faced with such reactions to their labors, the presidents have sought refuge in the likeliest of unlikely places—in rhetoric itself—thus responding to a primitive instinct to use human speech to fight an important fight.

Although the most recent presidents have sharply accentuated the amount of political listening required in the United States, there is some evidence that they have, in so doing, merely built upon a "rhetorical establishment" already existing in Washington. Figure 1.3, for example, shows that speechmaking is fairly evenly distributed across any presidential year not involving congressional or federal elections. There is a steady schedule of activities in the White House, with only slight rises in speaking during the heavily ceremonial months of May and June and the (locally) political months of September and October. Otherwise, the communicative effort required of presidents is constant (and unrelenting).

While figure 1.3 does not reveal individual presidential variations on this pattern, such variations were almost nonexistent. Also, the election-year curves for the individual chief executives differed only in the steepness of the peaks representing the "primary season" and "election season." The overall *shape* of the election-year curve depicted here remained constant for each of the presidents examined.

While some party-based differences in presidential speaking will be revealed later in this volume, there is more similarity than dissimilarity among the four Democrats and four Republicans studied here. Apparently, the rhetorical establishment requires that all presidents sacrifice their ideological and programmatic biases to regular discussion of a limited number of traditional topics. Table 1.4 illustrates that there have been only minor variations in the topics discussed during the last forty years; despite the very different personalities and political platforms involved, the last eight chief executives spoke about the same matters.[22]

As the historian William Leuchtenburg has observed, Franklin Delano
Roosevelt wrote the basic political hymnal used by his eight successors—no
matter what their party.[23] Thus, as the political scientist J. W. Prothro reports,
a careful inspection of even Dwight Eisenhower's speeches reveals an unmistakable legacy of New Dealism imprinted upon them.[24] As every junior
executive and international diplomat knows, it is the *agenda* that one initially
seeks to control in public discussion. Judging by the evidence presented here,
the presidential agenda is stable, a fact that serves to support the arguments
of third-party candidates (not to mention neo-Marxists) who complain that
Democrats and Republicans sound more alike than unalike largely because
they begin their discussions in the same places.

Table 1.5 continues this same theme—that presidential rhetoric becomes a way of governance because certain philosophical prescriptions have
been built into the American presidency. Admittedly, these prescriptions are
more implicit than explicit, and presidents do have some leeway in determining how they will sound. But, increasingly, they seem *not* to have the
option of remaining silent, and they seem *not* to be free to alter radically the

Table 1.5 *Alterations in Speaking Patterns within Presidential Administrations
(Reported in Percentages)*

	Period during Administration	
	First Half (N = 4,430)	*Second Half* (N = 5,539)
General location:		
Washington, D.C.	65.2	60.6
Domestic city	28.6	31.4
International city	6.1	8.0
Audience:		
Government employees	2.1	0.9
Local and/or press	50.8	51.7
National	8.1	7.7
Invited guests	14.4	16.7
Special interest group	24.6	23.0
Topic:		
Science	7.1	7.3
Economics	9.8	6.9
Governance	8.3	14.8
Human services	9.0	7.0
Human values	11.8	12.9
International cooperation	19.3	19.3
International conflict	5.5	6.8
Multiple	22.3	19.4
Other	6.9	5.6

matters to be discussed at the weekly press conference. As we see in table 1.5, the audiences being addressed, the topics being discussed, and the locations selected for presidential speech do not change appreciably over the course of the average presidency. Clearly, this hypothetical average is only partially instructive since, of the last eight presidents, three (Truman, Eisenhower, and Reagan) served virtually two complete terms in office, two (Johnson and Nixon) served what amounted to one-and-a-half terms, one (Carter) served one term, and two (Kennedy and Ford) served less than one complete term. On the other hand, the consistency found in table 1.5 seems less an artifact when one reckons with the thoroughgoing institutionalization that has taken place in the American presidency during the last four decades. This table reflects stability in discourse, a stability manufactured by the limited number of persons, issues, and political opportunities available to a modern president. Although many unexpected things happen to these presidents during their tours in office, it is not altogether inconceivable, given the basically conservative routines of American democracy, that had all things *been* equal for each of them, all things would have *appeared* equal for each of them. That is exactly what table 1.5 suggests.[25]

Later in this volume, we shall pause to consider what it means that the American presidency has become increasingly rhetorical during the middle of the twentieth century and what is implied by the considerable predictability in rhetorical form and function just observed. Why these patterns developed as they did is not altogether clear, although it is probably safe to say that they performed certain important duties for the American people. Both Jimmy Carter and Richard Nixon spoke about science and agriculture with equal frequency during their years in office because America has been, and continues to be, a land-grant nation with a technological bent. Similarly, they discussed foreign affairs equally often because the American people, or at least most of them, have long seen themselves as international guarantors of liberty. Even though Richard Nixon was the internationalist and Jimmy Carter the scientist, the job they took, and the rhetorical calcifications it has developed over time, pointed them in kindred directions. The substance of presidential discourse has a constancy to it because its purposes transcend its makers. As the communication scholar Lawrence Rosenfield observes, such discourse operates for the American people "like the rhythmical breathing of a living mammal . . . the steady din of familiar controversy, like the ocean's roar, serves to reassure us that things are normal and the public institutions remain healthy."[26]

The Kennedy Revolution

If FDR gave birth to the modern presidency, surely it was John Kennedy who became its adolescence. Throughout this study and in a variety of ways, it became apparent that it was he who shifted the rhetorical focus of the White House. Kennedy spoke more frequently, for a greater variety of purposes, and in a greater range of speech settings than did his two immediate predecessors. He imposed rhetorical solutions upon problems not normally admitting to such solutions; he spoke throughout the United States more often during nonelection years than most previous presidents had spoken on the hustings; when touring Europe, he did not just visit its historic battlements, he spoke there; and if he were presented with an anomalous political situation, JFK more often than not invented a rhetorical form suitable for dealing with it, a form attractive enough to soon become White House precedent (e.g., the live, televised press conference). Although we now know that Mr. Kennedy was remarkably reticent, some even say remote, in private, in public he was clever and articulate. He was also clever enough to see the advantages of being articulate.

John Kennedy spoke more often during the summer months than did any of the other presidents studied here (except Ronald Reagan, who equaled him).[27] An incidental finding, at first glance, but upon closer examination it suggests a person who could find both relaxation and profit in rhetoric. When most Americans think of their presidents on the road, they think of them speaking while the snow is melting during the primaries or during the autumn elections as the leaves are falling. But John Kennedy's busiest month in office came in June (of 1963), a month that would have found Harry Truman attending to a backlog of paperwork or Dwight Eisenhower testing a new fairway. During Kennedy's busiest month, he gave the graduation addresses at U.S. Air Force Academy, at San Diego State College, and (most memorably) at American University. During this same month he spoke to the annual meetings of the Young Australian League, the U.S. Conference of Mayors, and the International Congress of Medical Librarianship. He officiated at the Centennial Celebrations in Charleston, West Virginia, made remarks to the American Committee on Italian Migration, punctuated his signing of the Equal Pay Act with a short speech, spoke during lunch to Sponsors and Editors of Historical Publications, and then gave thirty-two speeches in Europe in one week's time. In addition, he found something to say to the members of the World Food Congress, to the scientists at the Missile Range in White Sands, New Mexico, to the sailors aboard the U.S.S. *Kitty Hawk*, to the gawkers at the Honolulu International Airport, and to a national audience of persons interested in civil rights.

This intensive and varied rhetorical schedule seems completely normal by modern standards, which is exactly the point: John Kennedy set the standard. During his short stay in the White House, he discovered that the American people were incredibly curious about their chief executives. He knew, unlike many of his predecessors, that their appetites for presidential words were just as ravenous in the Western states as they were in the banquet halls along the East Coast. And so he spoke in the West twenty-two times during his two nonelectoral years in office, even though Harry Truman gave only seven speeches there (in almost four such years) and Dwight Eisenhower only five (during his four nonelectoral years in office).[28] When speaking in Seattle in November of 1961, Kennedy described the technological changes the West had experienced and in so doing implicitly justified his taking the time to speak at what had only been a stop on the campaign trail heretofore. Lionizing the public service of U.S. Senator Warren Magnunson, Kennedy described the developments of the last twenty-five years:

> This State was half sagebrush. The Columbia River ran unharnessed to the sea. There was no atomic energy plant at Hanford, no aluminum plants, no dams or locks, no up-river navigation. Today there are more than a million acres of new fertile farmland, more than 50,000 men working in the aluminum plants, millions of kilowatts of electrical energy are produced by a vast complex of hydro-electric power plants—the Columbia has been largely tamed and great ships sail its waters.[29]

When making his own *rhetorical* discoveries of the West, John Kennedy proved that speechmaking could be used for vote insuring as well as vote getting, thus adding a new and valuable tool to a sitting presidency.

As anyone who reached the age of political reason in the early 1960s knows (the age of political reason being that sudden, curious moment when a youngster comes to understand that presidents, movie stars, and athletes are not employed in exactly the same ways), John Kennedy also brought his speechmaking to Europe and beyond, accenting a trend begun more tentatively by Dwight Eisenhower. Kennedy learned a curious thing about such traveling: because of the now-voracious mass media, the people he left behind at home would follow his every move while abroad just as avidly as they would follow his domestic trips during election time. Kennedy discovered that the *act* of speaking in foreign countries possessed as much, if not more, intrigue and grandeur for the American people as the actual words uttered in such locations (a distinction we shall pursue more fully in Chapter Two). Finally, Kennedy discovered, perhaps rediscovered, the quite tangible, political as well as symbolic, appeal of ceremony. In making this latter discovery, John Kennedy established what would quickly and powerfully become a habit for his successors in office.

Table 1.6 reports how frequently the presidents participated in international ceremonies, that is, ceremonies in which speaking played a major role. (This distinction is not an unimportant one, for it is perfectly possible, if politically inconceivable, for an American president to make international trips silently, operating as a private listener rather than as a public speaker.) The data show that while Eisenhower and Kennedy had different (propor-

Table 1.6   *Comparative Use of Presidential Ceremonies*

	International Ceremonies			Other Ceremonies		
President	N	N *as % of All Speech by This President*	*Yearly Average*	N	N *as % of All Speech by This President*	*Yearly Average*
Truman	1	0.0	0.1	226	16.1	29.1
Eisenhower	89	9.6	11.1	233	25.2	29.1
Kennedy	42	5.4	14.5	321	41.6	110.7
Johnson	49	3.0	9.6	841	51.4	164.9
Nixon	108	10.4	18.9	403	38.9	70.7
Ford	45	3.6	18.8	395	32.0	164.6
Carter	61	4.6	15.3	454	34.3	113.5
Reagan	49	3.0	9.8	420	25.6	84.0
Total (average)	444	(5.0)	(12.3)	3293	(33.1)	(95.8)

tional) instincts about such international speaking, Kennedy increased the absolute amount of ceremonializing and did so *early* in his presidency. (JFK went to Europe less than four months after having been inaugurated, while it took Dwight Eisenhower three-and-a-half years to get there after his first day in office.) It is interesting that most of Kennedy's successors maintained his use of such speech settings, even though to do so required that they add to an already-filled speaking schedule. Jerry Ford, for example, spoke as often in such settings as Kennedy, even though Ford's international speeches accounted for less of his total rhetorical effort (see proportion column of table 1.6).

The early interest shown in international ceremonies by Kennedy was attended by a new "international style" or, perhaps more precisely, by an Americanization of the international ceremony. When he visited Chile in March of 1960, for example, Dwight Eisenhower spoke in the formal cadences of diplomacy, a language well suited to his own somewhat cluttered speaking style[30] as well as a language he had had an opportunity to practice in his prepresidential years. Eisenhower's language is distanced; stilted by modern standards. It is a language replete with abstractions, a language that hides the personal intentions and feelings of its user, a language more likely to be read than spoken. Note, for example, some of Eisenhower's sentences containing the first person singular:

> May I say, Mr. President, that in the short time I have been here I have seen all the ingredients of progress. . . .

I was greatly encouraged to meet with large groups which are fostering Chilean-American understanding . . . for I deeply believe that genuine understanding is the foundation for all fruitful cooperation. . . .

And of special significance, I think I have sensed in all the people I have met a will to work—a faith in their ability to solve their problems in their own way—and in freedom.[31]

Progress, understanding, cooperation, freedom—these are the entities with which Mr. Eisenhower's "I" was associated. John Kennedy's energetic, personal style is in contrast. When he made self-references, Kennedy did so to link himself with specific people and actions, features of public discourse Americans especially appreciate. In speaking in these ways, Kennedy demonstrated the keystone of his "revolution"—that *all* presidential speech, no matter how specialized its subject matter or how international its location, is speech that can be bent to domestic, ultimately political, ends. John Kennedy charmed by being himself and by using himself:

I must say, that though we are far from home, you made us feel at home, so we want to express our thanks to you, and all of the citizens of your city and country. . . .

I am here today—the second American President to visit Columbia—in that same spirit of cooperation. . . .

In 1960, your distinguished President, Dr. Lleras Camargo, addressed the United States Congress of which I was a member. . . .

But I also want to talk to those beyond this dinner table, and beyond this room, and this old house. . . .

And tonight, here in this old city, I pledge to you the commitment of the United States of America, to that great cause [of freedom].[32]

John Kennedy's international speaking brought him garlands, a fact not lost on those who succeeded him in office. Even a "domestic man" like Lyndon Johnson utilized international ceremonies (roughly ten a year), largely because they seem to give an American president stature. Because of John Kennedy's ability to attract media attention, international traveling has become a reelection year staple, a recent example of which was Ronald Reagan's 1984 European sojourn. Kennedy melded American informality with foreign glamour, a combination that pleased his international hearers as well as his American overhearers.

Although he already knew a good deal about political matters, Lyndon Johnson was an especially attentive student of Kennedy's. Serving under JFK for almost three years, Johnson learned firsthand the potency of properly conducted international ceremony. As table 1.6 indicates, Johnson also followed up on another of Kennedy's inventions—the domestic ceremony. JFK quadrupled Truman's and Eisenhower's uses of such settings, but Johnson far surpassed even that total, sharply increasing the yearly average that Kennedy had established. In his five years in office, Johnson averaged almost three such rituals per week, over three-quarters of which occurred in Washington, D.C. (almost all of them held in the White House). Under Kennedy's tutelage, Johnson learned that people behave especially well during ceremonies, that they quickly defer to the individual conducting the ritual, and that ceremonies have a special ability to nurse political wounds and to bring together former adversaries in a spirit of (sometimes resigned) cooperation.

Knowing these things, Johnson ceremonialized constantly. Consider what he did in July of 1965, for example. He swore in LeRoy Collins as under secretary of commerce; he authorized the World Law Day proclamation; he waved goodbye to the American Field Service students; he shook hands with the British ambassador at the Magna Carta anniversary ceremony; he celebrated the Department of Defense's cost reduction program; and he signed ten major pieces of legislation. But before he did any swearing or authorizing or waving or shaking or celebrating or signing, Lyndon Johnson did some speaking. Mr. Johnson liked his celebrations filled with gushy, tendentious, thoroughly gesticulated oratory. Johnson's speechmaking was not something he put on, like a coat. It was something he *did,* something he *was.* And to be able to do it in the White House was a special treat indeed. He believed that a president's words were a kind of gift; it was a gift he kept on giving.

Once again, we find that quantitative changes in presidential speaking go hand in hand with certain stylistic alterations. When pressed, for example, Harry Truman would conduct a White House ceremony. But when he was required to, he would do so in his characteristically taciturn way, wasting no words lest his emotions be seen as contrived or, worse yet, as false. Thus, when he swore in Tom Clark as associate justice of the Supreme Court, the *entirety* of Mr. Truman's remarks were as follows:

> For the last time Mr. Attorney General, I hand you a Commission as Justice of the Supreme Court of the United States.
>
> We have had a great Attorney General for the last 4 years, and we will have a great Justice of the court from now on.
>
> I present you to your wonderful chief.[33]

Although Lyndon Johnson may not have felt that words were exactly cheap, he surely did not treat them as being particularly expensive. Ceremonial words were a particular bargain for him. Therefore, when he did his swearing in, even if only swearing in a Fifth Circuit Court of Appeals judge (who was, admittedly, a close friend), Johnson dug deep into his pocketbook of words. In contrast to Truman's, Johnson's speech was downright wordy, as were the 857 other ceremonial speeches he gave while serving as the nation's thirty-sixth chief executive:

> My friends:
>
> This is a very happy occasion for Lady Bird and me and all the members of our family.
>
> We are so pleased we could be honored with the presence of Judge Brown this morning, Judge Spears, and Judge Jones, who is a longtime personal friend of Judge Thornberry and a former partner of his.
>
> Homer and Eloise have been with us the last few days while they went through the necessary constitutional requirements of getting confirmed, and we have enjoyed their presence so much.
>
> I don't know of anyone that is missed more from Washington than this wonderful Thornberry family. But I know, too, that the people that they serve in this area of the United States are very happy that they could be here.
>
> We hated to see him leave the legislative halls, but we are glad to see him preside in the temples of justice. Because we know that there is no more courageous person, no better and finer human being, and no man with a greater sense of justice and fairness and feeling of equality for all human beings, wherever they live, whatever their color, or whatever their religion, than Homer Thornberry.
>
> So, it is a peculiar delight for us to come back here to the porch of our little home and ask the Thornberry family, and the Engles, and Thornberry children, to come here to see Homer administered the oath as Circuit Judge of the Fifth Judicial District, in the Fifth Circuit Court, in the presence of his neighbors here, and some of the best friends he has in the world.
>
> I now want to present one of those best friends—Judge Herman Jones.[34]

Mr. Johnson's sentimental tone was, assuredly, his special distinction. It was not a tone that John Kennedy would have countenanced, but the impetus for employing such a style probably can be laid at Kennedy's doorstep, largely because he redefined the presidency as an institution in which public rhetoric—of whatever variety—was to count a great deal more than it had in the past. Under Kennedy, rhetoric became a consistent presidential ally and the president both its nurturer and master. Kennedy would have disavowed Lyndon Johnson's plebian ritualistic instincts, but he could not have denied Mr. Johnson's appropriating the *role* of chief ceremonialist. For a variety of reasons, John Kennedy sensed that presidential talk had not been utilized to its fullest extent in previous presidencies, and he no doubt sensed that the advent of the electronic media would increase Americans' taste for presidential words well said. While his successors could not say words as well as John Kennedy, they could say them as frequently, thus giving the impression that they were governing even if they were only orating. What else, other than the Kennedy Precedent, could explain the leader of the free world sensing that he had something deeply philosophical to say when confronting the football team at the University of Michigan in September of 1976? What else, other than his memory of John Kennedy's triumphant globe-trotting and glamorous White House soirees, could have suggested to Mr. Ford that the business of the people is well served in musky locker rooms?

> The friends I made and the opportunities educationally and the whole atmosphere here was a great factor in the incentive and the drive to do as well as one could. I know that with the great record that you have—and I can say as a Monday morning or grandstand quarterback—I sit up there in the stands and watch on television—and I am very proud of the great record that you have and the way you play football. You play to win, and that's the only way I know to move ahead, whether you are on the gridiron or whether you are in classrooms or whether you are in politics or anything else.
>
> So, good luck, beat Stanford, and you've got nine more ball games before you go to the Rose Bowl.[35]

In academic circles, there is considerable controversy over whether speeches like Mr. Ford's were "required" by certain ongoing, response-demanding social situations or whether rhetoric is essentially "imposed" upon life's fluidity.[36] The "requirement" school of thought would have it that a wartime crisis necessitated FDR's fireside chats, so dire and omnipresent were the exigencies he and his people faced. Proponents of this viewpoint would also indicate that certain traditions built into the office require a president to speak on the Fourth of July, no matter how inconvenient or benumbing that prospect appears to him.

John Kennedy belonged to another school of thought. He saw all political situations (which, for him, were all situations) as being prone to rhetoric. Throughout his presidency, he found ways to provide a new kind of talk on state occasions that had become fossilized or that were ill-defined. He was, in short, rhetorically creative.

Table 1.7 demonstrates just how creative he was and how he and his two immediate successors (the imperial presidents?) invented new persuasive forms. Table 1.7 depicts the presidents' usage of what might be called

Table 1.7   *Presidential Use of "Miscellaneous" Speaking Situations*

President	N Miscellaneous Speeches (1)	Total Speeches Delivered (2)	(1) as % of (2)
Truman	193	1407	13.7
Eisenhower	89	925	9.6
Kennedy	180	771	23.3
Johnson	224	1636	13.7
Nixon	157	1035	15.1
Ford	82	1236	6.6
Carter	98	1322	7.4
Reagan	43	1636	2.6

anomalous speech, messages delivered on subjects lying outside the seven standard topics with which presidents deal (science and agriculture, international conflict, etc.) and on occasions that could not reasonably be called ceremonies, organizational meetings, briefings, or political rallies. These "miscellaneous" speaking situations reward the virtuoso rhetorical performer, the artist who can fashion an assemblage of unknowns into an interpersonal masterpiece. What does one say, for example, when standing at the City Hall in County Cork, Ireland, after being presented with a modest gift? What does one say to the Boys' and Men's Choir of Poznan, Poland, *before* they have sung? What does one say when Pablo Casals comes to dinner at the White House? In each of these cases, John Kennedy found something to say, arguably something masterful to say. His rhetorical gifts were such that he did not shrink from uncertain encounters but in fact sought them out, knowing that speech without precedent is speech that cannot be judged against precedent. In some of these situations, Kennedy probably sounded no more substantive than Jerry Ford and his linebackers. But in a greater number of them, Mr. Kennedy taught while he entertained:

> I also want to welcome those of you who are in the world of music. I think it is most important not that we regard artistic achievement and action as a part of our armor in these difficult days, but rather as an integral part of our free society.
>
> We believe that an artist, in order to be true to himself and his work, must be a free man or woman, and we are anxious to see emphasized the tremendous artistic talents we have available in this country.
>
> I don't think that even our fellow citizens are perhaps as aware as they should be of the hundreds of thousands of devoted musicians, painters, architects, those who work to bring about changes in our cities, whose talents are just as important a part of the United States as any of our perhaps more publicized accomplishments.[37]

Kennedy's success in untraditional settings was such that he increased his use of them throughout his short presidency—twenty-six in 1961, sixty-seven in 1962, and ninety-seven through November 1963. In doing so, Kennedy used rhetoric to punctuate political and social issues normally deprived of a regular presidential forum. Depending upon one's perspective, Kennedy can be seen as either creative or exploitative, but there can be little doubt that he welcomed public discussion on any matter in any situation. Although the 771 speeches he gave as president account for less than 8% of the presidential total, his "miscellaneous" speeches account for 17% of such speeches delivered between 1945 and 1985.[38]

Unlike all other modern presidents, John Kennedy almost never used "smorgasbord" speeches (i.e., those on "multiple topics") when touring the nation; only ten such addresses were found among the 148 he delivered regionally.[39] Kennedy preferred to tailor-make his remarks for the audiences and situations in question, thereby permitting sharper definition of the issues, greater control of the agenda, and, not infrequently, greater audience impact. By fine-tuning his speeches as he did, Mr. Kennedy (with the able assistance of his talented speechwriters) demonstrated an unusual ability to make rhetoric out of nothing. In doing so, he started a trend of viewing speechmaking as a primary, not a secondary, mode of presidential communication and, in addition, of presidential governance. Those who followed him in office would utilize different, more conventional, rhetorical forms, but the lesson he taught would not be lost upon them: when a modern president speaks, about anything, it will be regarded as important and, increasingly, as constitutively appropriate to the office. This was John Kennedy's revolution.

Consequences

Throughout this book, we will consider the many different ways in which Kennedy's legacy has been manifested. We will examine the uses of presidential speechmaking in electoral, ceremonial, and mass media settings and try to understand how public suasion has been bent to particularized political ends. But before doing so, let us consider the general social and political effects of this steady increase in presidential speechmaking. What has come of all of this talk? Are we now better informed by our presidents, better understood, better loved? Is the office of the presidency changing in fundamental ways or are presidents simply doing the same old things more often? Are the trends highlighted in this chapter likely to taper off or to continue unabated? Should any of this worry us?

Despite what it has done for presidents, speechmaking seems not to have heightened a sense of dialogue between the people and their leaders. As figure 1.4 reveals (tangentially, at least), between 1964 and 1978 the Amer-

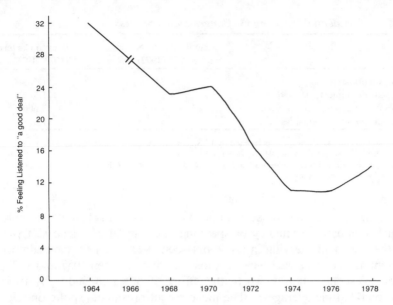

Figure 1.4. American voters' "sense of communication" with government officials across time. National survey responses to the question "Over the years, how much attention do you feel the government pays to what people think when it decides what to do?" Reported in W. E. Miller et al., *American National Election Studies Data Sourcebooks: 1950–1978* (Cambridge, Mass.: Harvard University Press, 1980), p. 261.

ican people felt increasingly ignored—spoken at but not listened to.[40] While public speaking should be an obvious, indeed prime, exemplar of human communication, the voters have felt more and more isolated each year, even though their presidents averaged almost one speech per day during that time period. Lyndon Johnson's White House ceremonies, Richard Nixon's addresses to special interest groups, Jerry Ford's marathon campaigning, Jimmy Carter's town meetings—none of these seem to have reversed people's feelings of being ignored by their elected officials. It is as if the American people were awash in a sea of talk and yet thirsty for recognition. Naturally, feelings of being ignored may be endemic to any citizenry at any time in history, but it is more than a bit ironic that these feelings would peak during an age of excessive presidential communication, an age in which America's chief executives spoke *regionally* once every five days.[41] They were among us, but we seemed not to have felt their presence.

If presidential speechmaking does not serve to buoy people's spirits, to accentuate what a political scientist would call their "senses of political competence," then surely there must be at least instrumental profit in speak-

Table 1.8   *Presidential Speaking vs. Congressional Success**

	Eisenhower to Nixon (1957–1972)	Nixon to Carter (1973–1978)
% victories on domestic bills	.732	.565
Speeches/year on domestic issues†	74.1	121.3
% victories on foreign and defense bills	.736	.600
Speeches/year on international issues	75.6	81.8

*Congressional votes on "key" issues as calculated by L. Sigelman, "A Reassessment of the Two Presidencies Thesis," *Journal of Politics* 41 (1979), pp. 1195–1205.
†Includes all speeches on science, economics, governance, and human services. Excludes all speeches on "multiple" and "other" topics.

ing a great deal. Alas, this too seems not to be the case, as is shown in table 1.8, which compares frequency of speaking and legislative success. Even though the presidents serving in office between 1973 and 1978 gave almost twice as many speeches each year as those serving between 1957 and 1972, their oratory seemed hardly worth the effort, if one may judge by their congressional batting averages.[42] The more recent presidents spoke on television more frequently than their predecessors (24.6 speeches/year vs. 12.8), held more briefings for the press (78.8 vs. 36.4), and lobbied special interest groups more intensively (101.5 vs. 61.1). Still, they could not match the legislative victories of those who preceded them in office. Naturally, it would be reductionistic to judge such presidential speech as failed speech. The differential congressional batting averages revealed in table 1.8 could have been the products of a host of historic, economic, political, or sociopsychological factors. Still, these data do indicate that speechmaking has been no panacea for presidents. It guarantees them neither a sense of closeness with constituents nor political leverage with legislators, but only that more words will be spoken to more audiences about more issues.

Public speaking makes one guarantee, however, and in a modern presidential era it may be the only sort of guarantee a president values. According to a study of the 1980 campaign conducted by the scholar Darrell West, a politician's speech is twice as likely to receive media coverage as any other campaign activity.[43] Comparing candidates' campaign logs with actual reportage in the *New York Times,* West found this effect to hold for the half-dozen or so candidates he studied. For example, even though John Anderson spent only 7.9% of his time in press conferences, the *Times* devoted 23.2% of its coverage to this feature of his campaign. For our purposes, however, an even more revealing finding reported by West is the following: whereas 80.2% of (incumbent) Jimmy Carter's public performances were covered by the press, only 68.9% of Ronald Reagan's activities were reported, while John Anderson's campaign received even less proportional coverage (31.5%). In short, speech talks; presidential speech talks even louder.

One need not be an Oxford don to discern the practical implications of West's findings: if media coverage is the key to an administration's success, and if speaking can insure news coverage, then speaking—of whatever sort, in whatever context—is an inherent, presidential good. This appears to be the modern political logic, a logic now so deeply entrenched in the presidential mind as to be law-like. Even though the speeches of presidents produce comparatively few other verifiable results, the attention—both good and bad— focused upon them by the mass media insures their perpetuation. Presidents have developed a rhetorical reflex, a tendency to resort to public suasion as an initial response to a political situation. Like any true reflex, the use of speechmaking by presidents is now an instinctual reaction rarely given conscious attention. When happy, Jimmy Carter spoke, as when he celebrated the Camp David accords. When angry, Jimmy Carter spoke, as when he went to the Naval Academy to warn the Russians. When hurt, Jimmy Carter spoke, as when he declared his love for (and tacit displeasure with) his brother Billy. When confused, Jimmy Carter spoke, as when he tried to plumb the depths of a national malaise. When tired, Jimmy Carter spoke, as when he gave 105 speeches in October of 1980. Always, he spoke, and the speaking justified its own continuance: if the coverage were favorable, it stood to reason that more speaking would generate even more flattering responses from the media; if the press disparaged him, more speaking would set matters aright. Action-rhetoric-reaction-rhetoric.

Table 1.9 reports highly incidental but nevertheless intriguing findings. Focusing exclusively on the seven weeks following incumbent-election campaigns, table 1.9 shows that for some presidents the rhetorical reflex lasts on and on. Presidents Johnson and Carter (and, to a lesser extent, Ronald Reagan) continued to speak even though the crowds had drifted away. Johnson's behavior makes a certain kind of sense: a continuing president with continuing executive duties, a celebrating president who would no longer have to live in John Kennedy's shadow, an ambitious president who harbored significant legislative plans. Ronald Reagan, too, had a continuing mandate. But

Table 1.9 *Postelection Speaking by Recent Presidents*

President	Year*	N Speeches
Truman	1948	9
Eisenhower	1956	7
Johnson	1964	30
Nixon	1972	5
Ford	1976	8
Carter	1980	24
Reagan	1984	18

*Election day through December 31 only.

while the other successful and unsuccessful incumbents gratefully stepped out of the public spotlight following their contests, Jimmy Carter kept up the torrid pace he had established during four tumultuous years in office.

Surely, the American people would have forgiven Carter had he been perfunctory when signing the Alaska National Interest Lands Conservation Act on December 2, 1980. Surely, they would have understood that he was deservedly tired after a difficult campaign, and they would not have expected him to conduct a full-blown Oval Office ceremony and make a fifteen-minute speech on that occasion. But history books yet to be written have always had a strange fascination for political leaders, and Jimmy Carter knew, as all chief executives know, that historians regard presidential speeches as "primary data." Thus, he spoke on that December 2, sounding not at all unlike a candidate for public office:

> In the decade past we've worked hard to build strong programs to protect the environment and, where there was damage, to clean our skies and waterways. We have made some progress. It has not been easy. Human greed is not an easy foe to conquer. As Governor and as President this has been one of my most difficult political challenges, and throughout my life in the future, it's a challenge that I will continue to meet.
>
> In the past 4 years we've strengthened the Clean Air and Clean Water Acts and the Coastal Zone Management Act. We've established strict Federal environmental standards for coal mining, provided for better control of pesticides and toxic chemicals. We have at least continued our protection of endangered species. Outside of Alaska, we've made vast additions to our National Park System. We've created new wilderness areas and designated new Wild and Scenic Rivers. We cannot afford to retreat from these efforts now. We cannot afford to look at the immediate financial profits and ignore the long-term costs of misusing the environment.[44]

Years of incessant public speaking can cause one to take oneself very seriously indeed. Over the years, the presidents have not only stepped into the public spotlight with increasing frequency but they have also done their own lighting work on many occasions. Figure 1.5 compares the rise in presidential speechmaking to data I have reported previously in *Verbal Style and the Presidency*, a book that examines microscopically the language patterns used by recent presidents.[45]

Clearly, the trend lines representing total speechmaking and use of self-references (I-statements) are remarkably similar. Not only have the recent presidents stood on stage longer than their forebears, they have also focused upon themselves—their viewpoints, their plans, their worries, their exaltations—more and more. Intriguingly, the strength with which they make their remarks (i.e., Certainty) is dramatically lower than that of the earlier presi-

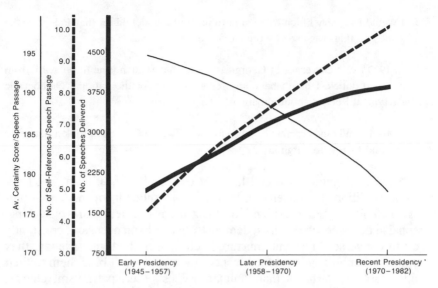

Figure 1.5. Frequency of presidential speechmaking vs. verbal measures of Certainty and Self-Reference. Based on selective sample of speech texts (N = 380) as reported in R. P. Hart, *Verbal Style and the Presidency: A Computer-based Analysis* (New York: Academic Press, 1984).

dents, the more recent chief executives often having substituted their own, partial perspectives on the issues of the day for ideological assurance. Perhaps this is why they now talk *so much*. Old international alliances can no longer be depended upon; party orthodoxies have become increasingly fluid; technological advances have caused military, industrial, and economic priorities to change rapidly and without prior warning. It is as if presidents are now using their (increasingly timid) speechmaking to stave off as best they can the speed and flux of the political world.

Perhaps this is also why their speeches reflect an increasing dependence on the self. The mass media, as well as a presidency-prone citizenry, are highly attracted to a dominant political personality. No doubt encouraged by such outlooks, and no doubt bedeviled by the uncertainties of their age, presidents now speak as if they were sunstreaked film stars being interviewed for *People* magazine. The stars chatter on and on, frequently making no particular sense, rarely taking an irrevocable stand on an important issue, but often appropriating the confessional style of one who talks for a living:

> I've always been proud of the fact that when I first came to Virginia to begin my campaign a couple of years ago and didn't have very many friends, I went to Henry Howell's home, and he and Betty were nice enough to . . .

I would like very much to be able to tell my grandchildren that I slept in the same bed that was used by the Governor of Virginia. . . .

In 1973 I was Governor of Georgia. I didn't have much time to be away from my own duties. I didn't have any responsibility for the national Democratic Party. But I heard about a man. . . .

I was a small businessman . . . as a farmer, I wanted . . . So, I took a Saturday off, and I came to Virginia . . .[46]

This is the sound of friendship, not leadership (or, at least, not leadership as traditionally conceived). It is not at all difficult for modern Americans to think of their presidents as their friends. Friends are easygoing, personal in their speech patterns, demonstrative only on occasion, constantly ready to converse. Presidents nurture such images, and, like friends, they continually demonstrate that they respect the verities that bind them to their friends. Table 1.10 shows that "human values" (i.e., patriotism, charity, beauty, etc.) is a highly popular topic in the speechmaking of presidents; of the seven main presidential topics listed, "human values" is the second most common focus for speeches; this comparative ranking holds for virtually all eight presidents surveyed. Within the various administrations, speeches on economics, international conflict, and other topics waxed and waned depending upon the events of the day, but political preachment (on such matters as human freedom, ethics in government, educational ideals, patriotic responsibilities, etc.) was never judged inappropriate. For presidents like Harry Truman (see figure 1.6), these speeches became increasingly attractive over time, in part because they allowed him to launch his political salvos from higher ground. Once, when presenting Medals of Honor to two soldiers who had served in the Korean conflict, Mr. Truman observed: "Wouldn't it be a

Table 1.10   *General Distribution of Topics in Presidential Speaking*

Topic	N Speeches	% All Speeches
Science	733	7.4
Economics	814	8.2
Governance	1181	11.8
Human services	785	7.9
Human values	1235	12.4
International cooperation	1917	19.2
International conflict	617	6.2
Multiple	2068	20.7
Other	617	6.2

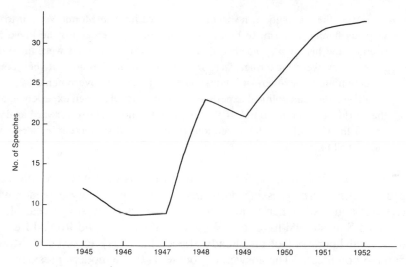

Figure 1.6. Harry Truman's frequency of speaking on human values (1945–1952).

wonderful thing if in our civic affairs we had fighters for the right like these two young men."[47] Medal of Honor ceremonies and the like allow the president to wrap himself in the mantle of the office; since the political winds can blow fiercely at times, that mantle has been used by all American presidents.

To Europeans, this American penchant for brandishing national values is a source of bemusement as well as irritation. They cannot understand why American politicians would spend 10% or more of their time talking about these pieties nor can they understand why there is always an ample supply of listeners for such issuances. Above all, they cannot understand why the *president,* of all people, is required to behave in such ways and why his speeches on these occasions can sometimes be so hackneyed:

> [George] Washington was gifted with the vision of the future. He dreamed America could be a great, prosperous and peaceful nation, stretching from ocean to ocean. He hoped the deliberations at Philadelphia would end with a declaration of our independence. He even designed and presented a drawing of the new American flag to Betsy Ross—13 stripes and a circle of white stars on a field of blue.
>
> When the war was going badly, his courage and leadership turned the tide of history our way. On our first Christmas as a nation in 1776, he led his band of ragged citizen-soldiers across the Delaware River through driving snow to a victory that saved the cause of American independence. Their route of march, it is said, was stained by bloody footprints, but their spirit did not fail. Their will could not be crushed. Washington kept them going . . .

After the Revolution, he wanted to return here to Mount Vernon to be
with his family, to farm, to hunt, to engage in commerce. But he loved his
country and his country needed him. The 13 former Colonies were impover-
ished. They were bickering. They needed a constitution so that they could
become a union of sovereign States joined to a central government.

The American political experiment was new to all human experience, and
the world expected us to fail. If Washington had not stepped forward again—
first at the Constitutional Convention, then as our first elected President, we
might well have failed.[48]

Europeans might argue forcefully that there is no news here, no fresh
approach to modern, pressing problems. They might decry a leader who
wastes his and his listener's time telling a story that any seven-year-old in
the United States could have told. Why, they might ask, did Ronald Reagan
take several hours out of an already speech-filled day to drive to Mount
Vernon to pontificate? The answer, of course, is that a modern president has
become jealous of all political roles *and of a great many social roles as well.*
Today's chief executives speak as frequently as they do because each speech
allows them to add "dimension" to their political selves. They become history teachers at Mount Vernon. They become chiefs of protocol at Dulles
Airport. They become masters of ceremonies at the Super Bowl in Miami.
They become media personalities in the broadcast booth with Dan Rather.
Modern presidents preside, award, debate, interrogate, announce, proclaim,
respond, evade, challenge, reflect, instruct, and celebrate. With each speech
act comes additional duties; with increased duties comes increased responsibility and, often, increased respect and power. Presidents gladly employ
themselves as priests because each new job they take on is paid in political
currency. Political currency, in turn, can be redeemed for legislative intimi-
dation, dominance over the media, stalemating of special interest groups,
and the admiration of the electorate. Americans like a winner. Any president
can seem a winner during a Fourth of July speech.[49]

No matter which category is examined, the rise in presidential speaking
has been nothing short of prodigious. Figure 1.7 compares the two earliest
and two most recent presidencies investigated and focuses on what one
would think of as slow months for speechmaking (December through February and June through August). These months were slow only for Harry
Truman and Dwight Eisenhower. While Ronald Reagan ought to have had
much in common with Dwight Eisenhower—they were both older chief executives, shared party affiliations, presided over economic recoveries, fought
cold wars, etc.—in terms of speaking behavior Mr. Reagan more closely
resembled his younger, Democratic, economically troubled, internationalis-
tic predecessor. By the time he entered office, Ronald Reagan was well

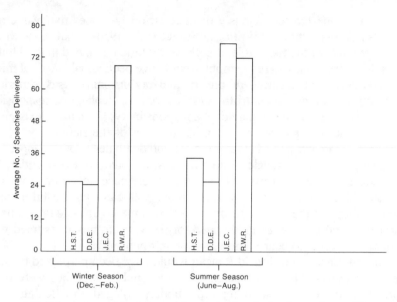

Figure 1.7. Selected presidents' speaking activities during "nonelectoral" seasons of the year.

prepared to cope with the "rhetorical reflex"; indeed, he may well have been chosen for office because he possessed this reflex. During his first four years in office, Reagan came to be known as the Teflon president—no political unpleasantness would stick to him—because of his persuasive ways. Like his most immediate forebears in office, Mr. Reagan understood that the mass media had come to expect a steady, virtually constant din from the White House. He knew that the act of talking had come to be equated with the act of leading (Richard Nixon's fall from grace, after all, was accompanied by a steady decrease in public appearances).[50] And he knew that no month of the year, no world event, no political personality, and no legislative possibility should be allowed to slip by without commentary by him. Mr. Reagan knew that he had comparatively little influence over events, personalities, and legislation but that he did control his time, and this he filled up with rhetoric.

One interpretation of figure 1.7 is that Americans have become, in Jacques Ellul's terms, "politicized." In *The Political Illustion,*[51] Ellul argues that postwar leaders have increasingly substituted talk for action and thereby become removed from the real needs of the real people they govern. Ellul asserts that political talk serves only to distract—leaders from acts of genuine governance, citizens from "full consciousness of the political reality as it actually exists."[52] According to Ellul, a "regime that talks most of some value is a regime that consciously or unconsciously denies that value and prevents it from existing."[53] Writing in France in the 1950s, what sense would Ellul have made of the rising tide of political rhetoric fashioned in the United States thirty years later? He no doubt would have been appalled. Ellul might have observed that a surfeit of presidential performing causes American voters to feel (1) that justice, truth, and freedom are "collective responsibilities" and, hence, no single individual's responsibility; (2) that the existential realities of the moment can be put aside in favor of the richer, mythic endowments of tomorrow; and (3) that the life and death needs of the oppressed are being fulfilled by a gaggle of political abstractions (a New Frontier, the Great Society, Free Enterprise, etc.) and therefore need not be dealt with by ordinary citizens in their localities. The more politicians talk, Ellul implies, the more they lull the voter into thinking that some great end-state is being approached and that there is little need for the voter to be "consumed with the desire to serve, to bear witness, to commit himself."[54]

Jimmy Carter and Ronald Reagan would have been perplexed by such esoteric warnings. They would claim that their public speeches were often informative to the press, soothing to the underprivileged, threatening to the nation's declared enemies. They might further claim that in a democracy politics can only be conducted in a public manner and, in a mediated age, only in a verbal manner. In these and other ways they would be correct; presidents often say both important and intelligent things. But they would be very hard-pressed, it seems to me, to explain why the needs to inform, soothe, and threaten have increased threefold during the last forty years. They would be hard-pressed to document exactly what it was that Jerry Ford found worth saying every six hours in 1976. They would be hard-pressed to explain what new set of political mores justified the many obvious or trite or opaque or foolish things they said in public. They would be pressed beyond recovery to explain why they have willingly contributed to what Jacques Ellul has called "politization." After all, with so much talk in the air, is not a voter now justified in thinking that governance is somehow being "taken care of" by their leaders? Apparently people do feel this way, because each decade's increase in presidential speechmaking has been accompanied by a corresponding (causal?) decrease in voter participation. There have been many more press conferences. Do people feel better informed about their government? There has been an increase in international ceremonies. Do Americans feel greater kinship with their allies? There is now an endless succession of regional political rallies. Are citizens now more trusting of their chief executives? Clearly, these questions cannot be answered in the affirmative. Although he states things in excessive ways, Ellul is not a thinker to be ignored. If government is drifting away from us, we should at least knowingly wave it goodbye, if not reach out for it.

Conclusion

When we listen to a president speak, he has, minimally, the psychological resources of any public speaker. He stands on a platform, above us. He is equipped with sound-amplifying devices; we have none. We sit huddled together, pressed by our fellow auditors; he roams the stage freely. He decides how long he will speak, who shall introduce him, what he will talk about, how he will conclude; we decide only if it is seemly to doze off. He may interrupt himself; we are enjoined to be quiet. Any public speaker has these advantages, but a speaker who is also the president of the United States moves even further above us and beyond us. Public speaking presumes deference on the parts of listeners. A president who speaks in public a great deal is thus tempted constantly by thoughts of kingship. Naturally, these temptations are sometimes squelched: the courtiers in the media may cavil; the peasants in the audience may shout down their monarch. But these are unctuous actions, actions normally censured by other courtiers, other peasants. In speaking as much as he does in so many different settings, a modern president constantly presumes upon us, soliciting our minds, our hearts, and, with double-digit inflation, our sacred fortunes. In a democracy we may resist these appeals, and we sometimes do. But there are always more speeches, more settings, more (and more complicated) issues than citizens can conveniently track. And so they often do what many listeners do: they defer.

It is this deference that worries Ellul, as it should concern any citizen living in a politicized nation. In this book we will examine the specific uses to which political speech is put by modern presidents. We will see how speech spoken by a president is sometimes treated as its own accomplishment. We will see how presidential speech can be made to have a benighting function, how it sometimes becomes a bauble over which pressure groups vie. We will study the intriguing relationships between presidential speech and the nation's mass media, asking ourselves who controls these relationships and what difference the answer should make to us. We shall examine the modern political campaign as an unusually perverse gauntlet from which even the victor staggers. Finally, we will ask what it means to say that the American presidency has become a "rhetorical presidency," specifically, what it should mean to those bothered by the political deference Ellul described. We can, if we choose, ignore Ellul. We can treat political communication as a harmless affectation having no impact upon us. We can regard the steady rise in presidential speech during the last four decades as signaling nothing more than changing fashion—from cream sodas to hula hoops to Rubik's cubes. Ellul would advise us otherwise. He finds it wise to study politics precisely because politics so often falls so short of its possibilities, and he finds it useful to examine communication because it frequently conceals more than it says.

Ellul's apocalypse thus has both political and rhetorical markings, and his voice should haunt us, at least for a time:

> If indeed we seek a place to make our fine feeling and our humanism count, let us not participate in politics: it is no longer capable of absorbing human warmth.
>
> If we do commit a political act or commit ourselves to a political enterprise we must first very seriously examine its actual effects and consequences, devoid of any illusory vocabulary: the insertion of values into the discussion of political acts is never more than just words. Liberty, justice, the right of peoples to self-determination, the dignity of the human person—these are no longer anything but pale justification for social conformity. I do not say that justice or truth do not exist. I only say that in the realm of political autonomy when these values are invoked today they are reduced to pure sound, they have no access to political decision-making, and no chance of being applied in practice (I see *no* chance, not just a reduced chance). Once invoked, they only serve to support an already existing political design. They become part of the propaganda apparatus, and often they are also used because political men like to delude themselves and give benediction to their action by attributing values to them.[55]

TWO

Speech and Action:
Building the
Presidential Image

W HEN HE MADE HIS FAMED CAMPAIGN TOUR (ACTUALLY, A SERIES OF campaign tours) in 1948, Harry Truman did more than just speak a great deal. The tour itself—the very fact of his making the tour—became newsworthy. No president had attempted such a feat in prior campaigns; no president had cut such a wide swath across the length and breadth of the United States; no president had spoken on so many different topics to so many different kinds of people, nor had an incumbent president done so with the fire and candor of a Harry S Truman. The individual speeches hardly constituted grand oratory. For example, the rear platform remarks he made on September 27, 1948, in Austin, Texas, would now be described by even the most ardent of Truman's admirers as tiresome, predictable political rhetoric. A public speaker is supposed to inspire during his introduction, and Truman was indeed inspired: "It's an inspiration to be in this city, which is named after a couple of pioneers from the great state of Missouri." A public speaker is enjoined to adapt appeals to the wants and desires of the audience, and Truman indeed adapted: "I know how Texas can fight for democratic ideals, and so I can understand why the Germans and the Japs in this World War II just past thought all the soldiers in the Army came from Texas." When concluding, a public speaker is advised to leave the audience with a pithy reminder of how they should behave, and Truman was, characteristically, pithy: "I have only one request to make of you—and I don't think I have to make that request in this district of Texas. I want you, on election day, to get up as early as you did this morning and go to the polls and vote a straight Democratic ticket.[1]

Mr. Truman's remarks in Austin were made at 7:35 A.M. and lasted approximately ten minutes. The *New York Times* of the next day devoted less than three column inches to the speech (and that on page 20); 90% of its coverage consisted of direct quotations from Truman's text.[2] The stories in the *Austin American* were markedly different. It carried extensive previews of the great event; it presented a self-consciously inflated editorial ("As President, he [Truman] is the supreme symbol of the government in a democracy"); and after the speech the local paper detailed every specific event contributing to this ten-minute happening.[3] Unlike the *Austin American,* the *New York Times* did not report that Austin schools would delay opening on that Monday morning or that the Pi Beta Phi sorority would present the president's daughter with a book. The *New York Times* missed the fact that Allan Junior High students—Patsy Hill, Ruth Fowler, and Carolyn Kirkland—would present a school pennant to the chief executive. The *New York Times* completely omitted the roles played by Fred Catterall (editor of the *Austin High Maroon*), Mrs. Edward Clark (chairman of the women's division of the reception committee), or Thomas E. Berry (captain of the National Guard). And the *New York Times* failed to report how Mr. Truman wore his Austin-presented ten-gallon hat throughout his speech; how he cheerily introduced "the Boss" and Miss Margaret; how the president asked, "Where's Beauford Junior?" (the governor's son); how Sam Rayburn, Lyndon Johnson, Tom Clark, and a host of lesser dignitaries almost crowded the president off the train's platform; or how traffic had to be blocked off on Congress Avenue between Second and Fourth Streets. Provincials that they were, the reporters of the *Times* no doubt found all of these details trivial, unrelated to the substantial business of electoral politics. They would claim that Truman had made no national news in Austin, that his speech was essentially the same one he would give a half-dozen more times that day, and that Austinites' reaction to his message were predictable and hence unreportable.

The reporters for the *New York Times,* however, would be wrong about one thing. *Voters do not react to messages; they react to messaging.* A public speech, because it is human and oral, can never be reduced to the *New York Times'* black marks on the *New York Times'* white pages.[4] A speech is a direct, personal exchange between living, breathing persons, persons like Patsy Hill, Mrs. Edward Clark, and Captain Thomas E. Berry. For them, the event of September 27, 1948, deserved far more than the three column inches the out-of-towners had given it. After all, they were *there.* They *heard* the speech. They *felt* the press of the little crowd assembled. They, or at least some of them, *saw* the president fumble with his new hat. For them, this presidential event began before it began and ended long after it ended. Patsy Hill had to pick out a new dress; Mrs. Clark had to search for the right sort of Texas history book for the president; Captain Berry had to rehearse his color guard until they performed flawlessly. Even after Mr. Truman had rolled down his railroad track on his trip to Waco, his speech had not really ended, for Patsy Hill still had the job of recasting the event for her seventh-grade classmates. Because speech joins people in "live" encounters, the

Truman address did not conclude until Patsy and her fellow Austinites stopped making it part of their interpersonal lives (a month, perhaps) or part of their memories (a lifetime, perhaps).

In Chapter One, we examined the tremendous quantitative jump in presidential speaking witnessed in this century. These numbers have been impressive, but it is all too easy to forget that each represents a speech *activity* (like that in Austin), an event with the human qualities sketched above. When anyone speaks, but especially when a president of the United States speaks, that speech is both message and event. When Harry Truman toured the country, his messages did not change substantially from town to town; but as each town donated momentum to the next town's event, the town itself began to make news and to generate in the public's mind a message about the messages. Truman not only decried the Republican Congress but he *decried* them. The very fact of his whistle-stopping became a decrying, and while he rarely said anything new his repeated sayings emboldened him and his listeners.

In *How to Do Things with Words,* philosopher J. L. Austin describes the nature of "speech acts," speaking events that *do* as well as say.[5] For Professor Austin and others, there are "performative" aspects to certain speech events which give them special status as accomplished human actions. When one says "I do" in the right circumstances, for instance, one communicates certain important sentiments, but, equally, one becomes married. Broadening Austin's conception a bit, we can view all speeches as having performative aspects, especially if they are the speeches of the most powerful person in the land. When a president speaks, doing is almost always being done. By giving an inaugural address, a president makes himself president. By presenting a State of the Union message, a president creates a legislative agenda. By describing activities in the Bay of Pigs, a president causes half an air force to run to its battle stations. And by speaking in Austin, Texas, a president gives that spot on the railroad line special status (greater than Uvalde's, greater than Bay City's) but, most important, becomes for his immediate listeners a flesh-and-blood creature (literally, "one of them") who by coming to their town acts in their behalf. It has been said that it is virtually impossible for an ordinary citizen (as opposed to an activist) to vote against a candidate whom he or she has talked to in person. Even a Republican city council member's Democratic neighbor is likely to split a ticket, since speech acts across the back fence cannot be dismissed as easily as the more abstractly communicated "messages" presented by the mass media or by campaign circulars. As we saw in Chapter One, presidents have increasingly operated on this premise during the last forty years.

In this chapter, we shall examine some of the duties performed by presidential talk, thereby examining the qualitative or "feeling" side of the speech act. We shall try to understand the implicit messages issued during

presidential speechmaking, messages bearing on leadership, political relationships, and power blocs in society. Because they are based in rhetoric,
these messages will not always be obvious. Subtle though they may be, Patsy
Hill knows they are indeed there, for every bit of her Patsy Hillness sensed
them when she gave Harry Truman her pennant.

The Politics of Leadership

When traveling among the Maori people of New Zealand, anthropologist
Anne Salmond discovered the interesting fact that the modern god of the
speaking ground is Tuu-te-isiihi, the god of war in the traditional cosmology.
Salmond also reports that modern Maori have established highly formalized
conventions for their political speaking, rules left over from the days when
all strangers were considered potential enemies and when "oratory was used
as a mechanism for managing encounters [with strangers] in peace."[6] For
modern Americans, political rhetoric is also a kind of war, and they too have
developed conventions useful for determining who is brave and who is not
brave. The primary convention established seems to be this: a given act of
speaking may not constitute an act of leading, but no act of leading can be
accomplished without an act of speaking. Politicians might deny this, but
their behavior suggests otherwise. And this is to say more than, as we have
said in Chapter One, that rhetoric has become governance. It is to say that
rhetoric may now be the primary means of personal assertion, the primary
means of *performing the act* of presidential leadership.

The great advantage of this political convention is that even if leaders
know not which direction to take, they can still speak in public, thereby
certifying an ability to at least search for leadership. With each speech act,
these certifications mount up, and, with enough of them, it quickly becomes
unclear which speech act leads and which only makes pretensions to leadership. The press presumes to help sort out the acts of genuine and feigned
leadership, but the press is also caught up in images of rhetoric and war and
political power. During the 1984 Democratic convention, for example, the
television cameras insistently sought out the faces of delegates being emotionally transported by the oratory they heard. For the home viewer, black
men grimaced when Jesse Jackson told them to, white women wept when
Geraldine Ferraro recounted her rise to power, and white men glowered when
Mario Cuomo described Ronald Reagan's policies of privilege. Almost never
were the cameras turned on the indifferent or the skeptical, as if the networks
were telling their viewers: "Pay attention. This is what leadership looks like."
Appropriately, the networks returned the compliment to the Republicans four
weeks later in Dallas, thereby redocumenting the notion that speechmaking
is bravery. Tuu-te-isiihi would have smiled.

The popularity of equating speech with leadership is evidenced by the quantitative information presented in Chapter One but also by numerous cases in which presidents have intentionally set up speech events rather than allowing such events to be imposed upon them by either exigence or tradition. Knowing that a sitting president has an enormous advantage over even hostile auditors, recent chief executives have sought the political monsters in their own lairs. George McGovern bravely addressed the Veterans of Foreign Wars to explain his antiwar stand in 1972. Ronald Reagan jumped at the chance to speak to the NAACP early in his administration. And Jimmy Carter ventured to Boston in October of 1979—right into the teeth of his Democratic nemesis, Teddy Kennedy—when he spoke at the dedication of the JFK Library at Columbia Point.

The actual words Mr. Carter spoke that day were in no sense war-like. Indeed, that was his very point: to demonstrate that he could venture into his enemy's encampment without the implements of battle, armed only with speech of the politest sort. He gave a perfunctory address, made no attempt to upstage his hosts, and yet by his presence certified that he was in charge. In reporting the event, *Newsweek* dutifully carried on the martial metaphor, noting that Carter and Kennedy were moving "to the brink of open combat for the presidency" after their "test match" in Florida. *Newsweek* noted that Mr. Carter had come to "fight for his survival" during his "encroaching war of succession with Kennedy." *Newsweek* also marveled at Carter's boldness in giving a speech to "men and women who had followed the colors" of Teddy Kennedy's late brothers and concluded that the president had acquitted himself well during "the truce of Columbia Point."[7] It would be difficult to determine who was led where and for what reason on that day in Boston, but there can be little doubt that Jimmy Carter's speech act was designed both to signal *and to constitute* leadership. Clearly, the press obliged him in this matter.

Speech is indeed a diary for a president, his way of recording for posterity the decisions he has made. It is also a means of documenting that he is a decision maker. American voters have been led to believe that if a president can speak in public he can lead in private *and* that he is unable to do the latter unless he can do the former. It was forty-seven days between Dwight Eisenhower's heart attack of September 25, 1955, and his next set of public speeches—one at Lowry Air Force Base in Denver and the other at Washington National Airport. As far as his health was concerned, Eisenhower could have left his Denver hospital earlier, but that would have meant being carried out of the hospital on a stretcher and, worse, being denied the opportunity of making a speech to display his fitness for office. Upon arriving in Washington after his hospital stay, Ike said: "To each of you who have come down [here], of course, we would like to thank you personally and thank you for the honor you have done us. That is impossible, and so, possibly in just saying thank you, we are grateful, you will understand what we would like to do and you will let the wish take the place of the deed."[8] Embedded within Mr. Eisenhower's wandering syntax is a fundamental misrepresentation of his speech act, for it was the rhetorical *deed* itself that reestablished his presidency in the minds of a concerned public.

By the time Lyndon Johnson had his gall bladder attack, the ante had been upped considerably, in part because of the torrid communicative pace Johnson had established for himself. He gave four speeches on the day before his surgery, and, eleven days later, he signed the Clean Air Act Amendments and the Solid Waste Disposal Bill in his hospital room. Naturally, because it was Lyndon Johnson who signed the legislation, a Lyndon Johnson speech had to be given as well. The next day, the day of his release from the hospital, Johnson spoke again, this time to his fellow patients at Bethesda Naval Hospital. His speech was vintage Johnson, filled with rugged derring-do, both its content and the fact of its delivery establishing that LBJ was coming back and coming back with vigor:

> But I know some of you must think that you got a bad break. And you have. But because of what you have done there are 3 billion people in the world that will get a better break, and their kids will live better, be happier, stronger, better educated, and eat more food, and have more freedom and more liberty.
>
> I just can't sum up in any words of mine how proud I am of the Marines, the Navy, the Army, the Air Force, and the Coast Guard, and the fellows that never look back. And when I feel pretty blue at night, and I issue the orders that you carry out, I do it with a heavy heart. But I never see one of your performances that I am not proud of you, and I wanted to come and tell you that before I checked out.
>
> Good luck to you. Tell all your families—your wives, your children, your mothers, and your fathers—that the President of your country is mighty proud of you.[9]

Gall bladder surgery is one thing, being shot is another. Then again, Lyndon Johnson was one thing, Ronald Reagan another. The assassination attempt on Mr. Reagan provided dramatic evidence of how central rhetorical dexterity can be to impressions of leadership: (1) the jokes he cracked to hospital personnel ("I forgot to duck") were cracked *before* his surgery; (2) a speech he had previously taped was presented the day after the assassination attempt during the (nationally televised) Academy Awards Ceremonies; (3) less than a month after John Hinckley fired at the president, Ronald Reagan spoke by telephone to the annual dinner of the White House Correspondents Association (a most appropriate group for convincing the American perople that Mr. Reagan still retained his prowess). Of special importance is that in this latter speech Mr. Reagan proved that he still possessed the sword of his special kingdom—his wit—the modern emblem of power in a savvy, subtle, sensual television era:

> *Mr. Pierpoint:* Mr. President, this is Bob Pierpoint at the Podium.
>
> *The President:* Bob, I hope you don't mind, but David Stockman is making me call collect. [Laughter]
>
> *Mr. Pierpoint:* Well, I do mind, Mr. President, but he's a hard man to talk out of it, so we'll take the call.
>
> *The President* **[laughing]:** Okay. Well, I'm happy to be speaking to the White House correspondents' spring prom. [Laughter] I'm sorry that I can't be there in person.
>
> *Mr. Pierpoint:* We're very sorry you can't also Mr. President.
>
> *The President:* Well, I'm up at Camp David. We're getting a little used to it now, but I have to tell you the first time I came to this place, to Camp David, Ed Meese sewed nametags in all my undershorts and T-shirts. [Laughter].
>
> But, Bob, I'm sure your fellow correspondents have already praised you or will soon do so for your year in office. Mark Twain is supposed to have said "there's nothing harder to put up with than the annoyance of a good example," and you certainly have been that to the White House press corps.
>
> *Mr. Pierpoint:* Thank you, Mr. President.
>
> *The President:* I know that Cliff Evans must be there somewhere.
>
> *Mr. Pierpoint:* Yes.
>
> *The President:* And, Cliff, let me send my congratulations to you as one new president to another. If you enjoy your office as much as I do mine, you'll be a very happy and fulfilled man.
>
> *Mr. Evans:* Well, you stay well, Mr. President, and we'll take care of the pressroom, Pierpoint and I and all of my colleagues. Stay well.
>
> *The President:* Okay. If I could give you just one little bit of advice, when somebody tells you to get in a car quick, do it. [Laughter].
>
> *Mr. Pierpoint:* Mr. President, we know now that you are really recovering. You sound terrific.[10]

Bob Pierpoint's closing comments are indicative indeed, for in the 1980s we do not need the head of surgery to tell us that a president is fit to lead; we only need the appropriate certification of media medicine men. Surely there is an ancient counterpart to this testing by rhetorical fire, wary poking followed by more strenuous physical assault, to see if the recovering warrior is still able to lead the tribe. As in ancient times, young braves continue to wait anxiously, ready to grasp the medallion of leadership should their chief fall (one is reminded of Alexander Haig's opportunism immediately after the attack on Reagan), so the first communicative act after The Challenge must be sage, deft, effortless. In a rhetorical age, a president can no longer take the risk Dwight Eisenhower took on January 8, 1956, when he subjected himself to a press conference focused on his health. Note his tentativeness: "First of all, the doctor tells me that what he calls my vital capacity is very much improved. I don't know the meaning of the term, and so there's no use asking me about it. But I feel very much better—stronger—and much more able to get about."[11] Sixteen pointed questions followed Ike's statement, all of which concentrated on his capacity to govern during a second term. It is noteworthy that Ronald Reagan took no such chances with the press—he raised the questions before they could raise them and thereby provided the answers as well. Today, when the going gets tough, the tough get talkative.

The traditionally masculine motifs invoked above (boldness, unconcerned with detail) tell only part of the story of presidential leadership, however. There is a maternal side to the presidency, too; modern presidents must nurture as well as establish their dominance. Indeed, the sharp increase in public speaking observed since 1945 is largely accounted for by major expansions in the ceremonial role of the president.[12] Throughout this chapter, we will observe how accustomed chief executives have become to the spotlight of political ritual. To stand in this spotlight is to risk comparatively little, for in such situations listeners' defenses are down, the press is prohibited by cultural mandate from being excessively cynical, and the institution of the presidency—its traditions and its emotional trappings—insulate the chief executive from attack by partisans. As we see in table 2.1, each of the presidents has had his favorite type of ceremony, but beginning with John Kennedy none has lacked the political acuity to use ritual and to use it often.

Presidents Ford through Reagan, the most recent presidents, have used the four types of ceremony with roughly equal frequency (Reagan tending a bit toward the celebratory) perhaps indicating that certain patterns have now become standard in the presidency, patterns suggested earlier in John Kennedy's administration. For Harry Truman, however, ritual was largely confined to the honorific and the celebratory—the clear, direct enunciation of basic American values. Richard Nixon, in contrast, rested his claim to leadership on his strengths in the foreign policy arena, and his days in the White House often ended in festive evenings honoring a visiting dignitary. Taking his cue from John Kennedy, Nixon averaged more than two welcoming rituals a month, demonstrating his ability to meet and greet the world's leaders. These ceremonies photographed particularly well since they featured both the familiar (the president) and the exotic (the president's visitor). They televised well also, with Mr. Nixon's international toasts providing cheery footage for the nightly newscasts. Nixon's natural stiffness became an enormous asset in such circumstances, allowing him to strike just the right balance

Table 2.1 *Presidential Usage of Ceremonial Types (1945–1985)*

President	Total Ceremonies		Initiating*		Honorific		Celebratory		Greeting	
	N	Monthly Average	N	%	N	%	N	%	N	%
Truman	227	2.44	45	19.8	53	23.3	112	49.3	17	7.5
Eisenhower	322	3.35	25	7.8	110	34.1	88	27.3	99	30.7
Kennedy	362	10.34	102	28.2	111	30.7	62	17.1	87	24.0
Johnson	890	14.59	290	32.6	301	33.8	169	19.0	130	14.6
Nixon	511	7.51	88	17.2	184	36.0	93	18.2	146	28.6
Ford	440	15.20	125	28.4	140	31.8	116	26.4	59	13.4
Carter	515	10.73	152	29.5	136	26.4	113	21.9	114	22.1
Reagan	471	7.85	107	22.7	91	21.8	186	39.4	87	18.5
Totals (average)	3738	(8.62)	934	(25.0)	1126	(30.1)	939	(25.1)	739	(19.8)

*See Appendix for appropriate definitions of categories used here.

Table 2.2   *Eisenhower vs. Johnson Legislative and Rhetorical Initiatives*

President	Bills Initiated (Yearly Average)	Initiating Ceremonies Held (Yearly Average)
Eisenhower	216.4	3.1
Johnson	380.4	56.8
Ratio (E/J)	1/1.8	1/18.3

between the cordial and the cautious. These rituals presented Richard Nixon at his best, and he managed them expertly, enhancing his own power by associating himself with powerful people.

As mentioned in Chapter One, Lyndon Johnson loved ceremony also, although his specialties were the "initiating" rituals which accompanied his signing of (typically domestic) legislation. LBJ conducted 290 such ceremonies in his little more than five years in office, approximately one ceremony for every six bills passed into law during his administration. No president exceeded Johnson's yearly average for such ceremonies (56/year), although Jerry Ford came close (52) and John Kennedy and Jimmy Carter (35 and 38, respectively) also understood the attractions of this brand of ritual. But it was Lyndon Johnson more than any of them who believed that even enacted legislation was never its own sufficient statement. And so he spoke—often.

Table 2.2 shows just how often. It compares the Eisenhower and Johnson administrations in terms of legislation and rhetoric initiated. The differences are stark, with Johnson holding a two-to-one edge in legislation proposed but an eighteen-to-one lead in the number of initiating ceremonies held. A slight portion of this difference could be explained by Johnson's 83% success rate in Congress (compared to Eisenhower's 70% average).[13] The real difference between them, however, lay not in the arena of power politics but in that of power rhetoric. Ike's philosophy of governance simply did not prize speechmaking the way Johnson's did. Moreover, it would have been difficult for Eisenhower to understand how chief executives could find relaxation in rhetoric, never mind intense pleasure in it. Lyndon Johnson figured things differently. He figured (1) that legislation did not speak for itself and that legalistic language needed to be translated for the people; (2) that no matter who authored a bill and no matter who pushed it through congressional committees, it was the speechmaker who would receive credit for the legislation being heralded; (3) that celebrations were useful politically because they helped to heal legislative wounds and exalt the art of compromise; and (4) that a new piece of legislation had to be "performed" for the mass media so as to give that piece of legislation a fair chance of being successful.

Throughout his administration, Johnson conducted such rituals both in the Oval Office and "on location." Mr. Johnson well understood the rhetoric of geography, as when he traveled to Liberty Island, New York, to sign the Immigration Bill in October of 1965, taking the time while there to lionize "men like Fernandez and Zjac and Zelinko and Mariano and McCormick" who were serving the cause of liberty in Vietnam.[14] Johnson traveled to Independence, Missouri, to sign the Medicare Bill in July of 1965 where, with Harry Truman at his side, he called off what he termed an "honor roll" of those in the Congress (fifteen in all) who had helped to pass the bill.[15] Listings such as these make for long speeches, but Johnson felt that rhetoric was like love—the more of it the better. And so he took his rhetoric to Southwest Texas State College in November of that same year and signed the Higher Education Act. In his long, rambling speech, he spoke of all the things he loved—his alma mater, hard work, "our own great Lone Star State of Texas," the Bible ("Ye shall know the truth and the truth shall make you free"), his former job selling "real silk socks," Thomas Jefferson, his grade school teaching in Cotulla, and Drs. W. T. Donaho and C. E. Evans (his mentors).[16]

There is little doubt that such ceremonies showed Lyndon Johnson at his best, for they centered on clear, empirical accomplishment, a perfect setting for a clear, empirical man. Press conferences made him stiff; televised addresses caused him to be pontifical, didactic, or both;[17] in international ceremonies he risked being untoward. But legislation was action, the best sort of action—accomplished action. And Lyndon Johnson liked action. That is why he spoke so often.

Throughout this book, we will observe how often and in how many different ways mass communication has affected presidential behavior. The electronic media, especially, have fascinated presidents, with the chief executives using them more often and more creatively each year. Table 2.3 shows one such use. The four most recent presidents have doubled, if not tripled, the number of speeches delivered on radio and television by their predecessors. (Ronald Reagan's totals are unnaturally inflated here because of his use of almost-weekly, radio-only homilies on a myriad of topics.) In

Table 2.3   *Presidential Use of National Addresses (1945–1985)*

President	N National Addresses/Year
Truman	11.3
Eisenhower	9.6
Kennedy	13.3
Johnson	12.9
Nixon	19.8
Ford	22.5
Carter	23.0
Reagan	52.8

part, this upsurge in mass media speaking may reflect the pattern of any innovation: if it exists, it will be used. But television is a special innovation and presidents its special clients. Television, after all, encourages the dramatic. Thus, presidents seek media exposure at every opportunity, using radio to familiarize themselves with the American people and television to impress them. This is not to suggest that the mass media remain inert, waiting to be exploited by presidents. Their representatives follow the president doggedly, hoping to snare him during an encounter requiring spontaneity of him. Largely, however, they wait in vain.

It should be remembered that *all* of the presidents listed in table 2.3 had large radio audiences available to them, and most of them had approximately equal access to television viewers as well. Thus, the changes seen in table 2.3 are not technologically based as much as they are based in an ever-increasing need to *display leadership*. For presidents, the attractive thing about television and radio is that they showcase symbolic action. These "actions" might include signing documents, visiting foreign capitals, scolding the opposition party, taking on the press, or going over the heads of the Congress to the people. In each case, television and human speech are conjoined, with the former extending the capacity of the latter.

Theoretically, the unattractive aspect of this marriage (for presidents) would be that speech, when encased in an electronic medium, will lose its ephemeral quality—the capacity of its user to "take back" what has been said. Oddly, however, this seems not to have been a major problem for presidents. Only rarely does one find the networks reaching into its files to contrast today's remarks to those of a year ago. During the Watergate affair, for example, viewers were never reshown Richard Nixon's Communist baiting or his "Checkers" speech or his ungracious concession to Pat Brown in 1962, even though such replays might have helped viewers contextualize Mr. Nixon's Watergate pleadings. Because they are so captivated by the new (they call it "news"), representatives of the mass media have a startlingly short memory. Thus, the more presidents speak via the media, the *less* likely it will be that any one set of their remarks will come back to haunt them and the *greater* will be their ability to direct the public's attention to the action of the moment.

The logic of media usage seems to be this: (1) mediated speech propagates itself, (2) presidential "action" has increasingly become metaphysical action, (3) the perceived difference between leadership and displays of leadership has been narrowed by radio and television; (4) the increased availability of the media has been a boon to presidents because it gives them access to the minds and hearts of the American people; and (5) presidents are a boon to the mass media because politics offers a dependable fund of stories having larger-than-life qualities. What all of this mediated talk has done for the American *people,* of course, is manifestly unclear.

Another way of examining how central rhetoric has become to national leadership is to examine what presidents talked about between 1945 and 1982. Figures 2.1 and 2.2 contrast the total amount of speaking on four general topics to the proportional emphasis given them by the various chief executives. (See the Appendix for details on topical categories.) Some of these differences will be examined in greater detail in later chapters, but some are worth mentioning now. For example, clearly depicted in figure 2.1 is the New Frontier–Great Society emphases of John Kennedy and Lyndon Johnson. Johnson's greatest stress (both absolutely and proportionally) was on the humanistic (i.e., social services, education, values, etc.). The steady diminution in this area after Johnson's presidency (and the steady rise in such "systemic" topics as science, governance, and the economy) makes his rhetorical profile all the more unique. Although Jerry Ford resurrected these themes during the Bicentennial, the sizable gap between his modest *relative* emphasis on such matters and the actual *number* of speeches he gave suggested that he hardly shared LBJ's emotional commitment to such topics. Even fellow Democrat Jimmy Carter emphasized the technocratic, a trend that hints at the changed constituencies or confused priorities of the Democrats in the post-Johnson years. Indeed, even Richard Nixon outdistanced Jimmy Carter's proportional emphasis on human services and values.[18] The times have indeed changed.

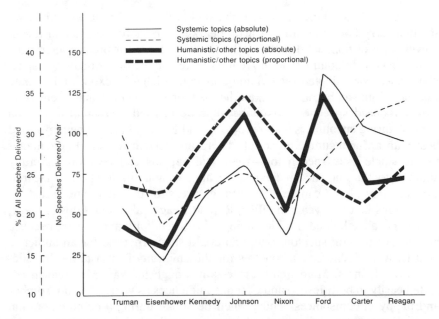

Figure 2.1. Absolute vs. proportional use of speech topics in presidential address: I.

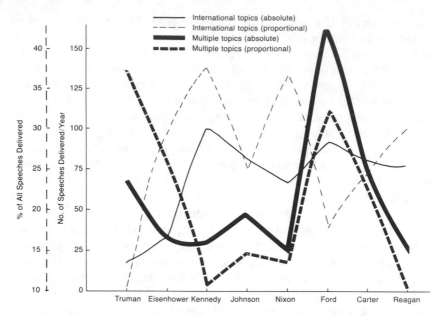

Figure 2.2. Absolute vs. proportional use of speech topics in presidential address: II.

Several important trends are revealed in figure 2.2. For one thing, we see that Jerry Ford and Jimmy Carter hearkened back to the Truman-Eisenhower style of political discourse—the multiple-topic (or press conference–style) speech. In contrast, John Kennedy's technique of spotlighting particular issues was adopted by Lyndon Johnson, Richard Nixon, and Ronald Reagan—Johnson because he liked the ideational and emotional intensity of tightly focused speeches, Nixon because he refused to relinquish agenda control during encounters with reporters, and Reagan because he performed best with an unencumbered script. There are certain technical advantages to the single-issue speech too—rhetorical appeals can be more carefully adapted to the audience receiving the appeal, and, in addition, a clearer, cleaner "news bite" can be offered to the press for the nightly newscast.

In his first two years in office, Ronald Reagan also noted this strategy, in part because he had trouble coping with serendipity and in part because he was such a craftsperson, one who could shape rhetoric for an audience as if he were fashioning silhouettes for the children of tourists on the sidewalks of Hyannis. Mainstream Protestant though he was, Mr. Reagan adjusted easily to both Jewish and Catholic audiences as well as to both somber and happy circumstances. Thus, when he spoke during a commemoration for victims of the Holocaust and when he spoke two weeks later during commencement exercises at Notre Dame, Reagan neatly blended personal reflections with the standard themes expected on such occasions:

> And I remember April '45. I remember seeing the first film that came in when the war was still on, but our troops had come upon the first camps and had entered those camps. And you saw, unretouched—no way that it could have ever been rehearsed—what they saw, the horror they saw. I felt the pride when, in one of those camps, there was a nearby town, and the people were ordered to come and look at what had been going on, and to see them. And the reaction of horror on their faces was the greatest proof that they had not been conscious of what was happening so near to them.
>
> And that film still, I know must exist in the military, and there it is, living motion pictures, for anyone to see, and I won't go into the horrible scenes that we saw. But it remains with me as confirmation of our right to rekindle these memories, because we need always to guard against that kind of tyranny and inhumanity. Our spirit is strengthened by remembering, and our hope is in our strength.[19]
>
> Now, if I don't watch out, this may turn out to be less of a commencement than a warm bath in nostalgic memories. Growing up in Illinois, I was influenced by a sports legend so national in scope, it was almost mystical. It is difficult to explain to anyone who didn't live in those times. The legend was based on a combination of three elements: a game, football; a university, Notre Dame; and a man, Knute Rockne. There has been nothing like it before or since . . . Having come from the world of sports I'd [once] been trying to write a story about Knute Rockne. I must confess that I had someone in mind to play the Gipper. On one of my sports broadcasts before going to Hollywood, I had told the story of his career and tragic death. I didn't have very many words on paper when I learned that the studio that employed me was already preparing a story treatment for that film. And that brings me to the theme of my remarks.[20]

It is interesting to note that in neither excerpt was Mr. Reagan sharing *actual experiences* he had had with the victims of the death camps or with Knute Rockne. (In both cases, he was responding to films he had seen.) Rather, his dexterity lay in his ability to share feelings and events separated by one or two removes from his own reality and to use them to manage the rhetorical situations he had entered.

Figure 2.2 also shows that, since the Kennedy administration, presidents have spoken regularly in international contexts, averaging roughly ninety foreign policy speeches per year since that time. Comparatively, Kennedy and Nixon were most attracted to international forums, but no president (not even Lyndon Johnson) could forego virtually constant discussion of these matters. Naturally, presidents have always been concerned with foreign policy, but, as figure 2.2 shows, it is now required, or politically profitable, or both, to *speak* about such matters. These findings will hardly surprise adult Americans, for beginning with John Kennedy their eyes and ears have been filled with the sights and sounds of Quemoy and Matsu, Cuba, Vietnam, Cambodia, Afghanistan, Iran, Grenada, and Nicaragua.

Although he was not required to be one, Dwight Eisenhower was also an internationalist at heart. Proportionally, he devoted much attention to foreign affairs even though (as the gap in figure 2.2 reveals) he spoke about such matters only modestly often in comparison to his successors. Today, Americans are accustomed to having their head of state jet off to some distant place at a moment's notice, but in the 1950s they knew little of a rhetorical presidency (save what they learned from Franklin Roosevelt) and were only beginning to learn about an international presidency. Thus, when Eisenhower addressed the nation prior to leaving on his first foreign visit, he was avowedly apologetic. There is an almost antique ring to his words. He spoke as if it were inconceivable that his successors would be able to expend much greater international effort without censure (indeed, *with approbation* in most cases). In July of 1955, Mr. Eisenhower was conducting a true rhetorical experiment:

> Good evening friends:
>
> Within a matter of minutes I shall leave the United States on a trip that in some respects is unprecedented for a President of the United States. Other Presidents have left the continental limits of our country for the purpose of discharging their duties as Commander in Chief in time of war, or to participate in conference at the end of a war to provide for the measures that would bring about a peace. But now, for the first time, a President goes to engage in a conference with the heads of other governments in order to prevent wars, in order to see whether in this time of stress and strain we cannot devise measures that will keep from us this terrible scourge that afflicts mankind.
>
> Now, manifestly, there are many difficulties in the way of a President going abroad for a period, particularly while Congress is in session. He has many constitutional duties; he must be here to perform them. I am able to go on this trip only because of the generous cooperation of the political leaders in Congress of both political parties who have arranged their work so that my absence for a period will not interfere with the business of the Government. On my part I promised them that by a week from Sunday, on July 24th, I shall be back here ready to carry on my accustomed duties.[21]

President Eisenhower gave only four sets of public remarks during that first trip to Geneva, but he gave forty-one speeches four years later during his tour of Europe, Asia, and Africa. Not only did he speak more often on this latter occasion but he did so with supreme confidence, for he had learned, as his successors would learn, that a traveling/speaking president is, in the eyes of many Americans, a leader. If speech is action, international speech is action-plus. Thus, one can sense a confidence, a curious blending of nationalism and internationalism, when Mr. Eisenhower set out on his journey in early December 1959:

> Good Evening Fellow Americans:
> I leave in just a few minutes, on a 3-week journey halfway around the world. During this Mission of peace and Good Will I hope to promote a better understanding of America than to learn more of our friends abroad.
> In every country I hope to make widely known America's deepest desire— a world in which all nations may prosper in freedom, justice, and peace, unmolested and unafraid.
> I shall try to convey to everyone our earnestness in striving to reduce the tensions dividing mankind—an effort first requiring, as indeed Mr. Khrushchev agrees, the beginning of mutual disarmament. Of course, I shall stress that the first requirement for mutual disarmament is mutual verification.
> Then I hope to make this truth clear—that, on all this earth, not anywhere does our Nation seek territory, selfish gain or unfair advantage for itself. I hope all can understand that beyond her shores, as at home, America aspires only to promote human happiness, justly achieved.[22]

Thrust as he was into the presidency sans mandate, Gerald Ford had little he could depend upon. It is interesting that he chose to depend upon speechmaking, for he surely was not gifted in that sense. But he had witnessed John Kennedy's international successes. He had seen Harry Truman handle himself comfortably, if not with aplomb, during press conferences. And he had listened to Lyndon Johnson preach and ceremonialize after he was abruptly ushered into the Oval Office. So Jerry Ford learned from his predecessors and attempted, in two-and one-half years, to recreate all five of the presidencies that immediately preceded his.

Gerald Ford did more of everything—more multiple-topic speeches than the obliging Harry Truman, more speeches on foreign affairs than internationalist Dwight Eisenhower (and almost as many as John Kennedy), more pragmatic speeches than Jimmy Carter, more speeches on human problems than even Lyndon Johnson. Sensing that the key to leadership in the United States was a rhetorical key, Mr. Ford spoke and spoke and spoke.

During his third month in office (October 1974), Ford traveled to Mexico, hosted the first secretary of Poland and the president of Portugal, and shared the spotlight with Henry Kissinger as he left for the Middle East. He spoke at fund-raising dinners in Michigan, Pennsylvania, Missouri, Iowa, Illinois, and Oklahoma. He gave briefer campaign speeches in those same states as well as in California, South Dakota, Nebraska, Kentucky, Indiana, South Carolina, North Carolina, and Ohio. He dedicated buildings for the Department of Labor and the *Anderson Daily Mail*. He addressed the annual conventions of the American Lutheran Church, the Future Farmers of America, and the National Council on Crime. He spoke while signing the Federal Election Campaign Act, the Energy Reorganization Act, the Emergency Home Purchase Assistance Act, and the Drug Abuse Prevention Week Proclamation. He participated in ceremonies for Calvin College, Richard Roudebush, Veterans Day, and Leslie C. Arends. He gave two press conferences, a speech on school desegregation, and explained why he vetoed a bill. Then it was November.

And October of 1974 was but Mr. Ford's seventh busiest as president. Throughout his term in office he used speech to fabricate a presidency out of humble raw materials. *Yet he sensed that public discourse was somehow emblematic of command* and that by acting presidential he would become presidential. These notions were reinforced in him by the press, by the audiences that applauded him, and by the sudden rise to power (through sheer doggedness of speechmaking) of his eventual Democratic rival. Ford's major challenge, therefore, became that of keeping up with the myriad texts his speechwriters produced for him (texts he seldom changed).

It is not surprising that few of his contemporaries would be able to quote a single line from one of the 1,231 speeches Gerald Ford gave while serving as the thirty-fourth president of the United States. (The closest they would come would be to hazily reconstruct some sort of gaffe he made about Poland during his debate with Jimmy Carter.) His quantity of speech hardly contributed to quality—of language or ideas. But Jerry Ford, like many other modern presidents, sensed, perhaps correctly, that the *act* of speaking in public often carries with it excitement and emotional satisfaction for listeners, admiration and influence for speakers. Jerry Ford was not ideological enough to stand upon a partisan platform to establish his inherited presidency, nor was he apolitical enough to shrink from seeking a full term in office in his own right. Thus, he chose rhetoric, a course that other modern presidents had chosen, a course useful for establishing a sense of direction when one lacks a compass, a course that in the views of many Americans, leads to leadership.

The Politics of Relationship

In the past, communication scholars have been quick to comment on the psychology of persuasion—how an Adolph Hitler mesmerized his audiences, what needs were fulfilled by those who listened to and later followed crazed evangelist Jim Jones—but only rarely have observers paused to consider the sociology of persuasion. Yet in politics, it is often the social forces operating in a speaking situation that tell the richest story. Even before speaking to an audience, for example, a speaker makes a commitment to the members of that audience by agreeing to address them. To speak to a listener is to choose that listener above all other listeners, to acknowledge that the attitudes of that audience are somehow important. Equally, when one agrees to become part of an audience at a political or religious gathering, one makes an implicit commitment to the organizers of that event. Even if one has come only to carp, one submits in part to the speaker's influence by allowing that speaker to interrupt other plans one might have made for that day and time. Thus, in any speaking situation a metastatement is made.[23] That statement is the product of who has agreed to speak and who has agreed to listen, what they have decided to discuss, for how long, and within what set of procedural constraints. In the political arena, decisions often turn on this sociology of persuasion, as when Communist China was finally made part of the United Nations' discussions, as when John Anderson was excluded from important presidential debates in 1980, as when John Kennedy faced the Houston ministers to address the religion issue during his 1960 presidential campaign, and as when the shape of the table for the Vietnam peace talks was finally decided upon. In each case, who agreed to talk to whom under what circumstances became the news of the day.

Throughout this book, we will examine the sociology of presidential persuasion. Presidents and their staffs become expert in this area, and much of their time is devoted to discovering the best social superstructure for insuring that a given rhetorical event will proceed smoothly and impressively. Like many sociologies, the sociology of presidential persuasion has both covert and overt aspects. For example, table 2.4 reveals unsurprising but nonetheless fundamental patterns of where presidents go when they wish to share something important. They go, for instance, to the Western United States when moved to discuss science and agriculture. (Or, alternatively, when they must head West, they must speak technically.) Harry Truman talked floods in Ehrata, Washington, in June of 1948. John Kennedy talked electricity in Hanford, Washington, in September of 1963. Jerry Ford talked

Table 2.4   *Selected Topics Discussed by Presidents in Various Regions of the United States*

Topic	East	Midwest	South	West
Science/agriculture	24*	71	58	74
Economics/labor	65	64	51	45
Human values	108	78	101	37
International cooperation	45	45	35	29
International conflict	40	40	28	26

*Figures = total number of speeches for topic/region between 1945 and 1985.

pollution in Seattle, Washington, in October of 1976. And Jimmy Carter talked volcanos in Spokane, Washington, in May of 1980. Clearly, these presidents' political philosophies, interests, and expertise on scientific matters differed. Still, given the ties they were attempting to build or salvage in the West, they knew what to talk *about* during their visits there.

Table 2.4 is rife with political stereotypes: talk of science and agriculture in the heartland with its powerful farm lobbies, talk of profits and losses in the East's corporate boardrooms, talk of anything but international cooperation in the isolationist South and West. These data are stereotypical (1) because these particular stereotypes hold true electorally, and (2) because political rhetoric is horribly uncreative. Politics follows votes; political rhetoric follows predictable audience responses. Topics like the Constitution (i.e., human values) sell well in both the liberal East and in the conservative South because both parts of the country are tradition bound, although it goes without saying that different features of this document are emphasized in Boston and Birmingham. These communicative patterns are breaking down somewhat as political relationships in the United States become less regionally based and more greatly affected by economic and symbological forces. But it is significant to note here that the content of presidential messages (i.e., the actual arguments made) are sometimes less important than the

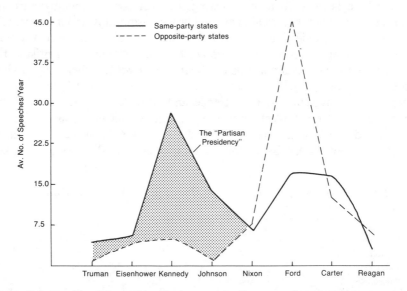

Figure 2.3. Presidential speaking during nonelection years in same-party vs. opposite-party states. In same-party states: Republican states, $N = 16$; Democratic states, $N = 16$.

Table 2.5   *Richard Nixon's Use of Ceremonial Events during His Administration*

	Phase of Administration		
	Triumph *(1969–1970)*	*Toil* *(1971–1972)*	*Trouble* *(1973–1974)*
N initiating ceremonies	39	25	25
N honorific ceremonies	95	42	47
N celebratory ceremonies	45	29	19
N greeting ceremonies	91	33	22

strategic bringing together of the right persons on the right topics in the right places.

Any human relationship will be affected by the needs of its partners. Any such relationship must respond (if it is to survive) to the changing needs of its partners; this is especially true if those changes threaten to discomfit the other partner. Political relationships must also adapt, a vivid example of which is presented in figure 2.3. This figure traces regional speaking during *non*election years in both Republican and Democratic states between 1945 and 1982. ("Neutral" states were excluded from the analysis.) The results are those one might predict, with one exception.

Generally, the presidents spoke to their own kind when the political heat was off, indicating, to no one's surprise, that political relationships are extraordinarily expedient. The one marked exception to this pattern was Gerald Ford's presidency. Figure 2.3 shows how sharply Ford veered away from the traditional pattern during 1975, his single nonelection year in office. He devoted unprecedented attention to the Democratic states, probably because he would be visiting them later and, this time, making more pointed requests of his listeners. Depending upon one's level of cynicism, one could argue that in speaking where he did (1) Mr. Ford was striving to be the president of all the people, (2) he was sensitively trying to guard against charges of political incest, or, (3) he was stealthily attempting to set up his marks for easy pickings during 1976. The most parsimonious conclusion seems to be that Ford's behavior was aberrant because he served without a mandate and that if he had been reelected he would have returned to the standard, political relationship with regional America.

Because relationships depend on communication, patterns of interaction can sometimes provide a gauge to the quality of a relationship. When attempting to diagnose a troubled marriage, for example, a counselor might ask a couple if they still enjoyed recreating together. This same sort of question could have been asked of Richard Nixon's treatment of the American people: as his relationship with them deteriorated, did he become less convivial? Table 2.5 strongly indicates that the answer is yes. Mr. Nixon exhibits a fairly steady drop in all of his ceremonial duties as Watergate approached. These data are particularly revealing when we remember that rituals, unlike press conferences (which he also curtailed), are normally insulated from political stress and that their agendas are largely controlled by the guest-of-honor/master-of-ceremonies (whichever the president happens to be). Thus, when a president absents himself even from the parties, he signals either a general reluctance to be with others or a growing preoccupation. In either case (and Mr. Nixon's case could have been either case), avoidance suggests trouble. No other president demonstrated this pattern (virtually all *increased* their ceremonial duties as their presidencies progressed). Changes over time in the content of Mr. Nixon's messages may have been nonexistant or subtle, but *the decisions he made to speak and not to speak* were themselves eloquent.

As Richard Nixon's situation indicates, it is sometimes instructive to inspect how political settings are framed and how these framing devices characterize a presidency. Subjectively, for example, no two presidencies could be more different than those of Harry Truman and Ronald Reagan—one a Democrat, the other a Republican; one an "early media" president, the other an almost "postmedia" president; one feisty, the other mellow. Although nothing definitive can result from contrasting these presidencies (that would be like comparing apples and oranges and concluding that they are different), such a procedure can point up different rhetorical styles and show how they can set the tone for an entire administration. After all, when one thinks about these two presidencies, one thinks of descriptions like hot-versus-cool, turbulent-versus-controlled, open-versus-closed, and plain-versus-sophisticated. Figure 2.4 supports these impressions by contrasting the audiences favored by these two presidents.

The differences between the two administrations are pronounced: Truman spending most of his time with "the people," Reagan talking primarily to intermediaries (or to the people via the mass media). Mr. Reagan's speaking situations are whole and preset, strategically built, while Mr. Truman's are more fluid, in process, ad hoc. The differences seen here are heavily affected (but not totally determined by Truman's 1948 and 1952 campaign trips, which were about as fluid as rhetorical events can be, an impression supported by virtually any intoduction to any speech he gave on the stump:

> Thank you, Senator, I appreciate that very much. We really didn't have a scheduled stop here, but I am so happy to see so many people turn out and have a chance to see what the President looks like and to hear something about what he believes in. You know, there has been so much publicity about your President not knowing where he is going or what he is doing or anything of the kind that people are surprised when they find that he does know where he is going, and he knows what he is doing.

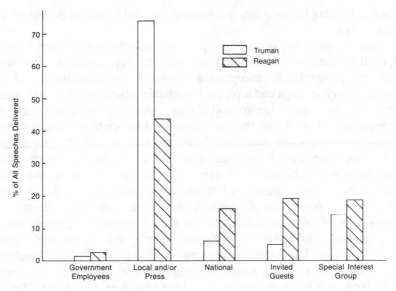

Figure 2.4. Comparison of audiences addressed by Harry Truman and Ronald Reagan.

This campaign has been a campaign of the people against special interests. And when you go to the polls to vote on November 2nd, just bear in mind that you are voting for yourselves. If you vote in your own interest, you can't do but one thing, and this is vote the Democratic ticket straight. . .

Now, just do one thing in your own interest. When election day comes, don't do like you did in 1946. You know, two-thirds of you stayed at home in 1946, and one-third of the people of this country elected that good-for-nothing, "do-nothing" 80th Congress.

Those of you who stayed home got just what you deserved. Now don't do that this time. Go out and vote your sentiments. Vote in your own interest. Then I won't have to be troubled with the housing shortage, I will still live in the White House for another 4 years.[24]

Even if he had found himself in Mr. Truman's political straits, Ronald Reagan could hardly have produced such ragtag rhetoric. The "sociology" of recent campaigning is more controlled and machine-like than the inspiration-driven rhetoric produced by Truman. As we shall see in Chapters Four and Five, presidential speech is now carefully choreographed, and this choreography is itself an interesting commentary on presidential relationships with the voters. Mr. Truman's improvisations are thus a throwback to the vaudeville era in which he was raised. Ronald Reagan learned his hoofing in that era, too, but his speeches more closely resemble the controlled artistry of rock videos.

Another, final way of examining the politics of relationship is to stand back from the behavior of individual chief executives and examine the overall contexts of presidential communication. Several things are important to note about the speech settings and topics contrasted in table 2.6. First, the obvious ones: (1) human values are overwhelmingly discussed in ceremonial surroundings rather than during the more business-like briefings; (2) conversely, ceremonies and economics apparently do not mix as well (from a *proportional* standpoint); and (3) specialized groups exist and are sought out by presidents (see Organizational Meeting) for virtually any important topic. These are the expected patterns, but others are more intriguing. For example,the political usefulness of ceremony becomes clear when the *absolute* numbers in table 2.6 are examined. There have been over 700 ceremonies in forty years on such pedestrian matters as science, economics, and bureaucratic governance. These data seem counterintuitive until we remember that, from the standpoint of role, Americans employ their chief executives just as peasant farmers employ priests to bless their plantings. Given their Puritan background and their understanding of the United States as a New Israel, Americans have little difficulty in seeing the essential rightness of their planting as well as of their tinkering and bartering. Presidents, then, often provide such blessings, and, if appropriate ceremonies do not exist, they invent them. Lyndon Johnson was particularly inventive:

On Money qua Money

We are gathered here today for a very rare and historic occasion in our Nation's history . . .

When I have signed this bill before me, we will have made the first fundamental change in our coinage in 173 years . . .

Table 2.6 *Domestic Topics Addressed during Presidential Messages on Selected Occasions*

	Ceremony		Briefing		Organizational Meeting	
	N	%	N	%	N	%
Science/agriculture	347	18.8	138	16.2	91	13.4
Economics/labor	188	10.2	279	32.8	192	28.3
Governance	186	10.1	202	23.8	83	12.2
Human services	385	20.9	110	12.9	145	21.4
Human values	738	40.0	121	14.2	168	24.7

I commend the new coinage to the nation's banks and businesses and to the public. I think it will serve us well.

Now, I will sign this bill to make the first change in our coinage system since the 18th century. And to those Members of Congress, who are here on this very historic occasion, I want to assure you that in making this change from the 18th century, we have no idea of returning to it.

We are going to keep our eyes on the stars and our feet on the ground.[25]

On Paying Government Employees

Of the many measures enacted this year, this legislation ranks near the top of the list in importance to the entire country. This is much more than just a pay bill. It is, as the title says, a reform measure, the Government Employees Salary Reform Act of 1964. For the first time this gives us the tools to identify and inspire, to reward and retain excellence in our Federal service. . .

America's challenges cannot be met in this modern world by mediocrity at any level, public or private. All through our society we must search for brilliance, welcome genious, strive for excellence. And this measure will help us to do that in our Federal Government.[26]

On Securities and Exchange

This afternoon, I am signing a measure to protect the prosperity of our people . . .

All Americans and all the world can take new inspiration and fresh faith from the example that this day presents . . .

Capitalism in America is what it is today because of the initiative, the enterprise, and the responsibility of our free system.

But it is also what it is because of the course that we have chosen for this Government to follow.

We rejected the idea that the role of government is either coercion or control. On the contrary, the proper function of government is to meet its responsibilities wisely so that people may have confidence in their future, in their system, and in themselves.[27]

There is more than a bit of LBJ's braggadocio here; for him, every breath he took was a historic breath. But all American presidents can become emotional about money (and spaceships, and agricultural subsidies, and hydroelectric dams, and trade deficits, and high technology, and diesel gasoline). What's more, they can make philosophy (if not poetry) out of such mundanities and discover, within the most humble sliver of reality, truths essential enough to buoy up a nation founded on equal parts pragmatism and transcendentalism.[28]

For some, the darker side of table 2.6 is that discussion of human services and values is largely excluded from formal briefings. Some might argue that with these important issues being relegated to ceremonial settings and to the closed conferences of special interest groups, they are thereby subordinated to more tangible and more capitalistic values. These same ob-servors might further argue that only briefings are treated as significant by the press, by government officials, and by foreign leaders and, therefore, that the data in table 2.6 strongly support Herbert Hoover's refrain that "the business of America is business."

Cooler heads might counterargue that 1,667 speeches exclusively devoted to human services and values during the last forty years is hardly insignificant, no matter in what setting they were delivered. They might claim that when a *president* talks about such matters, such matters will be treated seriously by all listeners (immediate as well as distant). They might also assert that some human problems—like ignorance, poverty, religious strife, racial prejudice, and family conflict—are so endemic to human society and hence so unresolvable in the short run that all a president can do is talk about these problems in a sensitive and hopeful manner until practical solutions can be found. Finally, such commentators might argue that these so-called human issues are, actually, economic, scientific, or bureaucratic issues at root and hence are dealt with constantly by presidents.

Clearly, no resolution to this debate is possible. The data support either interpretation. The answer may come down to how optimistic or pessimistic one is or how much regard one has for presidential rhetoric in the first place. In any event, discussions like these center on the metameanings of speech, meanings whose import can become quite tangible in the sphere of politics. For example, more than a decade after the Watergate affair ended, many Americans, perhaps most adult Americans, still felt insulted that Richard Nixon had not offered a clear, public apology for his misdeeds in office. They reason that Mr. Nixon had broken faith and that he further offended their relationship with him by not attempting to repair it. They know full well that such an admission of wrongdoing would not mean much substantively, but they feel that they would have apologized in like circumstances if they had done what Richard Nixon had done.

For his part, Mr. Nixon is perplexed by such statements. He argues, quite rightly, that his voluntary resignation from the highest office in the land is surely the most dramatic, albeit implicit, apology an individual could offer. It is the "albeit implicit" that sticks in the craws of many Americans. They still feel that their president took advantage of their trust and that a tight-lipped resignation is not the speech act designated to deal with ruptured social bonds. In so reasoning, the American people show how much stock they put into their relationships with presidents and how central rhetoric is to those relationships.

The Politics of Distraction

A phrase like "the politics of distraction" may seem an inherent redundancy and in some senses it is. Viewed from a distance, the political enterprise involves little more than sleight of hand—distracting citizens from their individual needs and pointing them toward the needs of the larger community; distracting the nation's enemies from their differences with us and pointing them toward beliefs and experiences we share. That is why rhetoric is so central to politics—rhetoric understands that a listener can think of very few things at any one moment. Rhetoric also understands that many forces compete for the attention of a listener during all moments. Thus, the job of political discourse is to open up the mind to new thoughts *and to fully occupy the mind with those thoughts*. Rhetoric gives us something to think about as well as something not to think about.

Presidents are enormously accomplished distracters. They direct citizens' attention toward the good and the just and the hopeful and away from the cruel and the shameful and the depressing. During war they talk of peace; during recession they talk of prosperity. In a more partisan vein sometimes, presidents emphasize the enormous advantages of their tax plan and attempt to shut our ears to the tax plans of their rivals. Thus, at the height of the Vietnam war, Lyndon Johnson returned from the Far East in time to deliver a Christmas message to the American people. In a masterful effort to distract his audience from a war in which they were feeling engulfed, he interspersed thoughts of conflict with yuletide themes and visions of a happier 1968.[29]

When he spoke on this occasion, President Johnson's popularity was at an all-time low (45%), so it is not surprising that he found comfort in an ageless distraction—public ceremony. As figure 2.5 indicates, presidents use ceremony more than any other forum. We have already seen some of the reasons why—the press is less hostile in such contexts, partisans are less

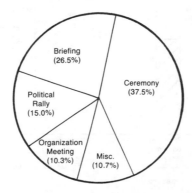

Figure 2.5. Apportionment of speech settings for modern presidents.

likely to nip at the president's heels, touchy subjects can be avoided. There are more positive aspects too—precedent suggests what to say, clear procedural ground rules normally eliminate unexpected interruptions, the president typically presides over such occasions and therefore receives most of the publicity, and the chief executive can be assertive or ponderous or sentimental without risking widespread censure.

Sensing these advantages, perhaps, Jimmy Carter also distracted, even though it was devilishly hard to distract his constituents during the latter part of his administration. Figure 2.6 presents a revealing look at Mr. Carter, showing how he increased his speechmaking about human values over time but how his discussion of the more tangible topic of social services declined considerably. In addition, the style of Mr. Carter's speeches changed. His language became more complex and abstract (i.e., it contained less realism), but it also became firmer and more patriotic in tone.[30] Thus, Americans who felt in 1980 that Jimmy Carter had lost touch with their everyday problems may have been responding to Mr. Carter's own behavior (or nonbehavior). Carter was a tolerably good preacher, and in that sense he may have been wise to seek out ritual as often as he did. But times change and people are fickle, and even Mr. Carter's best sermonizing could not prevent his steady drop in public opinion polls. Iran, inflation, and general irritability put the American people in no mood for church. And so they turned to a former

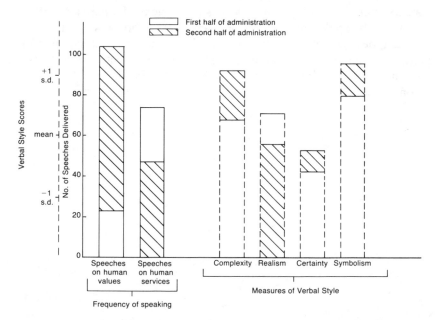

Figure 2.6. Frequency of speaking and verbal style in the Carter administration.

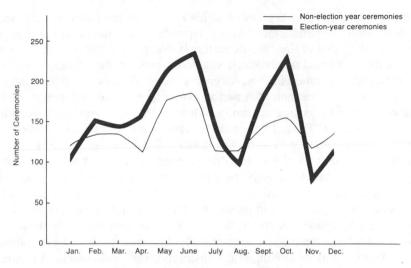

Figure 2.7. Use of ceremonies by presidents in nonelection and election years.

Democrat and former matinee idol because Mr. Reagan offered them a kind of distraction not heard before.

Presidents use ritual, therefore, for the reasons that elementary school teachers encourage their charges to take an active recess each day. During recess, the freneticism of an eight-year-old is, at least, freneticism within boundaries. Energy expended during a game of kickball is energy that cannot be used to climb on the top shelf of the bookcase during spelling lessons. For similar reasons, no president can resist ceremony. If a given ritual can keep even one major constituency in its seat and out of the president's hair, it is an opportunity to be seized. But recess is useful even for "good" children—as an insurance policy against their becoming restless later in the afternoon. Norwegian-Americans have been good children, but Jerry Ford sought them out just as actively as any ethnic group, especially when they offered to build a health spa in Minnesota during the Bicentennial. He praised them not only for the gift of the spa but for all their contributions as American citizens to the growth and progress of the country and grandly offered the gratitude of all America to them.[31]

This notion of "distraction" does not suggest that presidents try to dull the intellect via ritual. Quite the contrary. They attempt to fill up the mind with thoughts, and the heart with feelings, so that the national consciousness becomes supersaturated. They use ceremony not so much as an opiate but as a stimulant (a stimulant for "the right," of course). For this reason, presidents actually *increase* their use of ceremonies during election years, as can be seen in figure 2.7, which examines ceremonial usage on a monthly basis (through 1982). During September of his reelection campaign, for example, Lyndon Johnson used his incumbency to preside at a variety of rituals ranging from an inspection of SAC Headquarters in Nebraska ("the strength and the skill of this Command are absolutely vital to the peace of the Atlantic world"),[32] to an airport dedication in West Virginia ("West Virginia has given much to the land we love, the land of America. America must never forget it, and it will never forget it as long as I am President."),[33] to a university convocation in Rhode Island ("Today I am proud to have in my administration two men who served as deans at Brown—Dr. Robert W. Morse and Dr. Donald Hornig").[34] It is hard to distinguish this language from what one hears at a political rally. That is precisely the advantage ritual offers. Because he was a president, Johnson was allowed to stretch the rhetorical rules. Because his occasions were ceremonial in nature, he was not called on the carpet for his generic transgressions. A nonpresident would not have had quite these perquisites. During a campaign, it is better to be a president than not a president.

Another way of looking at the distractions of discourse is to contrast the realms of the practical and the theoretical in politics. That is, in some arenas it becomes difficult to actually *do* much, either because problems are so widespread that no short term palliative suffices or because problems are so personal and so local that government has neither the power of surveillance nor the power of enforcement to intervene effectively. In either case, political leaders speak in order to head off the short-term effects of the difficulty and to lay groundwork for a more permanent solution.

Figure 2.8 contrasts the amount of presidential speechmaking in five areas with the amount of federal legislation initiated to deal with those exigences. The resulting profiles are markedly different. Comparatively little presidential discourse is devoted to science/agriculture and social welfare, even though considerable legislation is put forward in both areas. Perhaps presidents are unable to generate much enthusiasm in their audiences in the former case and entirely too much in the latter instance. The picture is quite different when it comes to foreign defense or civil liberties. Presidents talk a good deal about these matters. Apparently, civil liberties is the kind of microscopic issue, and foreign affairs the kind of macroscopic issue, that resists simple legislative solution. And yet because both areas prove vexing for modern society, they require ample public discussion.

It is as if dialogue itself were being treated by presidents as the only long-term solution to these latter problems. The presidents seem to reason that women will be discriminated against in the work force and that Russia will rattle its sabers until the *attitudes* of Bendix executives and Politburo members are changed. Affirmative action legislation and strategic arms agreements can take us only so far, presidents appear to reckon, so they treat their rhetoric as surrogate action. Rhetoric has long been used in such

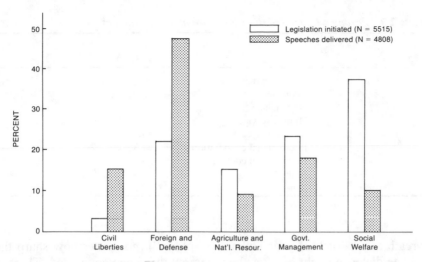

Figure 2.8. Presidential speechmaking and initiated legislation contrasted (1953–1975). Legislation initiated is from L. T. Le Loup and S. A. Shull, "Dimensions of Presidential Policy-making," in S. A. Shull and L. T. Le Loup (eds.), *The Presidency: Studies in Policy-making* (Brunswick, Ohio: King's Court, 1979), p. 9.

ways, as when Martin Luther King, Jr. shared his dream with American blacks in 1963 even though tangible progress in civil rights would not be made until many years later. As has been suggested elsewhere, speech can be a kind of "existential way station for the patient," a means of generating interim group strength.[35]

While not eliminating problems in an empirical sense, such discourse can hearten people until their problems are solved with finality. This, of course, is the optimistic picture. Liberals would argue that entirely too much rhetoric (and not enough action) exists on behalf of personal liberties and international harmony. Conservatives would object to the patterns just described on yet another ground—that producing so much talk overemphasizes the importance of minority rights and of getting along with foreign governments. Counterpoised between such sentiments, presidents behave as described above.

Given the complexities sketched here, it should come as little surprise that presidential ceremonies often focus on foreign alliances (see table 2.7 for how often). For a president, international ceremonies can do at least two things: (1) because they require careful planning, orchestrate a variety of (overt) human behaviors, and generate mass media attention, ceremonies become an obvious kind of social *action;* (2) because this action is behavioral, it carries its own metamessage ("We are not friends, but I will still lay a

Table 2.7   *Topics Discussed during Presidential Ceremonies*

	% (N = 3739)
Science/agriculture	9.3
Economics	5.0
Governance	5.0
Human services	10.3
Human values	19.7
International cooperation	34.8
International conflict	5.0
Multiple	2.4
Other	8.5

wreath at the tomb of your Unknown Soldier"), no matter how sharp the private dialogue might be after the ceremony has been concluded. There is often a Kafkaesque quality to such ritualizing—actions without "real" action, consequences that cannot be measured—but the only option seems to be to have no ceremony at all which, of course, means to have no dialogue at all.

Students of international relations often talk about the "signals" governments send one another via ideology-encrusted, highly stylized maneuverings ("It looks like this, but it really is that"), and they argue that experts are required to decode the meanings lying beneath many international moves. That may well be true, but it takes comparatively little effort to discover why international speech occurs in ceremonial settings: ceremonies isolate pan-human qualities.

Consider some of the times heads of state get together: when they are coronated, when their children are married, when one of them dies. These are, of course, rites of passage, times when one is distracted from politics as usual, times so essentially human that ideology must struggle to subsume more basic social instincts. Ideology always wins the tussle, but ritualistic discourse makes its claims for attention (rather, for distraction), as when Richard Nixon traveled to the People's Republic of China in 1972:

> The world watches. The world listens. The world waits to see what we will do. What is the world? In a personal sense, I think of my eldest daughter whose birthday it is today. As I think of her, I think of all the children in the world, in Asia, in Africa, in Europe, in the Americas, most of whom were born since the date of the foundation of the People's Republic of China.
>
> What legacy shall we leave our children? Are they destined to die for the hatreds which have plagued the old world, or are they destined to live because we had the vision to build a new world?

There is no reason for us to be enemies. Neither of us seeks the territory
of the other; neither of us seeks domination over the other; neither of us seeks
to stretch out our hands and rule the world.[36]

Conclusion

When he spoke in China, Mr. Nixon knew that he could not alter half-a-
century's worth of attitudes with one speech. But he probably sensed that
to have spoken in China was, at least, to have *done something* on behalf of
world peace. In this instance, at least, speech became unusually powerful
social action—in terms of Nixon's personal prestige and in terms of an important international relationship. Because speech acts possess meanings
beyond their messages, Richard Nixon helped the United States turn a corner
when he talked about his daughter in Peking. As Dean Acheson once noted
when commenting on presidential speechmaking, "This is often where policy
is made, regardless of where it is supposed to be made."[37]

Many observers, of course, would be alarmed by Acheson's cynical
claim. Writing in the *New Republic,* Charles Krauthammer decried the great
amount of political symbolism he sees in this country: "But just as religious
piety becomes hollow when it substitutes for goodness, and offensive when
it masks evil, in politics the symbolic act corrupts when it substitutes for
action, or worse, when it conceals contradictory action. Yet that is the use
to which political symbols are almost invariably put."[38] Krauthammer's argument has a certain appeal to it. Essentially, he is objecting to political use
of the performative and distracting aspects of speech, arguing that such features disguise real reality and thereby subvert the lives of the persons who
must live that reality. But, as we have mentioned before, it is also worth
considering what there is to governance other than the symbolic. As an
American president, Richard Nixon could "do" comparatively little. He
would not have accomplished much, for example, if he had gone to Vietnam
and fired an M16 himself, so he talked others into doing it for him. He would
not have been allowed to turn the nation's newspapers into propaganda machines for his administration, so he employed Spiro Agnew to harass reporters in hopes that they would become Nixon propagandists. It would have
been impossible for Mr. Nixon to go to China and personally dismantle its
nuclear weaponry, so he spoke of his daughter while there in hopes that the
Chinese would do the dismantling themselves.

The American presidency is a kind of symbolic cocoon because the
political traditions of the nation prohibit presidents from taking matters directly into their own hands. Despite their mandated constitutional powers,
presidents are often left with little other than speech. But this is hardly to
say that they are therefore left with nothing. Speech gives to presidents
personal influence they would not have had otherwise; it helps them build

and maintain important political relationships; and it helps them focus voters' eyes on matters the president deems important. In using speech as frequently as they do, presidents thereby may be tapping the very essences of their presidencies.

Throughout this chapter, we have seen presidents use ritual more and more often. Some authors, such as Stephen Hess, seem little concerned about this ceremonializing which he feels is "adjustable to fit the time he [the president] is willing to expend." Hess argues that these ceremonies "can serve a highly useful purpose in keeping him in touch with the people, in helping to create a sense of national unity, and in endorsing worthwhile undertakings."[39] It is not clear from Hess's commentaries if he is aware of the exact magnitude of White House ritual. Is he aware, for example, that in 1952 alone Harry Truman spent a total of ten hours and thirty minutes just with athletic teams, or that in 1960 Dwight Eisenhower devoted seven hours and sixteen minutes exclusively to youth groups?[40] These expenditures of time do not include the many more hours both presidents spent with veterans, with charitable organizations, with business delegations, with fraternal organizations, with church groups, and with military detachments, nor does it include the presidents' international or political ceremonies both in the White House and on the road. Moreover, as we have seen, these figures are modest indeed compared to those of Mr. Truman's and Mr. Eisenhower's successors in office.

To say that speech is political action is, for me, to make a technical designation and nothing more. It is surely not to endorse a presidential mindset which prizes symbolism above all else. Words can charm and captivate and exalt and soothe and befriend. They can also persecute and debase and alienate. It is worrisome, it seems to me, that presidents have developed a rhetorical reflex, that they think first of how an utterance will play in Peoria and only later, if at all, of what is best for Peorians. It is vexing, it seems to me, that so much stock is now placed in presidential words; in the summer of 1984, for example, the most common question raging in the newspapers was whether or not Geraldine Ferraro would, as a neophyte in the heat of political battle, make a verbal slip when campaigning. It is dangerous, it seems to me, not to heed the sobering observations of former speechwriter Harry McPherson:

> Political words offer a rationale for otherwise chaotic events. They help to unite people of very different sensibilities behind common policies, and thus they help government to function. But they rarely give an accurate reflection of reality. Their writers, joining in (and sometimes leading) the applause that follows their ringing phrases, can easily forget that. And communicating fairly and precisely is not the only question. Out beyond the convention centers and the Hilton hospitality rooms, beyond the cars pulling up with lobbyists and their clients, are citizens whose problems do not yield to any words at all.[41]

THREE

Speech and Power:
The Tools of
Presidential Leadership

T HE LINK BETWEEN SPEECH AND POWER IS AN ANCIENT ONE. IN EARLY
Rome, extensive instruction in rhetoric was provided to all young
patricians to help them preserve their privileges via careers in law and statecraft. At another time in another place, Dale Carnegie told a generation of
American plebians that they, too, could use speech to embolden their frail
selves and to further their philosophical or financial causes. Because human
speech makes an interior life public, it always involves a risk of the self, but
because speech is also the primary means for directing the lives of others,
many people choose to speak. The simplest speech act—say, a street-corner
greeting—is a primitive power move. It says that we, too, count in this world.
By noisily interrupting the (perhaps delicious) silence of the passerby with
our salutation, we have, momentarily at least, achieved dominance over him
or her. If we are clever, our domination will not be regarded as such; indeed,
it will seem gracious, a social favor. Therein lies rhetorical art disguised as
polite convention which, in turn, disguises a wanton imposition on the life
of another human being. Sometimes, a famous movie star or an influential
senator or a motivational expert will become so influential that audiences
will actuallly seek them out, openly inviting them to monopolize their minds
and sensibilities for an hour or two. Thus, it is not surprising that a list of
popular speakers on the national lecture circuit reads like a Who's Who of
literary, political, military, religious, and financial *power*.

Throughout time, writers have noted this connection between speech
and power. One author states the matter baldly: ". . . all great, world-shaking
events have been brought about, not by written matter but by the spoken
word."[1] He adds that the power to use speech effectively is not universally
distributed. He says that "by and large, a brilliant speaker will be able to
write better than a brilliant writer can speak"[2] because speech is especially

useful to those in touch with their primal instincts. When writing about speech, this author often uses power imagery, suggesting in one case that mere repetition alone can inspire "capitulation to his [the speaker's] arguments."[3] He claims, "False concepts and poor knowledge can be eliminated by instruction, the resistance of the emotions never."[4] He observes that at night, particularly, audiences "succumb more easily to the dominating force of a stronger will,"[5] and he goes on to observe that the success of the entire Russian Revolution can be laid at the doorstep of public speech:

> What has won the millions of workers for Marxism is less the literary style of the Marxist church fathers than the indefatigable and truly enormous propaganda work of tens of thousands of untiring agitators, from the great agitator down to the small trade-union official and the shop steward and discussion speaker; this work consisted of the hundreds of thousands of meetings at which, standing on the table in smoky taverns, these people's orators hammered at the masses and thus were able to acquire a marvelous knowledge of this human material which really put them in a position to choose the best weapons for attacking the fortress of public opinion. And it consisted, furthermore, in the gigantic mass demonstrations, these parades of hundreds of thousands of men, which burned into the small, wretched individual the proud conviction that, paltry worm as he was, he was nevertheless a part of a great dragon, beneath whose burning breath the hated bourgeois world would some day go up in fire and flame and the proletarian dictatorship would celebrate its ultimate final victory.[6]

If one experiences some discomfort when reading these metaphors of power—agreement as capitulation, audiences raped, opinions attacked, orators as hammerers, listeners likened to worms—one can be forgiven. Our commentator has been Adolph Hitler. Adolph Hitler, a person whose theoretical understanding of speech lagged just behind his canny ability to use it, knew a good deal about power. These reflections about speech were actually written *prior* to his seizing power, when he was imprisoned, when he had the least ability to use the spoken word. But Hitler evidences here an instinctual confidence in the power of speech, and that is precisely how he used it—instinctively, powerfully. Much has been written about Hitler's degradations of the human community via brute force, but he was even more successful in establishing through communication that his will and the will of a nation were isomorphic. He described why things were as they were and how they could be made better. He used speech to check the power of other powerful speakers—the church, the academy, the Prussian establishment—and only later persecuted them physically. Hitler knew, as all political leaders know, that power acquired through speech (as opposed to coercion) has a more favorable cost-benefit ratio and that it lasts longer as well. Prior to Hitler, there had been other madmen, other savages, but there had been nobody who could use words quite so well to disguise madness or to make savagery seem a virtue. Among the other vile things he was, Adolph Hitler was also a rhetorical criminal.

But he was simply the most excessive, not the only individual who saw an intimate connection between speech and power. Most American presidents, certainly the most recent American presidents, have observed this same connection, even if they deplored the Hitlerian lengths to which it could be carried. In this chapter, we will examine this connection. We will see that the spoken remarks of presidents exert influence not found in the speeches of others. We will see how presidents depend on speech when they feel insufficiently powerful, and we will see that, because they are presidents and not chancellors of the Third Reich, presidents normally feel insufficiently powerful. As a result, *presidents use speech to convince themselves and others that they are not impotent*.

One anecdote should suffice to make this latter point. At 4:35 A.M. on May 9, 1970, a restless Richard Nixon took himself to the steps of the Lincoln Memorial and visited with the knot of student protestors still awake at that unlikely hour. While there, Mr. Nixon seemingly used every appeal in his personal textbook of persuasion to reach the two dozen or so young people he confronted. Several things are significant about Nixon's speech/conversation. One is his use of fairly standard pro-war arguments: that the battle in Vietnam would insure peace in the region, that the American system itself demanded intervention, that widening the war was necessary for narrowing the war. Also interesting was the salad of non-Vietnam topics he discussed: his Quaker background, his admiration for Winston Churchill, his love of travel, the plight of Mexican-Americans, new developments in China, the drabness of Moscow, the danger of nuclear weaponry. The most interesting feature of Mr. Nixon's polylogue, however, was the inventiveness of his ingratiating tactics. He told one young woman that her hometown was his personal favorite. He told another that he had taken steps to preserve "the greatest surfing beach in the world."[7] He told yet another that if they were having trouble getting a visa to travel they should contact his office for help. (Mr. Nixon reported, "This seemed to get a little chuckle from them.")[8] And he invited "a bearded fellow" to have a picture taken with the president which, according to Nixon, produced "the broadest smile I saw on the entire visit."[9]

Admittedly, there is something surreal about an encounter between a stiff, formulary politician and a group of young radicals in the middle of the night outside a national monument dedicated to a radical Republican president. But what was even more surreal was the Nixonian impulse to get out of bed, drag his butler, his doctor, and a gaggle of nervous Secret Service agents to the monument, and to presume that his speech would be both appropriate and influential. Surely we are witnessing primitive forces in action here: a beleaguered president confronting his most severe domestic critics on their own turf, presuming that in just a few moments he could bridge chasms of age and ideology. But Richard Nixon was a rhetorical determinist. For him, the power of speech and the right, nay the duty, of the powerful to use speech, were notions that informed his entire administration (indeed, his entire career). Perhaps the most surreal fact of all is that Mr. Nixon took the time when he got back to the White House to record personally and in detail the entirety of his encounter at the Vietnam vigil. In Nixon's reconstruction, his pride about that speech during those wee hours becomes obvious. For him, the speech showed that he did not fear his detractors and also that he could conquer their every objection to his war and to his self. Pride, fear, conquest—unlikely themes for political speech, but because they are primitive themes they will be the themes of this chapter.

Necessity: The Mother of Discourse

The first proposition may seem overly obvious: presidents speak when they are in trouble. There are two ways of looking at figure 3.1, which reports the ratio of political ceremonies to party rallies in the regional United States between 1945 and 1985. One way would be to regard it simply as a reverse index of sobriety, with Presidents Eisenhower through Nixon preferring the

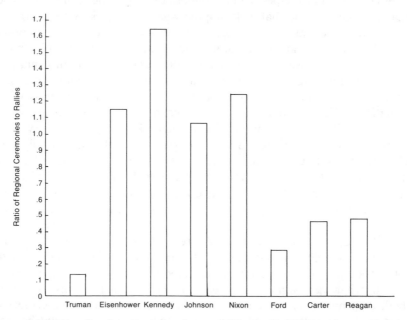

Figure 3.1. Ratio of regional ceremonies to political rallies for recent presidents.

convivial to the politically functional. Another, probably more accurate, interpretation is to treat the height of the bars as a rough indicator of overall political security. Remembering that these are ratios (and not absolute numbers), we can view them as indicating the relative need to focus on bottom-line politics, with Kennedy standing above such pettiness and Eisenhower, Johnson, and Nixon buoyed up by the landslides that would sustain their presidencies (until, of course, the latter Johnson and Nixon years).[10] Presidents Truman, Ford, and Carter, on the other hand, clearly felt the need to reverse these ratios; when they traveled to the hinterlands, they clearly had business on their minds. Presumably, Ronald Reagan's early second-term popularity relieved him of the necessity of being so business-like (these data only go through 1985) although, given the partisanship of American politics in the 1980s, one cannot be sure of this. In short, the more recent presidents still use ritual a good deal, but they buffer these activities with party politics, eschewing the role of King Richard holding court in favor of that of the good Sheriff of Nottingham, collecting their due at each hamlet.

These data seem ever so sensible, but it is useful to ponder why, given all of the things that a president could do when in trouble, he would choose to talk. Part of the answer has been hinted at before: the presidency is now a verbal, media-driven institution demanding speech in exchange for publicity. The presidency is now inundated by special interest groups that also carve out public, rhetorical turf, thereby inviting constant presidential response. It is worth noting that this mandate to speak is now unquestioned by presidents, even though there is virtually no hard data to suggest that an American head of state must speak in order to survive. But folklore binds the mind almost as tightly as physical instinct, and presidential folklore now has it that the chief executive must be first and foremost a talker.

The modern presidency treats forces like the goodwill of the media, adherence to political traditions, and personal charisma as the raisons d'être of presidential behavior. Speech, it is believed, secures these goods. To question this folklore, to be silent, is to admit to being powerless. There is something primitive about turning toward speech when the world favors others and not us. Ashley Montagu recounts that "speech was among the early tools originated by man during the early hunting phase of his evolution. Because of its highly adaptive value as the medium through which cooperation is secured, speech has played a seminal role in man's evolution. That it originated under the pressure of necessity, and was preserved by natural selection, is in conformity with all that we know concerning the evolution of man's other traits."[11] Presidents, too, use speech to hunt—votes, understanding, affection—and they jealously treat their rhetorical opportunities as their sustenance. Naturally, presidents will not die if they do not speak/hunt well, yet they operate as if they will. Like primitive religion, the folklore of presidential politics can be compelling.

Table 3.1   *Presidential Speaking in Response to Adverse Conditions*

Adverse Conditions*	% All National Addresses Delivered under These Conditions	% All Other Addresses Delivered under These Conditions
Opposition party controls Congress	57.9	37.5
High unemployment (>6.0%)	40.1	33.8
High magazine coverage (>100 stories)	48.0	36.8
Low legislative success (<69% passed)	30.8	20.9
Low popularity (<50%)	34.7	21.8

*Data not gathered through 1985 in all cases. See "Coding Procedures" in the Appendix for relevant dates.

Table 3.1 shows that folklore has consequences. It compares the use of national addresses by presidents under adverse conditions (e.g., high unemployment, too much publicity, low popularity, etc.) to the other speeches they gave under these same conditions. The pattern is clear: a president turns to the people when the political world does not suit him. There is also something primitive about returning to the tribe, rallying its support, when the enemy threatens. Obviously, not all presidents experienced each of these difficult conditions; some experienced none. But the data still indicate the powers thought to attach to highly publicized speech.

As we shall see later in this chapter, Richard Nixon was a president who operated, at times, under many of these adverse conditions, and he turned to mediated speech to cope with the difficult world he faced. For Nixon, the nationally televised address was useful because it insulated him from the very forces that inspired the address. When discussing Watergate on April 30, 1973, for example, Mr. Nixon could say, "Until March of this year, I remained convinced that the denials were true and that the charges of involvement by members of the White House Staff were false,"[12] even though, of course, he lied by saying so. He also claimed that "in the final analysis, the integrity of this office—public faith in the integrity of this office—would have to take priority over all personal considerations,"[13] even though facts later disclosed that Mr. Nixon was preoccupied with "personal considerations" when he spoke. For a clever president, a televised address uninterrupted by reporters presents a perfect opportunity to dissemble. When the legitimate power of the presidency is combined with the psychological power of the mass media and to that is added the charismatic power of a deft politician, anything is possible.[14] Such an address can cause facts not to seem factual (as in the Watergate case), or facts acknowledged as such not to seem important (e.g., spiraling budget deficits during Ronald Reagan's first term). When speaking to the nation on television or radio, a president need not mention the views of his critics, need not detail plans alternative to those he champions, need not recount his previous miscalculations or outright failures. The national address provides the president with an opportunity to get even under conditions that are themselves uneven. It is little wonder that such conditions are exploited by presidents when the world proves uncivil.

Between 1945 and 1982, the president's party has controlled Congress roughly as often as the opposition party has controlled it. It is useful, therefore, to see how presidents respond to these different conditions. A simple effect is revealed in figure 3.2, which shows where presidents speak when their party controls Congress and when their party does not. The effect is clear: presidents head for the hills—the Black Hills of North Dakota, the Hill Country of Texas, the foothills of Colorado—when they are frustrated by congressional behavior or, in Harry Truman's case, by congressional non-behavior. These regional tours show speech being used to goad. Here is speech removed from the political cauldron of Washington D.C. Here is "the speech of the people." Today, presidential trips are so widely publicized by the mass media that a speech that plays suitably in Peoria has a simultaneous chance of playing well in Pittsburgh or Pocatello. If "going over the heads of the Congress" is the appropriate metaphor for a president's nationally televised addresses, then "returning to the grassroots" aptly describes his other alternative. In more favorable circumstances, a president with a friendly Congress can "preside" in Washington, using the symbolic perquisites of the White House to further his personal political goals. In short, there seem to be different loci of rhetorical power—the Capitol and the heartland. Presidents play one against the other, or both against their opponents, signifying just a few of the advantages of incumbency.

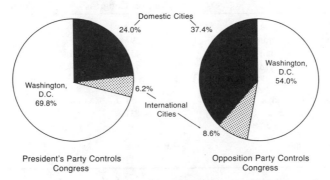

Figure 3.2. Locations of presidential speechmaking vis-à-vis congressional control.

By contrasting presidential behavior during periods of congressional control and noncontrol, table 3.2 presents an assortment of additional facts in this area, many of which conform to the shibboleths of modern athletics, modern business, modern war: adversity creates opportunity, the best defense is a good offense, you're only as good as the competition. Presidents do not use accountancy or bayonets or perspiration to fight their battles. Instead, when confronting a hostile Congress they present dismal analyses of the nation's finances and scathing denunciations of party politics or intransigent bureaucracies. Such presidents also work a longer day than their counterparts and are less likely to secret themselves behind closed doors when speaking. Obviously, Harry Truman's early presidency contributed a good deal to such trends, but so too did Gerald Ford's. Unlike many of their nineteenth- and early twentieth-century predecessors, Truman and Ford did not benignly use the perquisites of office. They aggressively pursued a persuasive campaign, rushing to any potentially supportive gathering and drawing upon the power that attends all presidential speech but that especially attends coordinated, hard-hitting, highly visible speech. This is a new turn in the presidency. Although American politics has never been genteel, only recently have the tools of campaigning been so extensively appropriated for governance by harried presidents. Today, even sitting presidents oftentimes sit on the edges of their chairs.

Perhaps table 3.2 adds data to something already known—that it is better to be loved than not loved. Clearly, it was enjoyable for Lyndon Johnson to visit Knoxville, Tennessee, in May of 1964 and tell his listeners (indeed, to guarantee his listeners) that their government-backed social services would be increased and that the Congress would help him do it. His

Table 3.2 *Presidential Speaking in Response to Congressional Control (1945–1982)*

	President's Party Controls Congress	Opposition Party Controls Congress
Speech topic:		
N speeches on economics	297	363
N speeches on human services	453	258
N speeches on governance	420	591
*Speech activity**		
% light-speaking days	51.0	49.0
% heavy-speaking days	31.8	68.2
Political rallies†		
N "open" rallies	148	726
N "closed" rallies	132	244

*Light = days on which three or fewer speeches were delivered; heavy = four or more speeches/day.
†Open = attendance by chance; closed = attendance restricted to organizational members.

speech on that occasion was not so much a solicitation as a verification, less
a request of his listeners than a promise to honor their requests of him:

> We have come here today on a very important visit. It does us good to get
> away from Washington and come out and see the people that we work for,
> talk to them, see how they live, recognize the sacrifices they make for their
> country and for us, and try to appreciate their problems . . .
>
> It was more than 30 years ago when President Roosevelt visited this State,
> and during that period of the early thirties, in trying to appeal to his country-
> men, he reminded them that more than a third of our people were ill fed and
> ill clad and ill housed. Today, apparently in the midst of plenty, we have reduced
> that one-third—that was ill clad and ill fed and ill housed—to one-fifth that now
> make up the poverty group.
>
> But that represents some 30-odd million people in this country. And this
> administration has decided and has determined that it is going to do something
> about it. We have put in our budget, funds for a poverty program that is headed
> by Sargent Shriver.
>
> We have put in our budget, funds for the Appalachia program that is headed
> by Franklin D. Roosevelt, Jr. And we, today, will visit 5 States in the Appalachian
> area, making a total of 9 of the 10 States in that area that we shall have visited.
>
> We want to listen and to learn.[15]

As Mr. Johnson shows us, there is a kind of power in promising. Although no incumbent president is without power, a politically weakened
position requires one to take chances. Because of an unfriendly Congress,
for example, Harry Truman was forced into this approach in 1948. As he
traveled throughout the country, he discovered what many speakers before
him had discovered—that castigating an opponent draws attention to oneself
as well as to one's opponent and thus one must also have a clear, positive
alternative to present. Truman seemed to realize that a bully, even a congressional bully, derives his real influence from the taunting—not the fisticuffs—
and so he taunted the 80th Congress from the Atlantic to the Pacific, being
careful on each occasion to legitimize his bullying with his oath of office and
to justify punishment of his opponent with a grand political vision. Thus,
whereas Johnson's power emerged from the more traditional reservoir of
self-interest, Truman's resulted from the aggressiveness of his personality,
from his readiness to take on an ostensible political behemoth. The resulting
rhetoric is hardly delicate, but it does have its attractions:

> It certainly is a pleasure to be in this wonderful City of Wilkes-Barre today.
>
> A Democrat ought to feel at home here, in a city and county which have
> supported the Democratic party consistently—except for a little mistake in
> 1946.

We can't afford to make mistakes this year. This election is too important.

Just one fundamental issue in this election this time, and that is the people against the special interests. And when you vote at the polls on November 2d, you will either vote for yourself or you will vote against yourself. Remember that.

I have just been telling your neighbors over in Scranton what the Republican 80th Congress has done to labor and what the Republican Party plans to do to labor, if it gets control of the 81st Congress and puts a Republican President in the White House.

You know, I exercised my power of veto oftener than any other President of the United States in the same time limit, except Grover Cleveland, and each of those vetos I felt was in the public interest. Suppose I hadn't been there!—the 80th Congress would have certainly fixed you sure enough, but they didn't have a chance to do all the things they wanted to do.

All you have to do to avoid a mistake like the 80th Congress is to come out and vote on November 2d.[16]

One of the most consistent findings of this study is that, in general, there is no relationship between how often a president speaks and how well he does in the public opinion polls. Dwight Eisenhower was one of the most popular presidents studied here, and yet he averaged only about ten speeches per month during his eight years in office. John Kennedy spoke approximately two-and-one-half times more often than Ike and yet garnered only five points more in the polls (approximately 70% vs. 65%). Lyndon Johnson spoke considerably more often than Kennedy but dropped fifteen points in popularity. Jerry Ford doubled his speaking between 1975 and 1976 (392 vs. 682 speeches) only to find himself ten points less popular in the latter year.[17] Clearly, simple frequency of speech is no key to political power, and yet presidents continually operate as if rhetoric alone can save them. Rhetoric, of course, is never alone during a presidency. It is accompanied by such contingencies as labor strikes, international flashpoints, party defections, legislative battles, and Billy Carters. Perhaps because presidents must cope with so many unexpected difficulties, they turn to public discourse since, by planning their rhetoric carefully, they can fully determine its content, style, and occasion for delivery. Full determination of *anything* may be a true joy to a bureaucratically constrained chief executive.

In some senses, rhetoric may have taken on totemic power for the chief executive. By wearing it around their necks (or on their sleeves), presidents seek to exorcise the evil spirits housed in budget deficits, oil shortages, and political scandals. With the exception of Richard Nixon, every president has spoken more frequently during the second half of his administration than in the first half, even though they would be hard-pressed to demonstrate scientifically the utility of having done so. On the other hand, the power of the totem lies not in its ability to eliminate all diabolical forces but to help one deal with them. The power of rhetoric may lie in the logic that *things would be considerably worse for the president if he chose to be silent*. Speech, after all, is behavioral, a doing, a bodying forth. The psychic peace that comes from rubbing an amulet (or vocalizing a prayer, for that matter) derives in part from one's ability to externalize through behavior the tensions one feels within. This is not to say that speechmaking does nothing. But it is to be reminded that how often one speaks is unrelated to standard, *empirical* measures of political success. Yet the amulet rubbing of presidents is greatly encouraged by the news-hungry, personality-based mass media as well as by White House staffs who often can think of no alternative method of coping with political life. So this may be one reason why presidents speak frequently. And this also may be why Roman Catholic expatriots from Haiti who have lived all of their adult lives in the most technologically advanced and most urbane city in the United States, make the sale of voodoo paraphernalia a multimillion-dollar industry in the side streets of Manhattan.

Another way of looking at the relationship between rhetoric and power is to conceive of the former as a means of simulating the latter. That is, because presidential speaking is an observable (thanks to the mass media, a highly observable) activity and because the presidency is such a respected institution in the United States, the continued oratorical presence of the chief executive may sometimes serve as a sharp, public denial of the standard measures of political success mentioned above. Given the whimsy known as public opinion, and given the oftentimes curious ways of measuring it, presidents may now be running (and publicizing) their own public opinion polls by choosing to speak constantly. In so doing, rhetoric becomes for them an antidote to the polls, a notion one senses when inspecting figure 3.3, which contrasts amount of speaking with personal popularity. Clearly, the alternating peaks and valleys of Jimmy Carter's discourse produced virtually no effect on the fairly steady slide he experienced in the polls. Seemingly, no matter what Jimmy Carter said or didn't say, his political position steadily worsened. Neither his international jaunts nor his domestic forays helped him substantially. The two brief exceptions to his steadily declining popularity were probably occasioned more by development in foreign affairs (the Camp David accords, the Soviet invasion of Afghanistan, and the Iranian hostage crisis) over which Mr. Carter had minimal control. As far as the opinion analysts are concerned, rhetoric was hardly Jimmy Carter's savior.

Surely Carter saw these same patterns. Why, then, did he speak so often? Numerous answers are available: because he personally believed in effort for the sake of effort; because speech released him from the tensions of the job; because the rhetorical routines of the White House have now become thoroughly institutionalized—he had no choice; because he regarded reclusiveness as cowardly; because appreciative audiences (and a president's

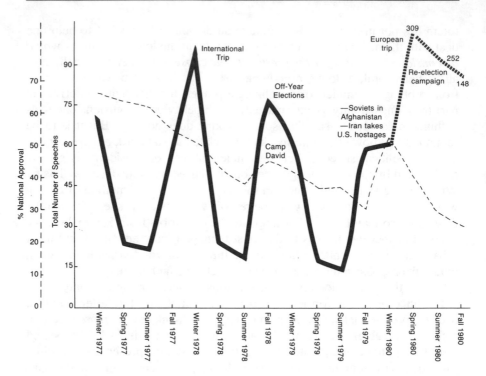

Figure 3.3. Jimmy Carter's frequency of speaking vs. his national popularity (1977–1980). Percent national approval from CBS/*New York Times* opinion poll. Partial summary included in *New York Times* of August 12, 1980, p. 2.

audiences are normally appreciative) are heartening; because he was a dogged ideologue, a preacher with a message.[18] From what we now know about him, all of these could have been Jimmy Carter's reasons. There is yet another reason: hope. For its practitioners, political rhetoric is constantly new. When a president approaches listeners, he, not they, knows what he will say. Because his speech has never been given before to this particular audience at this particular time, his speech may just reinvigorate his entire presidency. Politicians know, or think they know, that a well-received speech can create momentum and that several well-received speeches can create an avalanche of it. They know, or think they know, that the political world is ever new, that change is its only stabilizing force. In this schema, rhetoric is seen as the only constant, the one controllable force. In Jimmy Carter's mind, even his reelection eve speech—his twelve hundredth as president—may have been the one to turn the tide. Most political discourse focuses upon things yet to be, upon policies not yet in force, upon visions not yet made manifest.

Politicians are prognosticators; they peddle the future. The world their rhetoric creates is always grander than listeners' present worlds; for the politician, this new and better world holds personal promises too. Jimmy Carter spoke and spoke and spoke because he believed that rhetoric permitted renewal.

The popularity of Camp David registers in figure 3.3, as does an increase in Mr. Carter's persuasive efforts. The fall of 1978 was a busy one for him as he made extensive campaign trips to North and South Carolina, Pennsylvania, West Virginia, Minnesota, New York, Massachusetts, and other states. He signed into law several pieces of legislation as well, providing a speech with each signature. On many occasions, and during most of the ten news conferences he held in that time period, Jimmy Carter mentioned the Camp David accords:

In Asheville, North Carolina
I'm glad to be back home in North Carolina—even if I am 1 week late. It is partially to your credit that we finally ended the Camp David summit with success, because I was eager to come back to North Carolina . . .[19]

At the Kennedy Space Center
I learned this morning that while I was at Camp David with President Sadat and Prime Minister Begin, that scientists at Cal Tech discovered a new mini-planet whose orbit . . .[20]

In Buffalo, New York
We have become the champions of human rights. We are not scorned and despised as we formerly were. The United States has become an object of admiration. And we have had some success, as you know, at Camp David recently . . .[21]

In one sense, there is nothing more here than the standard political boasting one expects to hear on the campaign trail. But in another sense, the Camp David accords are being reified, given a kind of immortality so that the entire Carter administration can be refurbished. In a crass sense, Mr. Carter is using an international event for domestic political ends. In a more abstract sense, Mr. Carter is attempting to extend in time an empirical event that is no more. In a rhetorical sense, Mr. Carter is using discourse as a divining rod, searching for a wellspring of hope for his faltering administration. For Jimmy Carter, and for many of his predecessors, the power of rhetoric lay not only in what it could do but also in what it could prevent, not only in its mathematical effects in the polls but also in the less quantifiable feelings it generated inside people, not only in its proving but also in its promising. The power of rhetoric is therefore a myth that persists.

The Johnson Solution

Lyndon Baines Johnson was larger than life and so it was appropriate that he have two presidencies. His first presidency—a domestic one—was a roaring, brawling drunk. He pushed more legislation through Congress on human services (education, welfare, medical care) in a shorter period of time than any president before him. He harangued and threatened and promised and wheedled until his former colleagues in the House and Senate fell in line. This legislation, Mr. Johnson's Great Society, was legacy enough for any president. But he also created another legacy, one he would share with Richard Nixon, and it spelled ruination for Johnson. It sounds like a cliché two decades later, but "Johnson's War," as it would come to be called, did indeed tear apart a nation, and it spawned so much controversy that LBJ was required to relinquish a job that he clearly, grandly loved. Lyndon Johnson's second presidency—an international one—was less a drunk than a painfully slow process of detoxification since Mr. Johnson became fully addicted to his war.

Lyndon Johnson's involvement in the Vietnam War is a matter of public record. Very public record. By contrasting his international speeches with his domestic speeches, figure 3.4 depicts his two presidencies: the first became the second, roughly, in June of 1965. Vietnam became a preoccupation. He did not just manage the war; he sold it as feverishly as he had peddled his Great Society. In retrospect, one can admire his openness in publicly

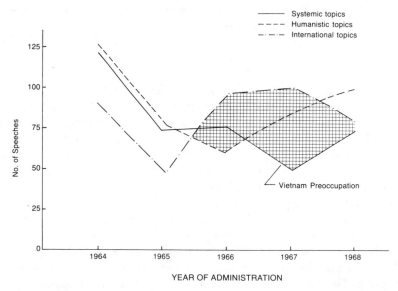

Figure 3.4. Lyndon Johnson's topical alterations over time.

accepting responsibility for prosecution of the conflict, but it is also true that his pro-war campaign may itself have been the major cause of both the war's continuation and of his commitment to its continuation. When one speaks, after all, one also listens to the self. As behavioral science studies have shown repeatedly, to speak in behalf of a proposition is to engage in autopersuasion largely because it is not easy to rationalize double-mindedness ("I feel this but I do that").[22] Social scientists report that even dissemblers rearrange their attitudes in the direction of the lies they tell in order to keep cognitive tension in check.[23] In Lyndon Johnson's case, it would have been impossible to be put on the line before so many audiences for so many months without his becoming more and more committed to his commitments in Vietnam (commitments that were, admittedly, strengthened by America's reverses in that part of the world).

Who, for example, could have uttered the following remarks in August of 1964, remarks with such clarity, resolve, and personal investment, and then abandoned them later when the political winds began to blow harshly? Lyndon Johnson, for one, could not do so:

> The Gulf of Tonkin may be distant, but none can be detached about what has happened there.
>
> Aggression—deliberate, willful, and systematic aggression—has unmasked its fact to the entire world. The world remembers—the world must never forget—that aggression unchallenged is aggression unleashed.
>
> We of the United States have not forgotten.
>
> That is why we have answered this aggression with action.
>
> America's course is not precipitate.
>
> America's course is not without long provocation.
>
> For ten years three American Presidents—President Eisenhower, President Kennedy, and your present President—and the American people have been actively concerned with threats to the peace and security of the peoples of southeast Asia from the Communist government of North Viet-Nam.
>
> President Eisenhower sought—and President Kennedy sought—the same objectives that I still seek:
>
> That the governments of southeast Asia honor the international agreements which apply in the area;
>
> That those governments leave each other alone;
>
> That they resolve their differences peacefully;
>
> That they devote their talents to bettering the lives of their peoples by working against poverty and disease and ignorance . . .
>
> Finally, my fellow Americans, I would like to say to ally and adversary alike: let no friend needlessly fear—and no foe vainly hope—that this is a nation divided in this election year. Our free elections—our full and free debate—are America's strength, not America's weakness.

There are no parties and there is no partisanship when our peace or the
peace of the world is imperiled by aggressors in any part of the world.
We are one nation united and indivisible.
And united and indivisible we shall remain.[24]

The power of presidential speech is thus both psychological and political. Johnson became obdurate about Vietnam. His speech fed upon itself as
he sought out audiences likely to applaud his applause lines. Table 3.3 contrasts his insistence in this regard to that of other presidents. As we see,
Johnson made a special attempt to be among the people; the television screen
was never large enough, nor the televised Johnson subtle enough, to project
adequately his oversized emotional intensity. On the road, he delivered thirty-
one complete speeches on Vietnam and mentioned it prominently in approximately 150 other (multitopic) addresses. He sought out friendly audiences
wherever they could be found, devoting almost 25% of his speeches in Republican states to discussion of his war, a figure representing (1) three times
his Vietnam speaking in Democratic states and (2) four to five times other
presidents' speeches on international conflict in Republican states. These
figures reveal a president seeking reinforcement from his listeners, not dialogue with them, a president using predictable speech situations to counteract
the volatility his wartime visions provoked in other quarters. These figures
also show a president using rhetoric aggressively, in some senses defiantly.
He tried to browbeat his critics into silence by creating a string of successful
stump speeches. In Lyndon Johnson's hands, rhetoric often became a blunt
instrument.

If the issues had not been life and death ones, some of Johnson's
machinations almost would be comical. Many of his Vietnam addresses made
political sense: a Navy League luncheon in Manchester, New Hampshire;
dedication of the Amvets National Headquarters; a speech before the 101st

Table 3.3   *Locations for Presidents' Speeches on International Conflict
(N = 617)*

	Washington, D.C.		Domestic U.S.		Outside U.S.	
President	N	%	N	%	N	%
Truman	34	7.7	21	14.5	1	3.1
Eisenhower	38	8.6	8	5.5	1	3.1
Kennedy	26	5.9	15	10.3	0	0.0
Johnson	67	15.2	31	21.4	12	37.5
Nixon	60	13.6	17	11.7	3	9.4
Ford	29	6.6	15	10.3	3	9.4
Carter	59	13.4	15	10.3	5	15.6
Reagan	127	28.9	23	15.9	7	21.9

Airborne Division at Fort Campbell. Others were more opportunistic. Within the first three minutes of his address marking the hundred and fiftieth anniversary of the State of Indiana, for example, Mr. Johnson found himself saying things like this: "In order to have peace we must have strength," "We are going to have to keep our guard up," "The stakes are much too high to be negligent."[25] At a groundbreaking ceremony at an industrial site in Pryor, Oklahoma, Mr. Johnson spoke neither ceremonially nor industrially: "I do know that if we fail in Vietnam, they [the enemy] will have good precedent for trying to gobble up a lot more territory."[26] At a nuclear testing station in Arco, Idaho, Johnson began by offering perfunctory observations about peaceful use of nuclear energy and then used the following transition to launch into a very different kind of speech: "But there is another, and there is a darker side of the nuclear age that we should never forget . . ."[27] Finally, even during remarks presented in honor of Franklin D. Roosevelt at Campobello Island, New Brunswick, Mr. Johnson could not resist linking his goals in Vietnam to those of his political idol:

> No man loved peace more than Franklin D. Roosevelt. It was in the marrow of his soul and I never saw him more grieved than when reports came from the War Department of American casualties in a major battle.
>
> But he led my nation and he led it courageously in conflict—not for war's sake, because he knew that beyond war lay the larger hopes of man.
>
> And so it is today. The history of mankind is the history of conflict and agony—of wars and rumors of wars. Still today, we must contend with the cruel reality that some men still believe in using force and seek by aggression to impose their will on others. And that is not the kind of world that America wants, but it is the kind of world that we have.
>
> The day is coming when those men will realize that aggression against their neighbors does not pay.[28]

Lyndon Johnson's concentration on Vietnam was not unique because he tried to rally his fellow citizens behind something he believed in deeply. It was unique because he was willing to unleash all of his rhetorical power on this one issue and to sacrifice completely the political credits he had earned with his domestic initiatives. Lyndon Johnson understood that speech could be used belligerently. He needed no training in assertiveness. In private, he was a coaxer and a cajoler, but he also enjoyed intimidating others.[29] In public he was little different. He considered presidential speech a lethal weapon, and, at least as far as Vietnam was concerned, it was a weapon he used knowingly.

Speech can be powerful in two ways, then—for audience and for speaker. But all presidents do not necessarily find their primary solace in rhetoric. Some, like Richard Nixon, find theirs in brooding. Others, like Dwight Ei-

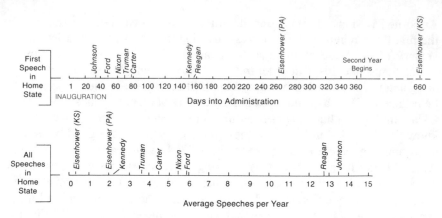

Figure 3.5. Timing and frequency of presidents' speeches in home states.

senhower, find theirs in relaxation. Lyndon Johnson, however, had an oral personality. When the pressures of the job mounted for him, he looked for an audience of friendly faces. Therein lay his power to continue.

Figure 3.5 reveals the various rhetorical uses the presidents made of their home states—how quickly they returned there after assuming the presidency and how often they visited after that. Clearly, Lyndon Johnson was at home on the range. He gave ninety speeches in the State of Texas while president, and he began doing so immediately upon taking the job. In contrast, John Kennedy spoke in Massachusetts only eight times during his administration, and Dwight Eisenhower, who alternately claimed that his roots lay both in Kansas and Pennsylvania (and occasionally in Texas) spoke at home even less frequently. On average, Johnson spoke three times more often at home than all the other presidents except Ronald Reagan (one who also enjoyed his home-state visits, no doubt more for social and political reasons rather than for psychological ones). Although his career had truly made him a creature of the District of Columbia, Lyndon Johnson's basic instincts were Texas instincts, features he displayed during his first speech back home:

> Mr. Chancellor, Mr. Foreign Minister, Mr. Secretary of State:
>
> It is with the greatest pleasure that we bid you welcome to the United States and to my home State of Texas—as a good friend, a great European, and as Chancellor of the Federal Republic of Germany.
>
> You have come to a part of our country where there are many Americans whose forebears came from Germany. So while all of us are your friends, there are many who feel a very personal relationship and who look forward to meeting you.

> We shall be working hard while you are here, but there will also be time
> to meet some of our neighbors, to see us as we are, and to join us in a Texas
> barbecue.[30]

Several questions need to be asked about Mr. Johnson's habits in this
regard: Why did he go home so often? Why did he speak publicly when doing
so? And why did he speak so frequently? Without engaging in long-distance
political psychology, it seems clear that these speeches provided a haven for
LBJ. Any public speaker, after all, would be overjoyed to know that his or
her audience would treat virtually anything said as a provocation to applaud.
When that speaker also happens to be the president of the United States,
the applause will come even more quickly. If that president has been experiencing political stress back in Washington, the applause at home will sound
even louder to him. At home, an audience will permit shirt-sleeve philosophizing, anecdotalism, maudlin emotionality, and talk for the sake of talk. In
his address to the graduating class of the Johnson City High School (his alma
mater) in May of 1964, Mr. Johnson displayed all of these qualities:

> I want you to know that some of you may have to wait 40 years to get something
> this beautiful, but I hope it comes to you as it did to me.
>
> I see in the audience tonight some of the members of the graduating class
> that finished with me a few years ago. I won't specify again how many. But I
> would like to ask them to stand so I can see how they look tonight. I would
> like for all of you to meet them.
>
> Louise, stand up over there. Here is Kitty Clyde. Someone said that she
> had to work as hard this year to get you graduates through this school year as
> she did 40 years ago to get me through. I remember Louise had to copy my
> themes and Kitty Clyde had to help me on other things, and somehow or other
> we managed.
>
> Is there anyone else here tonight from that graduation class? Georgie, are
> you here? Is John Dollahite here? John was always shy of the girls. There were
> just two of us, and I took his part, and somehow or other was about to take
> care of the four, although I guess John must have heard the girls were going to
> be here tonight and that is why he didn't come.
>
> Thank you.[31]

Home, as the expression goes, is a place where they have to take
you in when you go there. Lyndon Johnson found that his Texas speeches
provided precisely this sort of reception, and he also found that their pomp
and circumstance certified to the home folks just how important he had
become. He was no longer "Landslide Lyndon" who had eked his way
into the U.S. House of Representatives in 1938. He was now president of

all the people, welcomer of chancellors, and the most famous graduate of
Johnson High. These speeches reenergized him even though they must have
been enormously time consuming. On February 27, 1968, for example, he
gave two speeches in Texas, departed for the White House to give six more
speeches in three days, and then returned again to Texas on March 1 to
preside over a political testimonial, to sign an old age home proclamation,
and to visit with the staff at NASA in Houston. He flew to Georgia the
next day.

When visiting Texas, Mr. Johnson spoke at the entire range of rhetorical events—press conferences, bill signings, patriotic ceremonies, building dedications, and party rallies. Only some sort of crazed revisionist
would suggest that it was politically necessary for LBJ to have done so
once every other week for five years. He spoke in Texas because it felt
good and because he could speak with all of his emotions there. He used
these speeches to defend his administration as well as himself, confident
that his audience would vindicate both. He did not speak like Dwight
Eisenhower, who once said that he was "so swept with waves of emotion
upon returning to Kansas that he had thrown away his speech text" (but
who almost never spoke there again).[32] He did not speak like John Kennedy,
who once told a Boston audience that he took "special satisfaction in this
day" and was "particularly pleased to be with all of [them] on this most
felicitous occasion," but who offered not a single personal reflection in his
speech.[33] Johnson was not the rootless world traveler that Eisenhower was
nor did he have the ironic cast of mind or emotional restraint of a John
Kennedy. When an emotional Johnson spoke in his home state about American soldiers in Vietnam and their privations and their sacrifices for all of
us, he was expressing his deepest feelings without fear of being declared
insufficiently urbane by Eastern reporters. These Texas speeches permitted
purgation and thus they empowered him.[34]

The Nixon Solution

Speech and power were linked for Richard Nixon as they were for Lyndon
Johnson, but they were linked in fundamentally different ways. Although
psychologizing about presidents is always risky, anecdotal evidence suggests
that Johnson spoke as he felt, that he had no compunctions about using
speech aggressively, but that as a person he also needed clear, public reinforcement of what he said (hence his Texas speeches). Richard Nixon needed
reinforcement also, but he seemed not to savor the responses of live audiences. For Nixon, rhetoric was more a chess match than a boxing match, an
affair of the mind rather than the heart. His legalistic training made him
appreciate the strategy of argument, and he was a knowing analyst of both

political posturing and of press reactions to such posturing. Whereas Lyndon Johnson cast his pearls before all, Richard Nixon husbanded his. He knew how prized the spoken remarks of an American president were, and, knowing that, he spoke only when it suited him.

Table 3.4 shows how differently Nixon and Johnson behaved. Focusing on the point in their (and Jimmy Carter's) administrations when things looked undeniably bleak for them, this table reports the dependence of the presidents on the spoken word. No matter which piece of data is examined, Mr. Nixon's approach is distinctive. While the other presidents badgered their listeners, Nixon enlisted his selectively. This is not to say that he eschewed rhetoric. Rather, he depended more on timing than on quantity, more on drama than on familiarity. Nixon felt that there was power in silence, especially if it were a presidential silence. He spoke only when it seemed appropriate *to him* to do so.

As we see in figure 3.6 (which contrasts his speech frequency with his popularity), this period of relative silence did not improve Mr. Nixon's image, even though it may have, in a curious way, demonstrated that a chief executive who can keep his own counsel is a political force to be reckoned with. In the latter part of 1973 and early 1974, Nixon only dabbled at rhetoric, signaling that he did not need John Kennedy's ceremonies or Lyndon Johnson's stump speeches and that the ultimate key to power for him was how carefully a thing was said, not how often. In one of the rare press conferences

Table 3.4   *Selected Presidential Speaking in Response to "Crisis" Conditions*

	Johnson	Nixon	Carter
Total months in office	61	68	48
Months with 20 or fewer speeches:			
N	15	58	15
%	24.6	86.6	31.3
N speeches during last 12 months in office	309	181	435
Administration's "crisis" point*	Nov. 1967	Nov. 1973	Nov. 1979
Approval rating at "crisis" point	38%	25%	31%
N speeches surrounding "crisis" point†	171	68	155

*Month during which the president reached his penultimate low point in popular approval (Gallup poll ratings).

†Includes all speeches delivered three months before and three months after "crisis" month.

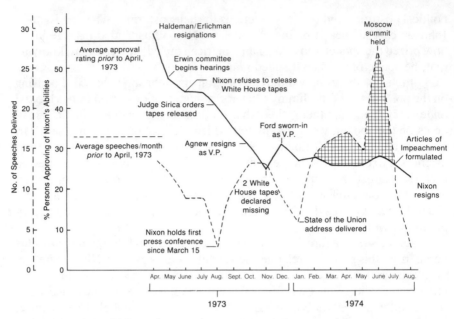

Figure 3.6. Richard Nixon's speech effort and public approval during the Watergate affair. Percent persons approving of Nixon's abilities adapted from R. G. Lehnen, *American Institutions, Political Opinion and Public Policy* (Hinsdale, Ill.: Dryden, 1976), p. 84.

he gave during this silent period (on October 26,1973), he demonstrated the power of being circumspect:

> *Question:* Mr. President, would the new Special Prosecutor have your go-ahead to go to court if necessary to obtain evidence from your files that he felt were vital?
>
> *The president:* Well, Mr. Cormier, I would anticipate that that would not be necessary. I believe that as we look at the events which led to the dismissal of Mr. Cox, we find that these are matters that can be worked out and should be worked out in cooperation and not by having a suit filed by a Special Prosecutor within the executive branch against the President of the United States.
>
> This, incidentally, is not a new attitude on the part of a President . . .
>
> *Question:* There have been reports that you felt that Mr. Cox was somehow out to get you. I would like to ask you if you did feel that, and if so, what evidence did you have.

> *The president:* Mr. Lisagor, I understand Mr. Cox is going to testify next
>   week under oath before the Judiciary Committee, and I would suggest
>   that he perhaps would be better qualified to answer that question.
> *Question:* Mr. President, I wonder if you could share with us your thoughts,
>   tell us what goes through your mind when you hear people, people
>   who love this country and people who believe in you, say reluctantly
>   that perhaps you should resign or be impeached.
> *The president:* Well, I am glad we don't take the vote of this room, let me
>   say . . .
> *Question:* Mr. President, in 1968, before you were elected, you wrote that
>   too many shocks can drain a nation of its energy and even cause a
>   rebellion against creative change and progress. Do you think America
>   is at that point now?
> *The president:* I think that many would speculate—I have noted a lot on the
>   networks, particularly, and sometimes even in the newspapers. But
>   this is a very strong country, and the American people, I think, can
>   ride through the shocks that they have . . .[35]

Mr. Nixon's footwork here is dexterous. In response to the first question he uses a combination of qualified language, the passive voice, and third-
person references to imply that he had answered a question he had not
answered and taken a position he had not taken. He passes off the second
indelicate question, impugning the character of Archibald Cox but humbly
admitting that he was not qualified to respond to the reporter's query. The
third question elicited stiletto-like humor, and the fourth question is, by and
large, answered with innuendo. Four pointed questions asked, none answered, and yet Nixon acquits himself well—powerfully. His remarks on this
occasion were described as virtuoso by many seasoned observers, a reaction
that reinforces Richard Nixon's notion of public speaking as performance,
not communication, of cleverness as its measure, not clarity. Lyndon Johnson's public persona was also powerful, but his power derived from the gut,
not the head, from shouting down his questioners, not trying to finesse them.[36]

Although Richard Nixon did resurface, rhetorically, in February of 1974,
he never again reached his pre-Watergate speech frequency, apparently presuming that a presidential message not heard is a presidential message that
cannot be picked apart by the press. The one major exception to this pattern
was his tour of Europe, Asia, and the Middle East in the early summer of
1974 which, in hindsight, seems more an attempt to rally domestic support
than to make progress in foreign affairs. A speaking trip of this sort was,
from Richard Nixon's standpoint, an ideal one, for the rhetoric of diplomacy
is a tightly controlled rhetoric in which speaking roles are prescribed, messages scripted, and media coverage dependent upon presidential whim. To a

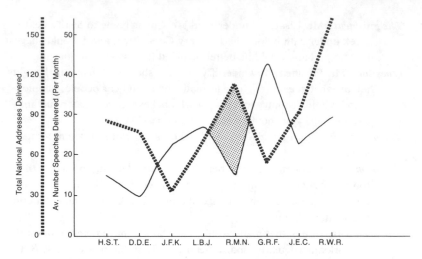

Figure 3.7. Richard Nixon's vs. other presidents' uses of national addresses.

slight extent, the trip succeeded in diverting attention from Watergate (see figure 3.6), but even Richard Nixon's iron control could not save him at this point. Yet the attempt to do so was thoroughly Nixonian because it built upon his essential communication theory: (1) speak for the institution, not for oneself; (2) speak in controlled settings, not those permitting interlocutors; (3) speak for the ages, not for the tempestuous moment. In accordance with this theory, Mr. Nixon addressed a luncheon of the National Citizens' Committee for Fairness to the Presidency before setting out on his trip. To his mind, it was an ideal reason to break his silence. Again, he spoke of the role of the president, of the office of the presidency, which "is much bigger than one man or one President." And the great goal: to build "a peaceful world for our children and our grandchildren and for those of others who have been our friends, and even those who have been our adversaries and our enemies."[37]

One of the most curious things about the Nixon presidency is that his old nemesis, the mass media, ultimately became his most trusted ally. This is certainly not to say that media *personnel* befriended him. Rather, the media themselves, radio and television especially, were enlisted even though they had deserted him earlier—during his debate with John Kennedy in 1960, after his loss to Pat Brown in California in 1962, during his early stump speaking in 1968. But television had given birth to his career too—the "Checkers" speech—and so Richard Nixon came to see the media as a troublesome but necessary ally. As we see in figure 3.7, Mr. Nixon made ample use of radio and television addresses throughout his presidency. They provided him with precisely the features he desired most in a rhetorical situation: attentional focus for him and minimal (or no) distractions from others. Whereas Lyndon Johnson was in many senses too powerful a stimulus for the coolness of television, Mr. Nixon, while unpretty, was crisp and pellucid under almost all media conditions.

The electronic media have an ambivalent relationship with human emotion, not unlike Mr. Nixon's own relationship with it. Raw emotion, Lyndon Johnson's kind of emotion, does not televise well, and uncertain emotion (perhaps Gerald Ford's problem) often has a problem of focus. Richard Nixon was hardly an emotionally expressive creature, but he knew how to talk about emotional topics, and he knew how to make other people respond to these topics emotionally. In this sense he was something of an emotional surgeon. He could show empathy without losing his professional detachment. This ambivalence precluded him from seeming heroic, but it did make him appear both competent and influential.

Figure 3.7 reveals that the gap between his overall rhetorical effort and his use of the media was quite large. Many of these speeches were broadcast only on radio and, as figure 3.8 shows, a great number of them were delivered during Mr. Nixon's reelection campaign in 1972. Radio might have been Nixon's ideal medium. It eliminated his personal stiffness, his uncertain eye contact, and his frequently discrepant facial cues. On radio, he could talk

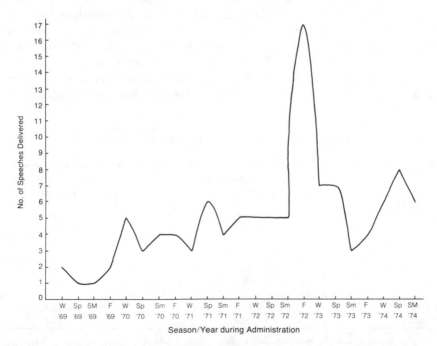

Figure 3.8. Richard Nixon's use of national addresses across time as president.

movingly about the plight of the farmer even though he hardly looked like a tiller of soil. He could talk about his personal experiences in Vietnam and his concern for the elderly without his audience being able to scan his face for the sign of genuine feeling. He could talk piously about governmental responsibility without appearing ministerial. Between October 21 and November 6, 1972, he spoke daily about these and many other matters. Although the air time for these addresses was purchased by the Committee for the Reelection of the President, that fact did not become as apparent on radio as it would have become on television. Mr. Nixon naturally chose to confuse matters even further, using the prerogatives of incumbency to make all of his rhetoric seem apolitical. He presented his radio talks as a kind of continuing dialogue with the American people, frequently referring in his paid addresses to remarks he had made in his unpaid addresses[38] and more than once using these radio talks to make an official announcement unofficially (e.g., a report of new grain shipments to China in his October 27, 1972, address).[39]

An incidental, but nevertheless interesting, feature of Richard Nixon's use of the mass media is reported in table 3.5; it shows that he, more than any other president except Ronald Reagan, made heavy use of value-based messages removed from the everyday business of government. All presidents, naturally, relish the opportunity to light the Christmas tree on the White House lawn or to sing the nation's praises on the Fourth of July. But Mr. Nixon made something of a fetish of such opportunities, perhaps because the American people had so often questioned his own ethics ("Would you buy a used car from this man?"), perhaps because such issuances dovetailed with his conservative political philosophy, or perhaps because it was extraordinarily hard to go wrong when talking about such matters. Another force

Table 3.5   *Presidents' National Addresses Exclusively Devoted to Human Values**

President	% All Speeches By This President (N = 9969)	% National Speeches on Values (N = 107)
Truman	14.1	12.3
Eisenhower	9.3	9.3
Kennedy	7.7	5.6
Johnson	16.4	14.0
Nixon	10.4	19.6
Ford	12.4	9.3
Carter	13.3	2.8
Reagan	16.4	27.1

*Speeches broadcast over the mass media which "heralded the overarching importance of philosophical commitments, ethical responsibility, and creative genius." See Appendix for further information.

recommending these sermonettes was that they allowed Mr. Nixon to deploy his very favorite verbal strategy—the invocation of disembodied (hence, nameless) voices bent on undermining the nation. Richard Nixon was never really strident, but he was at his best when he had a clear, definable opponent against which his rhetoric could struggle. In the practical political world, it is sometimes unseemly to identify these opponents too directly, but in the world of value-centered speaking, such demons can be summoned and delivered a deathblow without partisan blood being spilled. The combination of these features produces a speaker whose standard is true, an audience whose values are preserved, and an ill-defined enemy who has been soundly defeated:

> Recently we have seen that work ethic come under attack. We hear voices saying that it is immoral or materialistic to strive for an ever-higher standard of living. We are told that the desire to get ahead must be curbed because it will leave others behind. We are told that it doesn't matter whether America continues to be number one in the world economically and that we should resign ourselves to being number two or number three or even number four. We see some members of disadvantaged groups being told to take the welfare road rather than the road of hard work, self-reliance, and self-respect.
>
> It is not surprising that so many hard working Americans are wondering: What's happening to the work ethic in America today? What's happening to the willingness for self-sacrifice that enabled us to build a great nation, to the moral code that made self-reliance a part of the American character, to the competitive spirit that made it possible for us to lead the world? . . .
>
> Let the detractors of America, the doubters of the American spirit, take note. America's competitive spirit, the work ethic of this people, is alive and well on Labor Day, 1971.
>
> The dignity of work, the value of achievement, the morality of self-realization—none of these is going out of style.[40]

In both Richard Nixon's and Lyndon Johnson's cases, it is unclear that speech gave them the power they thought it did. But what is clear is that *they acted as if it did*. This power was political as well as psychological, political in that both presidents relied upon speechmaking to establish their authority over their opponents and psychological in that it made them feel safe from their opponents and better about themselves. In one sense, it seems odd that anything as public as public speech could meet such private needs. Yet when we consider how fundamental speech is to one's status as a human being (never mind to one's status as a president), it seems less odd. Speech is but a modality, a way of extending one's humanness, of reaching the humanness of others. Therefore, to observe that speech has power is, in some senses, merely to observe that people wish to be powerful.[41]

Speech as Commodity

To say that politics is dehumanizing is to sound hackneyed, but this seems truer now than it has ever been before. In a very real sense, presidents are less flesh and blood persons than they are widgets in a political machine—cut, shaped, planed, and polished until the machine hums smoothly. Presidents are described in the press as making moves and countermoves, as if they were but blinking lights in a video arcade game. Citizens cynically associate the president with "government" in general and presume that he is enmeshed in a cavernous political system devoid of human feeling. Foreign governments view the president less as an individual with unique fears and hopes and more as simply the current emanation of a Western democracy. Given the political constraints placed on the president of the United States, each of these viewpoints has credence.

But there is an even more fundamental way in which presidents become dehumanized—they sell their speech. A presidential speech is now a prize bought and paid for with political capital. The right to host the president when he speaks is a right purchased either with monetary contributions or with votes (at the polls or in Congress). How long a president will talk ("a major announcement," "just a few brief remarks," etc.) is also a point of negotiation, as is the time of day for his speech, its location, who will introduce him, what access the local press will have, and so forth. The White House is thus the nation's most active, most expensive, and (undeniably) most powerful lecture bureau. This all makes a certain amount of sense for, as an officeholder, a president has little to offer but himself and his words. He can make some political appointments, favor this federal contractor over that one, call up the marines rather than the National Guard. But the more frequent decision he makes is rhetorical—to involve himself or not involve himself in a congressional squabble, to favor a visiting dignitary with a formal banquet or a working dinner, to travel North versus South in the off-year elections. The political costs of each of these potential contracts are calculated when the president makes his decision. The political contractors themselves do all that they can to sweeten the deal, hoping against hope that they have political funding sufficient to "get Reagan" for their fundraiser (as opposed to Bush, or Baker, or Kemp, or worse).

When most Americans think of their president, they imagine him delivering a televised talk from his desk in the White House or facing media personalities during a press conference. But as table 3.6 demonstrates, over 40% of the president's speeches in Washington are delivered to special interest groups or to invited guests (a good many of whom also represent special interests). Americans may choose to think of the nation's Capitol as a counterpart to the Roman agora, and they may choose to think of Richard

Table 3.6   *Audiences for Presidents' Washington, D.C., Speeches*

Audience	N	%
Government employees	106	1.7
Local/press	2797	44.9
National	688	11.0
Invited guests	1147	18.4
Special interest group	1496	24.0

Nixon's chat with the student protestors at the Lincoln Memorial as normal presidential activity. But a great deal of the chief executive's public speaking is really private public speaking, speech acts designed to woo or placate or impress or apologize to a politically influential group.

To some extent, a president thus becomes known by his audiences. In one month, for example, Ronald Reagan addressed the Associated General Contractors, the National Association of State Departments of Agriculture, the Conservative Political Action Conference, the Sister Cities International Program, the White House Correspondents Association, the Young Republican Leadership Conference, and a National Conference of the AFL-CIO.[42] Depending upon their relative political clout, these groups received either a general speech or one carefully adapted to their organizational goals and procedures. Collectively, the above groups point toward the constraints imposed upon an American president by business, labor, bureaucracy, party politics, the media, and political activists. The following peroration was offered by Mr. Reagan to the AFL-CIO, but it is clearly composed of interchangeable words. From an audience's perspective, the power of a presidential speech is binary power—he speaks to them or he doesn't. Very few groups demand more than boilerplate:

> I'm here today because I salute what you've done for America. In your work you build. In your personal lives, you sustain the core of family and neighborhood. In your faith, you sustain our religious principles. And with your strong patriotism, you're the bulwark which supports an America second to none in the world. I believe the American people are with us in our cause. I'm confident in our ability to work together, to meet and surmount our problems, and to accomplish the goals that we all seek.
>
> Now, I know that we can't make things right overnight. But we will make them right. Our destiny is not our fate. It is our choice. And I'm asking you as I ask all Americans, in these months of decision, please join me as we take this new path. You and your forebears built this Nation. Now, please help us rebuild it, and together we'll make America great again.
>
> Thank you very much.[43]

It is not hard to see why a presidential speech is such a high-priced commodity in the political world. Reporters may scoff at most of the speeches they hear by a chief executive, but that is because they hear them all. Most listeners are meeting their president for the first time. Even though they may not sit close to the speaker's podium, they sense that they are very much "there" and that some important bit of news might be shared with them and them alone. Moreover, the presidency is a major repository for the nation's history and sacred truths, and that also makes speeches by the head of state— even in a massively public setting—highly attractive.

Perhaps the most "expensive" presidential speech of all is the special appearance, the "miscellaneous speech"—fluid in structure, spontaneous in appearance and comparatively rare (6.2% of all presidential speeches). It should not be surprising, then, that such speeches (there were roughly 600 of them between 1945 and 1985) are often delivered to members of "invited" audiences. As we saw in Chapter One, speeches of this type were heavily used by Presidents Kennedy, Johnson, and Nixon, each of whom had special talents as public flatterers. These speeches are particularly valuable political tokens for distribution *because they seem so apolitical.* Consider, for example, the remarks Richard Nixon made on March 16, 1974, at the Grand Ole Opry in Nashville, Tennessee. His performance that evening was unusually well received because (1) he had not been making public appearances up to that point; (2) he wandered from topic to topic during the speech, signaling that he was relaxed, among friends; (3) he mixed somber and lighthearted moods and formal and informal language; and (4) even played the piano and put on a yo-yo exhibition for his enraptured audience. One snippet from his speech indicates why listeners regard these speeches as more than worth the price of admission:

> *Mr. Acuff [handing the president a Yo-Yo]:* Now let it come over this way. Hold your hand like this. [Laughter] We are not in any hurry. He don't need to get back up there quick anyway. [Laughter] We need him down here for a while.
>
> Now, turn your hand over and let it ride. Now jerk it back.
>
> *The president:* I will stay here and try to learn how to use the Yo-Yo. You go up and be President, Roy.
>
> *Mr. Acuff:* That is just what it takes to be a great President, is to come among people and be among we working people, we common people, and then be one of us. That is what it takes to be a real President . . .
>
> Mr. President, do you belong to the union, the musician's union? You will get some talk on this if you don't. Come on up here. I want you to take the piano.

The president: I am an honorary member of the musicians union in New York City.

Mr. Acuff: That is great. There will be no argument.

The president: No, but I don't pay dues.

Mr. Acuff: He says he is an honorary member of the union in New York City.

The president: Roy, because of the remarks that I made, it occurred to me that what would be most appropriate at this time on this opening evening—and you still can play in the key of G?

Mr. Acuff: Yes.

The president: Okay, fine. You will know this song when I start playing it—I think they will know it when I start playing it. [Laughter] But anyway, you remember on that prisoners-of-war affair, that dinner, that one of the highlights was when Irving Berlin who had been very ill, came down and brought the original score of the great song that he wrote that everybody sings since then—

Mr. Acuff: Yes, I remember.

The president: I thought possibly we would try that one.

Mr. Acuff: Oh, do, that would be great. "God Bless America."

[The President played "God Bless America" on the piano.][44]

Presidential speeches like these are gifts, but such gifts are earned by their recipients. During his administration, Jimmy Carter made three different trips to the State of Iowa (in *non*electoral years) to pay back in speech a debt he had incurred in votes. On his first visit back, he reminded Iowans that they had helped launch his campaign for the presidency ("When I was lonely you took me in. When I needed support, you gave it to me")[45] and that his gratitude had not abated after the election. Such speaking trips were, quite clearly, good politics, for they showed that Mr. Carter paid his debts with the coin of his realm—his time, his voice. Mr. Carter's speeches in Iowa were hardly exalted (a radio call-in show, a town meeting in Burlington, a speech from the deck of the *Delta Queen*), but he knew the rhetorical rules attendant to such gift giving: (1) *indicate that the speech is being given freely, with no ulterior motives* ("I feel like I'm coming home"); (2) *show that the gift has been purchased with this, and only this, audience in mind* ("Iowa is number one in corn production, number one in hog production"); (3) *allay suspicion of opportunism by linking the giving of the gift to the larger relationship shared* ("You introduced me to your friends. I got to know you. You got to know me"); and (4) *designate the gift/speech as but a token of the relationship, a mere bauble when contrasted to the larger truths shared* *by speaker and audience* ("If you'll stand with me . . . I'll try to . . . work with you to make sure that we keep our Nation as it has always been—the greatest country on Earth").[46]

Although it is not frequently recognized as such, the giving of a gift can itself be an exercise in the use of power. When giving another a gift, we sometimes engender in them a sense of obligation to us, enhance our social image by appearing munificent, and, in general, constrain how the other person will relate to us in the future. This is not the pretty side of gift giving, but it is a real side—especially in political circles. Thus, when analyzing the motives of a political benefactor, it is important to know how much the gift really cost him or her. During the first six months of his administration, for example, Richard Nixon spoke to such groups as the Department of Housing and Urban Development, the National Association of Broadcasters, the American Cancer Society, the League of Women Voters, the Organization of American States, and many other groups. During his *last* six months in office, however, Mr. Nixon's largess was considerably more circumscribed: the Young Republican Leadership Conference, the Veterans of Foreign War, the U.S. Chamber of Commerce, the Daughters of the American Revolution, and, naturally, the National Citizens Committee for Fairness to the President. What the president giveth, he too can taketh away.

In connection with this latter point, to deny another a gift can also be an exercise in power relations. One political curiosity demonstrates this: between October 30, 1964, and April 17, 1975, no president spoke in the tenth largest state in the nation—Massachusetts. No other state could boast (or be ashamed) of such a record. During this period Utah had three speeches, as did South Carolina and Vermont, and even the citizens of Wyoming had a chance to meet their president. In fact, *no* state was deprived like Massachusetts.[47] Lyndon Johnson declared in his first speech there that he was part of an "Austin to Boston" pact, that Massachusetts would henceforth be known "as the home of the Kennedys and the Johnsons," and that he had "more men from Massachusetts in the White House than from all the other States put together."[48] Despite his professions of ardor, however, Lyndon Johnson never came back "home."

As we see in figure 3.9 (which plots the New England speaking of the two presidents), Mr. Johnson did manage to return to Windsor Locks, Connecticut; Lewiston, Maine; Manchester, New Hampshire; Kingston, Rhode Island; and Burlington, Vermont. We see that Richard Nixon also visited every New England state except its most populous one. Not until Gerald Ford returned in April of 1975 did Bay Staters hear a president speak in person. This is not to say, of course, that the good citizens of Massachusetts felt particularly deprived during this decade of presidential reticence. Neither Presidents Johnson nor Nixon were especially loved there—after all, one of its native sons tried to remove LBJ from office in 1968, and it was the only

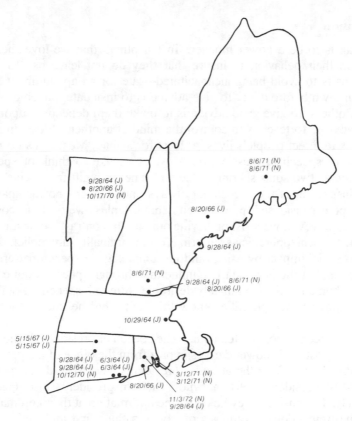

Figure 3.9. Speechmaking in New England by Presidents Johnson and Nixon.

state to vote for Richard Nixon's rival in 1972. From the standpoint of political economics, the citizens of Massachusetts clearly deserved their fate.

It would be gross speculation, of course, to suggest that there was something truly conspiratorial about all of this, but given what we now know about the personalities of the presidents involved (Johnson felt inferior around Harvard men; Nixon detested student activists; both had a "Kennedy complex"), their behavior seems understandable. After all, the media in Massachusetts are notoriously vigilant as well as notoriously liberal, and its citizens are not known for suffering in silence when a president they do not like comes to address them. Were Presidents Johnson and Nixon intentionally snubbing the people of Massachusetts? Were these presidents flaunting the authority of their office by traveling everywhere but there? Clearly, no definitive answers are possible here, but the questions raised about speech and power are fascinating indeed. To speak to another is, in some small way, to honor that person. To refuse to speak, to have forgotten to speak, or to be too busy to speak, makes a statement of a very different kind.

Conclusion

To speak is to be a power monger. To tell others that we love them is to constrain their behavior, to insure that they do not leave us. To ask for directions is to avoid being incapacitated—late for an appointment, unable to reach town before dark. To give advice is to insinuate ourselves into the lives of others; to give good advice is to make them dependent upon us for future advice. To teach is to control the mind of another, at least in part; to preach is to direct people's lives, at least for awhile. Most of us do not like to think of speech in these ways. Most of us like to think of speech as mutuality, as two souls sharing space and time, as a gift freely given. But a closer inspection of the speech act always finds power—power unacknowledged, power disguised, power even denied. Unless we wish no control of our lives, however, we insist on having our say. In contrast, some authorities describe the schizophrenic as suffering from marginality, an implicit decision to forgo social impact by using random, unintelligible speech patterns. The corollary is that the impulse to be influential through speech is quite normal and, in a human society, ultimately desirable. After all, speech is not the only route to power. Adolph Hitler knew this route, but he knew other routes too.

All speech is not created equal. The speech of presidents is more powerful than most. This power derives in part from the office of the presidency, but it also derives from the attitudes presidents have toward the speech act itself. Most presidents, certainly most modern presidents, use speech aggressively. The position they hold and the information at their command give them the tremendous advantages of saying a thing first and saying it best. Modern presidents engage in repartee with the press, knowing all the while that such polite jousts are really struggles for attitudes and hence votes and hence money and hence might. Modern presidents can be as stern as a deacon in the pulpit or as frivolous as youngsters rolling Easter eggs, but whether silly or serious they are always serious. Modern presidents play politics, a game about the distribution of power. Speech is how they play.

FOUR

Speech and Drama:
The President versus
the Mass Media

T HIS CHAPTER FOCUSES UPON THE TWO MOST POWERFUL ENTITIES IN THE contemporary United States. The American presidency, arguably the most unique political institution yet devised by any civilized polity, reaches directly into the lives of the American people on a daily basis largely through the efforts of a second great institution—the mass media. Two other powerful institutions, corporate America and organized religion, seem to founder when they lose the support of presidents and journalists. Likewise, the potential influence of government bureaucrats, members of Congress, and military leaders is sharply curtailed should they lose the confidence of network anchorpersons and the nation's chief executive. Alone, the president and the press are influential. Together, they are invincible.

And they are almost always together. As Michael Grossman and Martha Kumar claim, "The President represents the single most important story that the network follows on a continuing basis."[1] Indeed, although nobody has yet done the research, it surely must be the case that some story about the president of the United States has appeared in every issue of the *New York Times* printed in this century and on every CBS Evening News program telecast during the last three decades. No matter how pedestrian his day may have been, no matter what other matters of great moment may have imposed themselves on the nation that day, an American president will be seen, heard, and read every twenty-four hours. After discharging his public duties for the day, the president will retire to his private quarters to stare at the electronic self he created and to read the news in which he figures so prominently. This press/president relationship is probably more mutually parasitic than it is truly symbiotic—John Kennedy canceled newspaper subscriptions, CBS refused to televise some of Jerry Ford's speeches—but neither organism could sustain life without the other's nourishment.

Nowhere, perhaps, is this parasitism more apparent than when the president and the press come face-to-face. Nobody, perhaps, was as keenly aware of the interpersonal and political dynamics of press relations as Richard Nixon. Several things are noteworthy about the following exerpt from Mr. Nixon's press conference of June 29, 1972, the most subtle but most important of which is that relationships between the mass media and the chief executive have now reached tertiary levels of consciousness. That is, while presidents have always monitored their relationships with the mass media and while many presidents have been self-conscious when appearing before the press, only now are we seeing the sort of superconsciousness that allows presidents to *talk about such relationships while taking part in them*. Although Richard Nixon was unusually crafty and hence almost metastrategic, he probably spoke for all presidents when asked to comment on press relations. It is noteworthy that Nixon's answer to the following question was longer than most of those he gave during that press conference, longer than his comments on the Supreme Court, longer than his response to questions about the bombing of North Vietnam, longer than his speculations about a vice-presidential choice for the upcoming election. The length of Mr. Nixon's response alone signals the importance he placed on his relationship with the Fourth Estate:

> *Question:* Mr. President, this is kind of an in-house question, but I think it is of interest.
>
> *The president:* You would not ask an "out-house" question would you? [*Laughter*]
>
> *Question:* I am not sure what an out-house question is.
>
> *The president:* I know.
>
> *Question:* Nevertheless, I think this is of interest to our viewers and listeners and readers, and that is that you seem to have done very well tonight, you are certainly in command of this situation, and yet this is the first time in a year that you have been willing to meet with us in this kind of forum.
>
> What is your feeling about these types of press conferences?
>
> *The president:* It is not that I am afraid to do it. I have to determine the best way of communication and also, and this will sound self-serving and is intended to be, I have to use the press conference—I don't mean use the reporters, but use the press conference—when I believe that is the best way to communicate or inform the people. Now, for example, I had to make a decision—it may have been wrong—but I concluded that in the very sensitive period leading up to the Peking trip and the period thereafter and in the even more sensitive period, as it turned out to be, leading up to the Moscow trip and the period immediately there-

after that the press conference, even "no-commenting" questions was not a useful thing for the President of the United States to engage in.

I felt I was, of course, on television enough in that period anyway, if that was the problem. As you know, I have met the press, not perhaps as often as some members of the press would like, but I have met them in other formats than the televised conference.

The other point that I should make is this: I know that many members of the press have been discussing the press conference and they feel that perhaps the President, this President, is tempted to downgrade the press or downgrade the press conference. I am not trying to do that. It is useful, it is important. It requires hard work in preparing for it, I can assure you. But I think I can best put it this way: Every President has to make a decision when he enters the office about his relations with the press and about his job. I mean, I am as human as anybody else, I like to get a good press. But on the other hand I had to determine, and I did determine, as I am sure most Presidents do, that what was most important at this time was for me to do a good job because the stakes were so high, particularly in foreign policy, and also in some areas of domestic policy.

Now, if I do a good job, the fact I get a bad press isn't going to matter; if I do a bad job, a good press isn't going to help. When November comes, the people will decide whether I have done a good job or not and whether I have had so many press conferences is probably not going to make a lot of difference.

I trust I can do both because it is essential for a President to communicate with the people, to inform the press who, of course, do talk to the people, either on television, radio, or through what they write.

I hope perhaps in the future we can avoid the feeling on the part of the press that the President is antagonistic to them. I can't say whether the President thinks the press is antagonistic to him, but that is another matter.

Mr. Cormier: Thank you, Mr. President.[2]

The theme of the present chapter—that the relationship between the mass media and American presidents can best be viewed dramatistically— is amply in evidence here. The opening scene is a mild joust between king and courtier, with coy humor by the former generating coy innocence in the latter. The reporter then observes that the president has "done" (i.e., performed) very well that night and suggests that he appear on stage more often. Mr. Nixon next launches into a long and rambling soliloquy, a soliloquy as disjointed as any of Hamlet's and one equally filled with the Dane's under-

stated passions and dark reflections. Virtually every statement by Nixon
contains a self-reference, suggesting how close to the bone the media's
parries and thrusts can be for a president. Like Hamlet, Richard of Whittier
was no mean swordsman himself, admitting in paragraph 7 that he had to
"use the press conference" ("I don't [heh, heh] mean use the reporters")
as best he saw fit and that he was not, above all, "afraid" of his opponents
in the press. It is revealing that Mr. Nixon *began* his soliloquy with these
sentiments and that he later bolstered his argument ("I have met them [the
media] in other formats"), even though nobody had suggested that Mr.
Nixon's viscera were lacking.

In paragraph 7 of his reply, Nixon acknowledges something we will
investigate in some depth in this chapter—that the press conference is but
one way to bend the media to the will of the president. Presidential staffs
have now become adept at arranging tours, building stages, selecting scripts,
and costuming their star so as to best display his (not the media's) talents.
The dramatic tension one senses between press and president is therefore
tension related to social control: Who shall direct the minds and hearts of
voters? To be fair to the dramatistic metaphor, then, it is best to think of
both king and courtier as vying for the footlights at all times ("I am as human
as anybody else, I like to get a good press"), and who sense that no lighting
is probably ample enough to embrace two such portly egos ("I can't say
whether . . . the press is antagonistic"). As we shall see here, it is not yet
possible to tell which player is strong enough to send the other reeling into
the upstage shadows. In earlier times (e.g., during the Truman and Eisenhower administrations), the president clearly had the upper hand. Today,
however, reporters themselves are "media personalities," and the best of
them are now interviewed by still other reporters (e.g., Dan Rather soliciting
the views of Walter Cronkite during the 1984 party conventions). Image has
become issue. The president of the United States now tells reporters what
they are thinking, tells them, moreover, what they are thinking about what
he is thinking, and tells them, in the third person, that all is not as it appears:
"I know that many members of the press have been discussing the press
conference and that they feel that perhaps the President, this President, is
tempted to downgrade the press or downgrade the press conference. I am
not trying to do that."

"Of course you are, Mr. President" implied every important news
commentator later that evening on the network news programs, thus making
their reviews of the president's speech a kind of production itself. In this
chapter, we shall examine, first, how representatives of the mass media treat
a presidential speech and how reporters thus become extraordinarily busy
political actors themselves. Then we shall consider how presidents try to
interrupt the psychological momentum of the mass media by staging politics
on their own terms. Needless to say, this public tussling between press and

president is marvelously entertaining stuff for the American people in their front-row seats. But it is most unclear that any of this teaches in the way that great drama should teach. There is, in fact, every reason to suspect that such shenanigans do little more than divert—presidents from their jobs, reporters from their better selves, and voters from important political realities. All too often the president merely plays Punch to the mass media's Judy.

Words about Presidential Words[3]

Although there has been comparatively little systematic research about how the press treats the presidency, there has been a good deal of scholarly speculation about such matters. Figure 4.1 captures the rival positions. The first relationship described ("No Bias") is the simplest but least favored. It maintains that the media merely pass along—faithfully and without distortion—what the president has said. This "straight-news hypothesis" holds that there is a one-to-one relationship between a speech event and its reportage. Numerous studies have cast doubt on such a hypothesis, but the journalistic community stoutly embraces it. Says Walter Cronkite: "We newsmen are not jugglers, dancers, ventriloquists, singers or actors seeking applause. We are not in the business of winning popularity contests. It is not our job to entertain, nor, indeed, to please anyone except Diogenes."[4]

Diogenes and Walter Cronkite are seemingly alone in their reasoning about politics and the press. Many more hold to the views expressed by Spiro Agnew and Edith Efron who launched blistering attacks on the mass media for their alleged liberal bias.[5] Agnew and Efron argued (to many, persuasively) that journalists are socialized in a left-leaning media fraternity, that the editorial gatekeepers in most newspapers and television stations in the United States systematically prohibit conservative views from being heard, and that a Republican like Richard Nixon did not stand a chance of being treated fairly by the American media. Numerous fact-finding groups (e.g., Accuracy in Media) have sprung up to redocument Agnew's claims, and the 1980s witnessed the inauguration of entire television networks (e.g., the Christian Broadcasting Network) whose avowed purpose was to offset the radicalization purportedly encouraged by traditional media outlets.

A somewhat less histrionic perspective holds that critics like Agnew and Efron have it all wrong, that the American media subtly support corporate capitalism, that media representatives are stooges for reactionary, worker-exploitative values, and that American politicians are forced to the Right by the implicit ideological routines of newsgathering in the United States. In a popularized account, Robert Cirino maintained that important matters like corporate pollution, world hunger, and a variety of "establishment crimes" are systematically excluded from public inspection by media moguls.[6] In her detailed inspection of news production, the sociologist Gaye Tuchman arrives at a similar conclusion, arguing that "the act of categorizing is an act of theorizing" and arguing also that reporters have little psychological choice but to emphasize the views of those who sign their paychecks.[7]

Option no. 4 is different still. It holds that the mass media are powerless in comparison to a sitting president and that, despite their protestations, modern journalists have little choice but to do the ultimate bidding of the nation's chief executive. Denis Rutkus recounts how frequently modern presidents have availed themselves of free air time and how infrequently such privileges have been denied them.[8] Terry Buss and Richard Hofstetter detail

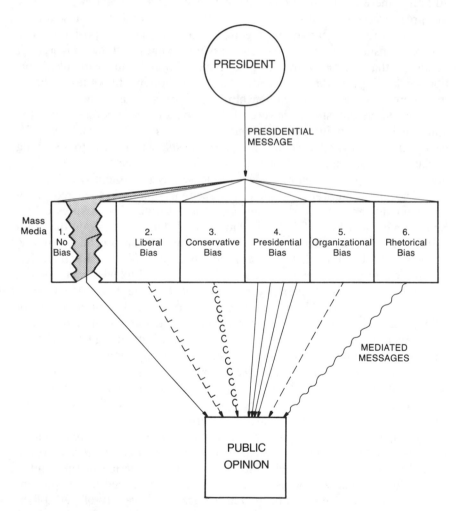

Figure 4.1. Alternative views of the presidency/press relationship.

the many subtle and not-so-subtle ways in which the president can intimidate the news media (e.g., by selectively providing backgrounders, by staging media events, by manipulating journalism's "star system," etc.) and hence insure that he is covered on his terms.[9] As Grossman and Rourke phrase it, ". . . the terms of the exchange relationship are still fundamentally in the president's favor."[10] Clearly, this would come as a surprise to many recent presidents.

A more "sociological" explanation of press/president relationships is depicted as the fifth main option in figure 4.1. This explanation shifts the emphasis from the presidency to the mass media, holding that certain organizational realities central to the gathering and writing of news dictate much of what will eventually be presented as news. Thus, for example, one observer found evidence that Henry Luce's personal political philosophy affected how *Time* covered Presidents Truman through Kennedy,[11] while another argued that the economic/geographic fact that newsgathering is centered in New York City and Washington, D.C., largely determines what is *seen* as newsworthy and hence what is *reported* as newsworthy.[12] Researchers Paul Arnston and Craig Smith reason that both the informal expectations and the more formal, bureaucratic procedures found in any business will necessarily transform presidential inputs into media-stamped outputs.[13] One set of authors even goes so far as to suggest that sometimes presidents use their knowledge of these media traditions to help them determine what news they, the presidents, should make in the first place.[14]

A sixth and final perspective holds that all mediated messages, including the news, grow out of certain generic (or class-bound) rules. These rules "not only place constraints upon how ideas are expressed but they also constrain what kinds of ideas are likely to be expressed. Over the years, these generic structures become entrenched (if they are socially rewarded), and messages emanating from them become self-reflective and, necessarily, formulaic."[15] This rhetorical viewpoint argues that the "no bias" perspective is naive, the political-bias perspectives too labyrinthine, and the other theories of news bias too functionalistic. The rhetorical viewpoint concerns itself with the fantasy themes implicit in news content, the "melodramatic imperative" needed to make news interesting, the various strategies used to render news anchorpersons credible, and the tonal features required to make televised news suitably memorable.[16] This perspective regards the president as a muse, his speeches as a plot to be exploited, and the reporters who cover presidents as playwrights. It is this perspective my research best supports.

To get an idea of how the news media react to presidential speechmaking (thereby extending, counteracting, or reconstituting what the president has said), I and two associates completed an in-depth content analysis of some forty-five newscasts devoted to major presidential addresses delivered between 1969 and 1978. (These "stimulus speeches" are recorded in table

4.1.) In all, some 5.7 hours of compiled videotape were studied for both their verbal and visual features. The average presidential news story lasted 7.7 minutes, and almost all of the stories were broadcast during the first half of the nightly news shows (presidents normally get top billing).[17] All three networks were represented equally in the study as were the three presidents focused upon—Richard Nixon, Gerald Ford, and Jimmy Carter. The longest news story lasted seventeen minutes (ABC's coverage of Nixon's Vietnam speech of November 3, 1969) and the shortest less than a minute (Gerald Ford's second State of the Union speech). The topics of the presidents' speeches ranged across the domestic and international scenes. Thus, although the sample used was just that, a sample, it was broad enough to suggest the general approach reporters used each night when representing (i.e., re-presenting) the activities of the chief executive.

The importance of conducting such analyses cannot be gainsaid. Because many Americans tune in more faithfully to the nightly news than to the president's speech of the previous evening, the network's recapitulations/ interpretations of the president's speech may be even more influential politically than what the president himself said originally. In a sense, then, a study

Table 4.1   *Network Commentaries Analyzed*

Speech Topic	Date of Newscast	Network
Nixon		
Vietnam	Nov. 4, 1969	ABC, CBS, NBC
Cambodia	May 1, 1970	CBS, NBC
Economy	Aug. 16, 1971	ABC, CBS, NBC
Watergate I	May 1, 1973	ABC, CBS, NBC
Watergate II	Aug. 16, 1973	ABC, CBS, NBC
State of Union	Jan. 31, 1974	ABC, CBS
Watergate III	April 30, 1974	ABC, CBS
Ford		
Economy	Oct. 8, 1974	ABC, CBS
Energy I	Jan. 14, 1975	ABC, CBS, NBC
State of Union I	Jan. 15, 1975	ABC, CBS, NBC
Energy II	May 28, 1975	ABC, CBS
State of Union II	Jan. 20, 1976	ABC, CBS, NBC
Carter		
Goals	Feb. 3, 1977	CBS
Energy I	April 19, 1977	ABC, CBS, NBC
Bert Lance	Sept. 21, 1977	ABC, CBS, NBC
Energy II	Nov. 9, 1977	CBS
State of Union	Jan. 20, 1978	ABC, CBS, NBC
Mideast	Sept. 19, 1978	ABC, CBS, NBC

of network *echoes* may be a study of the only presidential voices many Americans ever hear.

Each newscast was inspected for how often and how long certain general features were portrayed: How much of the president's speech was reshown? Where did the action take place? (At the White House? On Capitol Hill? In the network's studio?) Were voter's reactions to the president's speeches solicited? Were some politicians' viewpoints featured more often than others? Were geographical areas in the United States represented proportionally? Also coded were the kinds of statements reporters made in broadcasts—explanatory, evaluative, or generally interpretive. We examined the focus of the newscast, determining whether it had a policy orientation, a primary concern for the president's style, a congressional emphasis, etc. Finally, we did a careful analysis of the pictures shown during the newscasts, distinguishing between a presidential and a voter's focus, noting what sorts of activities had been filmed for airing (e.g., a bill signing, students protesting, etc.), and monitoring the use of "action" versus sedentary shots. In other words, we analyzed the news shows as if they were carefully written, graphically elaborate works of electronic art (which they are), and we also took pains to determine *how* the networks built dramatic intensity into even the most prosaic presidential event. Our results indicate that such effects are achieved by restricting the role portrayals of (1) the president and (2) personnel in the news media. Generally speaking, we found very little variation in the "scripts" analyzed primarily because the "dramatis personae" were so consistent.[18]

For example, the *president's role* in the newscasts varied insignificantly. Although Newton Minow and his colleagues have argued, "Because of who he is, newsmen and their editors allow the president to speak for himself. The remarks of an opposition spokesman may be summarized in television news reporting or analysis; the president's views usually are given in his own words,"[19] this is not the case. Figure 4.2 indicates the relative amount of time accorded the cast of characters on presidential newscasts. Clearly, the president is least often seen, even though it is the president, of course, who had provided the stimulus for the news occasion. Consider the facts:

1. Presidents were *shown* in only forty-one of the 173 major thematic units.
2. Twenty-four of the forty-five newscasts *never* depicted the chief executive.
3. President's words were *heard* in only eight of the forty-five broadcasts studied (for a total of 27.2 minutes of air time).
4. But presidents were *seen* speaking (voicelessly) in fourteen of the forty-five newscasts (for a total of 65.3 minutes).
5. The ratio between total presidential speaking and total broadcast length was 1:13.

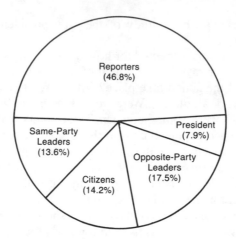

Figure 4.2. Speaking during presidential newscasts (minutes allotted).

In short, presidential newscasts are presidential only in the sense that the chief of state provides the "news peg" upon which the show hangs. Critics of the imperial presidency who worry that networks give sitting presidents an unfair second helping of media exposure after delivery of a major address may thus be comforted by these findings. Generally, the networks depict a silent president: viewers are two-and-one-half times more likely to *see* a president speaking (with voice-over provided by news commentators) than to *hear* that president. Thus, even though ABC devoted fifteen minutes to its coverage of Jimmy Carter's speech on the Mideast on September 19, 1978, the only portion of this speech quoted was the following: "After the signing of this framework last night and during the negotiations concerning the establishment of the Palestinian self-government, no new Israeli settlements will be established in this area."[20] These twenty-nine words were a considerable improvement over Gerald Ford's treatment at the hands of the media on January 20, 1976. Not one of the three networks included a single excerpt from his hour-long address of the previous evening.

Generally, then, the president plays a bit part on such news shows, ostensibly because he performed the evening before—alone on stage. It is fascinating, though, that the networks felt the need to *depict* the president speaking (silently), thus making him a ghostly presence called up to add color to the evening news' proceedings. Indeed, if a viewer watched nothing but the evening news shows, he or she might well view the president of the United States as both inert and inept.

But if the president is not speaking on such newscasts about his speeches, what then is he doing? Largely, he is providing an opportunity for dramatic conflict. Reporters love a fight, and they are not beyond starting one, given their ardor for the sport. In recent times the dialectical formula for political newscasts has been well worked out, and reporters often play a game the psychiatrist Eric Berne once labeled "Let's you and him fight."[21]

Turning to table 4.2, we can find such anecdotal evidence of this long-standing contest: twenty-two newscasts from the White House juxtaposed against twenty-two from Capital Hill, a perfect balance between the neutral "explanations" and the more opinionated "evaluations/commentaries," congressional or lay interviews (far more than half of which was critical of the president) in virtually every news broadcast, emphasis on "presidential policy" more than equaled by reactions to the president-as-leader. Thus, one gets the sense that the networks see it as their duty to remind the president on a nightly basis that, in America, it is the people—establishment politicians, laypersons (occasionally), and professional commentators—who govern.

Much of the networks' time is spent setting up these ferocious struggles, goading Combatant A with remarks made about him or her by Combatant B. Ideally, of course, the contestants are placed in the same ring (e.g., during presidential debates). If the combatants have not shared the same physical space, the networks insure that they square off at roughly the same time (e.g., via instant commentaries or by "equal time" arrangements). If even this is not possible, presidents and their adversaries can—through the magic of television—be spliced together in such a way that the literal constraints of space and time are dissolved. By prompting and promoting such political wrangling, news commentators dramatize the institutional dialectic that keeps viewers attentive. Thus, for example, on the evening following Richard Nixon's announcement of his Cambodia operation, CBS presented a full two-minute excerpt of a speech made that day by Senator Edward Kennedy. To do so, CBS had to go to the trouble of arranging a feed from Boston, but the result was a passionate, hard-hitting speech by Kennedy decrying "five years of nightmare" and concluding with, "This is madness, and this must be said. It is also demeaning to a great nation to attempt to justify it in the name of patriotism and honor and glory."[22]

Richard Nixon and Edward Kennedy were naturals for such a skirmish. They played their political roles flawlessly and consistently, thereby insuring the things that stereotypes always insure: simplicity, predictability. Thus, because of his own pugnacious personality and because of the media's (in some senses, perverse) attraction to such a personality, Mr. Nixon's speeches generated twice as many lay responses as did Jimmy Carter's, three times as many as Jerry Ford's. Moreover, he provoked twice the number of reactions from *both* Republicans and Democrats than either of his immediate successors in office. Nixon led the field in generating reporters' "general evaluations" as well.

Table 4.2   *General Features of Presidential Newscasts (N = 45)*

	Total Duration (in Minutes)	%	N Newscasts	%*
Topics:				
International affairs	100:55	29	8	18
Domestic policy	195:50	57	26	58
State of the Union	47:50	14	11	24
Presidents:				
Nixon	165:45	48	18	40
Ford	76:10	22	13	29
Carter	102:40	30	14	31
Networks:				
ABC	113:50	33	13	29
NBC	105:40	31	15	33
CBS	125:05	36	17	38
Reportorial type:				
One reporter	113:10	33	37	82
More than one reporter	226:55	67	38	84
Reporter purpose:				
Explanation	167:15	49	32	71
General evaluation	140:45	41	35	78
Official commentary	35:05	10	18	40
Reporter activity:				
Summarizes	62:20	18	24	53
Extrapolates	75:55	51	33	73
Introduces	69:45	20	17	38
General discussion	35:05	11	18	40
Reporter focus:				
Presidential policy	89:00	26	23	51
Presidential style	34:00	10	15	33
Presidential action	26:10	8	7	16
Congressional reaction	44:35	13	19	42
Lay reaction	49:10	14	15	33
Background information	89:30	26	3	7
Miscellaneous	10:40	3	4	9
Lay response:				
Individual	7:20	15	5	11
More than one	40:50	85	15	33
Republican response:				
Individual	25:55	59	12	27
More than one	18:10	41	7	16
Democratic response:				
Individual	27:55	45	12	27
More than one	33:40	55	14	31

Table 4.2   (*continued*)

	Total Duration (in Minutes)	%	N Newscasts	%*
Visual background:				
Natural (e.g., rivers, people)	232:05	70	41	91
Artificial (e.g., studio logo)	101:50	30	28	62
Visual focus on citizens:				
Everyday behaviors	27:40	38	10	22
Verbal reactions to president	45:30	62	13	29
Visual focus on president:				
Public speaking	65:15	68	14	31
Ceremonial exchange	16:10	17	6	13
Casual conversation	15:00	15	5	11
General location:				
Network studio	70:25	21	32	71
White House	79:20	23	22	49
U.S. Capitol	79:35	23	22	49
Other U.S. city	58:20	17	17	38
International	28:40	8	6	13
Miscellaneous	26:15	8	15	33
Domestic location:				
Washington, D.C.	176:00	73	35	78
Urban North	32:50	14	13	29
South/West	21:10	9	7	16
Mixed	9:50	4	3	7

*Need not total to 100% since subcategories may appear multiple times in a newscast.

An especially popular technique used by the media when dealing with Richard Nixon was to travel to some comparatively remote site to interview, serially, large numbers of the nation's citizens; 46% of these lay interviews were based on the remarks of five or more people, such as black leaders in Mississippi (November 4, 1969, ABC), Chicago commuters (August 16, 1973, ABC), and students at Georgia State University (May 1, 1973, ABC). Exactly why Mr. Nixon received such treatment is open to question. Certainly the issues he dealt with—Vietnam, Cambodia, Watergate—were more volatile than those faced by Presidents Ford or Carter. Also, Spiro Agnew may have been correct in espying a virulent anti-Nixon strain in the established media. Perhaps the best interpretation, however, is that Mr. Nixon's personality and policies stimulated the electronic media to do what they do best—keep a fight going.

A third major feature of the president's role on the nightly newscasts is that his behavior is made to stand as evidence of certain myths the mass media perpetuate about professional politicians. On virtually every newscast watched, presidents were described as cunning strategists who did all in their power to build and protect a political image. In this scenario, the newscaster's job is to (1) uncover such strategies and (2) hold up the president's image to public inspection. The scholar Thomas Benson had observed this phenomenon before: " . . . political talk is often [portrayed as] a matter of image building, but television penetrates the mask and reveals the inner politician."[23] Researcher David Swanson had observed it too: "[Politicians'] actions and statements are presented as contrivances designed solely to win votes and power."[24] Constantly on the evening news we are reminded of such things, with the media taking a rhetorical game like politics and making it a metarhetorical game.

At Jimmy Carter's press conference announcing Bert Lance's resignation, for example, one of the first questions Mr. Carter was asked by a reporter (and the one question selected for rebroadcast that evening) was if he thought that the Lance affair had damaged Mr. Carter's personal credibility. Some years earlier, matters of strategy were also called to the surface by David Snell of ABC news when he asked a cynical college student if "the public will respond well to 'God Bless America' at the end of the [first Watergate] speech." The young woman responded to the question quickly, appropriating the expected dramatistic metaphor: "It was almost, almost a comedy last night watching him try to be so sincere. I mean it really was. It was typical Nixon like I'd never seen him before."[25] An even more instructive example of metacriticism occurred when Dan Rather opened his description of public reaction to Nixon's Silent Majority speech with, "The president spent much of today convincing himself and trying to convince others that his Vietnam policy speech is an overwhelming success" and, then, after suggesting none too subtly that much of the positive reaction to the speech had been managed, concluded on an innocent note: "How many of the letters and telegrams are spontaneous and how many are part of the carefully orchestrated Republican party publicity campaign, it is too early to say."[26]

Reporters have long enjoyed proving that the emperor had left home without his underwear. Eric Sevareid was particularly fond of this approach, and his commentaries often dwelt on the strategic, thereby bringing the president down to (or below) the level of his constituents. Sevareid's commentaries were not so much *political* criticism as they were *rhetorical* criticism. Commenting upon Jimmy Carter's second major speech on energy, Sevareid began by stating that "there was a certain empty symbolism about the plan" by Mr. Carter to conserve fuel supplies. Sevareid went on to comment on the generic features of the speech ("It was neither a cozy chat, equipped with fireplace or sweater like last spring, nor was it a spell-binding appeal to the emotions"); he analyzed Mr. Carter's nonverbal appeal ("He was like a businessman in a Brooks Brothers suit reading the quarterly profit and loss statement to the stockholders"); he picked apart the chief executive's supporting material ("Even in print, statistics stir few glands, save those of economists"); and he even went so far as to make a metarhetorical event doubly metarhetorical: "He [Carter] did not get the morning headlines in various important regions, including New York, New Jersey, Virginia, even Washington itself. State and local election returns nearly shoved him off page one."[27]

Fed a steady diet of such innuendo, the American people have little choice but to see their elected officials as powerful but as essentially duplicitous as well. Depending upon one's viewpoint, fostering the image of president-as-manipulator either serves the ends of democracy (by fostering iconoclasm) or it subverts it by precluding pure-hearted, but thin-skinned, leaders from entering the turbulent world of mediated politics. When the details of the president's role on televised newscasts are examined carefully, then, the leader of the free world is found to be little more than a prop for the news of the day, but a prop that generates dialectic and reminds us of the perfidy of political life. The newstellers summon the president, require that he mumble a few (drastically edited) lines, and then that he roam their stage while bit players comment aloud about his meanderings and his dramatic flaws. The effect is fast-paced and pleasing, surely not intellectually taxing. Presidential newscasts do not tell us a great deal about the complexities of the office, about the nation's policy options, nor even very much about the president's speeches. They therefore leave us with a patina of understanding, but they rarely leave us bored.

If the president is devil on such newscasts, who then is saint? As we saw in figure 4.2, it is not the American public; they are rarely heard from. More commonly (as we see in table 4.2), the networks depict powerful persons doing powerful things. Some examples: (1) in *none* of the forty-five newscasts was a lay reaction ever solicited *before* a reaction from the political establishment had been recorded; (2) almost three-quarters of the action televised occurred in the citadel of American power—Washington, D.C. (vs. 9% for all of the Southern and Western states); (3) almost half of the action filmed occurred at either the White House or the U.S. Capitol; (4) the nation's citizens were interviewed in only twenty of the forty-five broadcasts studied, and these interviews were only *shown* in thirteen cases; (5) roughly 40% of the footage devoted to ordinary people depicted their "everyday behavior" (e.g., standing in an unemployment line) rather than their spoken opinions about presidential policy.

But this is not to say that the presidents' congressional critics and supporters are, alternatively, moved to heroic status on the nightly news. Typically, their views are counterbalanced (Jim Wright vs. Bob Dole) and their motives, like those of the president himself, are constantly questioned. No, only media personnel themselves are allowed to audition for the role of protagonist.

Reporters' roles on evening news shows are both consistently and carefully managed. Like all good persuaders, television reporters argue mightily
that they represent the world as it is, that they make no conscious attempt
to build and nurture an image. But one cannot examine forty-five newscasts
closely without becoming suspicious of such claims. If nothing else, television journalists are two things: (1) seers and (2) guardians-of-the-right.

Evening newscasts are, perceptually, a kind of seam between the past
and the future. They are designed to help viewers bridge from the nowness
to the unknown. Network reporters presume to do just that when they read
tea leaves or re-read presidential speeches for their audiences. One of the
things that equips them to foretell events is that they know *which portions*
of present-day reality contain the seeds of the future. Reporters know (or
presume to know) that interviewing members of a Kiwanis club in Park
Ridge, Illinois, for example, will best predict how the Silent Majority will
respond to Richard Nixon's speech on that topic. Other reporters know that
chatting with the patrons of the Brothers One Bar in Cudahy, Wisconsin,
will reveal the future of the Watergate affair because that bar "is a working
man's hangout in a working man's town."[28] Still other reporters can discern
in one student riot the seeds of yet another: "Tomorrow, students say that
they will try to prevent people from going to work at M.I.T.'s Instrumentation
Laboratory and the police say they will be there in force."[29]

Naturally, a seer does not become a seer simply by making predictions.
A real seer is one who can speak in such a way as to make one *believe* that
he or she has cornered a piece of the future. Among the ways one can do so
is to speak in an unqualified manner, use the passive voice, or quote from
public opinion polls. This latter strategy is particularly effective in the United
States because it contains more than a touch of scientism. Howard K. Smith
combined all three of these techniques in one of his commentaries on the
Bert Lance affair, and, by adding to them the manner and bearing of a kind
of ersatz senior diplomat, Smith's words seem truer than true: "Still, the
damage to Carter is indubitable. The polls show his loss of standing with the
people and the way his energy plan is being picked to pieces by his own
Congress may show his loss of it on Capitol Hill."[30]

Another effective technique used to make predictions plausible is to
evidence a firm grip on the past. Even the average citizen, after all, implicitly
acknowledges the truth of Santayana's axiom that to live only in the present
is to be victimized by the future. Throughout his career, Eric Sevareid punctuated his prognostications on Richard Nixon's invasion of Cambodia with
implicit references to American history: "In its dramatic tone and rhetoric,
the president's statement of last night resembled a presidential performance
on the outbreak of a new war . . . " He gave historical perspective to current
difficulties: "The generals have got what they have long wanted, so has the
Thieu government in Saigon . . . " And he blended the past with the future:

"The dice in this gamble are still rolling. If they come up wrong, then this war has no even approximate terminal date and this president quite probably will go the way of his predecessor . . . "[31] There is an almost irresistible sense of authority about such historically tinged predictions, especially when spoken by a dean of network correspondents. In the presence of such authoritative words, it is difficult to remember that Mr. Sevareid, like Mr. Nixon himself, was nurturing an image.

Network reporters are not foolish seers. They often do not comment on either the complex or the truly opaque. For example, virtually nobody enjoys a State of the Union address. Typically, they are long and detailed, often boring. Presidents probably do not enjoy delivering them any more than members of Congress enjoy listening to them. Clearly, television reporters hold them in even less regard, allotting them only one-third of the coverage devoted to speeches on international affairs (see table 4.2). From the State of the Union address, the media extract what they can, focusing on the policy implications of the speech, summarizing the address rather than extrapolating upon it (perhaps because its density precludes clear-cut implications from being drawn); and confining themselves to Washington, D.C., for reactions. Indeed, in the eleven stories (by three different networks) studied here, *not a single lay reaction to a State of the Union address was solicited.* Instead, the media salvaged from the address what pomp and circumstance it could and spent the rest of their time on the president's style (22% vs. 9% for international speeches and 7% for domestic speeches). Because there is comparatively little drama in the typical State of the Union address and because no serious confrontation can be expected until after Congress has had a chance to think about the president's several proposals, the networks dismiss the speech, making but a nod to its institutional importance.

A second major task of network reporters is to remove the scales from their viewer's eyes, to point them toward the truth. The truths they envision are not ideological truths (like the politician's) nor are they abstract truths (like those of the theologian). Rather, television journalists inform their audience about practical truths based on fact. When explaining presidents, reporters go the great lengths to make their truths accessible and to protect their images as tellers-of-truths.

For example, especially when dealing with political matters, the networks are fond of conducting polls. Polls are useful for the reasons mentioned earlier (i.e., they sound scientific and dispassionate) and also because the data they contain can be *shown* to viewers, thereby having their validity as data enhanced ("I saw it with my own eyes"). What is particularly interesting about such polls is that most of the reporters studied felt compelled to mention, ostensibly in passing, that such statistics were notoriously unreliable. By thus apparently falsifying their own data, they and their data took on even greater credibility. Numerous examples abound in the telecasts studied:

> *David Brinkley:* "Our poll is unscientific but interesting."[32]
> *Virginia Sherwood:* "Any opinion-sampling like this is necessarily arbitrary.
> But of the more than thirty blue-collar workers questioned here, the
> ratio was 5 to 1 against the president."[33]
> *David Henderson:* "From our unscientific sampling, a higher cost of gaso-
> line will not affect driving habits here."[34]
> *Frank Reynolds:* "I hesitate to apply the word typical to any group,
> but . . . "[35]

These disclaimers function not unlike the minute warning from the surgeon
general on a package of cigarettes: it protects the image of the manufacturer
without cutting into sales of the product. And like the cigarette manufactur-
ers, network reporters *do not stop manufacturing the polls* even though the
polls are ostensibly dangerous to their viewers' intellectual health. It is significant that, despite their collective hesitancies, Frank Reynolds, David
Henderson, Virginia Sherwood, and David Brinkley eventually told their
viewers exactly what they had always intended to tell them.

There is something vaguely disconcerting about analyzing reporters as
persuaders. Cultural stereotypes about the honest journalist in the threadbare
suit die hard. The media lobby is an influential one, and newscasters go out
of their way to promote themselves as public sentinels. Presidents, of course,
know better. Presidents understand (especially after four years in office) that
television reporters are a well-paid, ego-protective lot who peddle a party
line and who compete with the president for the respect and affection of the
American people. Until recently, presidents have been at a distinct disad-
vantage in this contest of reputability for they are, after all, politicians. But
as news reporters move ever closer to the status of "media personality,"
their images as seers and guardians-of-the-right will also be opened to public
inspection. Surely that is a good thing.

The relationship between presidents and television newscasters is obviously bilateral. Thus far, we have focused upon the networks' resources in
this dramatic war of words and pictures. Clearly, presidents have ample
supplies at their disposal as well: media specialists on their staffs, the power
to withhold information, an ability to put pressure on obstreperous reporters,
etc. Perhaps the most interesting comment yet made about the president's
resources was made by a former aide to Gerald Ford who said, in the spirit
of these findings, "You can predict what the press is going to do with a story.
It is almost by formula. Because of this they are usable."[36] In the next section,
we shall examine such uses.

Orchestrating the Media

Throughout my studies of presidential discourse, I looked for a single, simple
explanation for why presidents spoke as they did. I searched in vain. As we

have seen in the first three chapters, presidents' personalities, the peculiar issues they faced, the political circumstances that afflicted them, and several other important variables collectively produced the speaking patterns described. But one, simple, law-like proposition about presidential persuasion can be offered: the electronic media condition (at times totally determine) how, when, where, and why a president will speak. A corollary is this: presidents make no rhetorical decision (perhaps not even very many policy decisions) without gauging likely media responses to that decision. Knowing how the nightly news commentators habitually behave, a president will now structure his personal activities with an eye toward the media and attempt to calculate how he sounds even before he speaks.

The traditional way of looking at presidential communication is to regard the president's message as the stimulus that elicits feedback from the people and the mass media. This model is becoming dated. Now, presidents calculate feedback *before* it exists, using estimations of this "feedforward" to determine who they should speak to and about what. For example: since 1945, no American president has spent even 3% of his time talking to government employees. Most chief executives averaged only three or four such speeches a year, and some, like Richard Nixon, spoke even less often. Why would recent presidents pass up opportunities to address audiences that could be culled at will from among three million federal employees? Gerald Ford's experience of July 10, 1975, suggests why. On that day, he spoke to a federal regulatory agency, then to government officials on the general revenue, and later to members of the military at a hospital groundbreaking. Admittedly, Mr. Ford said little that was newsworthy in those speeches, but even his "hometown" newspaper, the *Washington Post,* made not a single mention of Ford's exertions.[37] It seems that government workers may be intelligent, they may be highly professional, but they are also notoriously diffident, unlikely to respond to even the president of the United States with the kind of wild abandon that makes for interesting film footage. Career bureaucrats protected by civil service are obligated to nothing more than polite applause in such circumstances, hardly the stuff out of which drama is fashioned.

Meg Greenfield, however, knows about such stuff. In an op-ed piece entitled "Invented Politics," Ms. Greenfield described the kind of political speech most likely to capture the attention of the media and, as a result, the attention of politicians:

> I spent a day with Gary Hart's campaign in Alabama recently. We went with the senator to a college, a high school and a city hall rally in Birmingham, to the Redstone Missile Arsenal in Huntsville, to a restaurant (over the border in Augusta, Ga.) where ribs and iced tea were to be consumed by the candidate, and to a session of the state legislature which he addressed in Montgomery.

There were dozens of reporters traveling with Hart. Most of the time we seemed greatly to outnumber the locals who assembled to greet him. For purposes of truth in packaging, I thought we should have been wearing a badge that said "Crowds R Us."

I don't mention this by way of starting one of those tiresome arguments over crowd counts in which the police chief says he estimates there were about twenty thousand people there and the campaign manager reports that he personally counted half a million. These crowds were not by any stretch of the imagination or by anyone's definition even crowds. They were miniscule— mostly little knots of people. For this, given the shortness of notice and the newness of Hart's prominence, there was ample reason. But what interested me was that, in viewing the day's proceedings on television later and also in reading about them in the papers, I saw where you could get an entirely different impression.

Let me be plain. No one lied. No one cropped the photograph or deliberately falsified what was there. It was just that given all the agitation and disruption and noisy *thronginess* the traveling party itself created in a series of fairly small settings, complete with the accurate, if portentous-sounding commentary ("Sen. Gary Hart, fresh from another New England triumph, brought his campaign to the South today . . ."), the sparsely attended and rather uneventful progress through Alabama took on the aspect of a crush. That's what it looked like on the screen. That's what people think happened.

In fact the Hart trip was less a series of speaking engagements than a series of "photo opportunities," as they are called in the trade. It wasn't so much what the candidate did or what he said to anyone that was the fact; it was the recording of these things, or snippets of them, to be shown on the nightly news and chronicled in the daily press that created the different set of apparent "facts." This is the new political "reality" in which we are operating.[38]

In the first part of this chapter, we saw why the television coverage Greenfield witnessed seemed so odd: the electronic media peddle drama on a daily basis—during game shows, on the soaps, as well as during the news— and thus they will seek out the visually captivating and emotionally stimulating scene wherever it can be found. It often makes little difference to the media whether joy or sorrow, conflict or celebration are shown, only that they are showable. Sensing the media's attitudes, presidents structure their schedules to take advantage of the press's passion for passion. Clearly, the data pertaining to topical choice and state politics in table 4.3 are in no sense surprising—presidents of both parties know that Democratic voters respond appreciatively to clarion calls for increased human services, that urban Republicans enjoy hearing about science and technology and rural Republicans about agriculture, and that undecided voters will listen attentively to a speech on the economy. This is stock politics. But it is also stock media engineering.

Table 4.3   *Regional Speaking on Selected Topics by U.S. Presidents**

State Politics	All Speeches (%)	Human Services Only (%)	Economics Only (%)	Science Only (%)
Democratic	27.2	38.1	19.1	26.9
Republican	16.1	9.0	16.0	24.5
Neutral	56.7	40.2	64.8	48.6

*Through 1982 only.

There is a difference in approaching voters as voters and approaching them as members of an audience. There is an even greater difference in speaking to one (live) audience in the hope that they will, in turn, perform adequately for another, more removed audience.

It is for this latter reason that recent American presidents have turned the map of the United States into a kind of giant political game board, with speeches as the tokens and with media coverage as the payoffs. Presidents eat up the mileage hungrily, attempting not so much to reach voters' minds (there are other, local agents better equipped to target appeals) but to *create a scene,* a scene having what the media people call "production value," a scene that itself argues in behalf of the president's arguments. Emotion is now central to presidential politics as it has never been in the past. The electronic media expect as much presence from the chief executive as from one of their own anchorpersons. It is not surprising that reporters mercilessly pilloried Walter Mondale in 1984 for having committed the most heinous political crime—being dull. In practical terms, being dull means being unable to generate even thirty seconds of usable crowd material per day. Unlike Meg Greenfield, television personnel are not overly interested in the ontogeny of this material, but they willingly savage a politician incapable of providing it. The American people, dullards as so many of them are, probably would not mind having a dull president in the 1980s, all things being equal. But with the electronic media, all things can never again be equal.

The rhetoric of the presidency is therefore a rhetoric of solicitation, with the president striving to create speech situations that appeal to the electronic heralds upon whom he depends so greatly. The key ingredient lies not so much in the message itself—that often tends to be somewhat invariant for an administration and hence unworthy of daily news coverage. Rather, the key is to serve up a fresh, warm *audience* each day, an audience that recognizes an applause line when it hears one. To provide a ready supply of such audiences, presidents over the years have increasingly turned toward special interest groups and invited guests (table 4.4).

The dramatic rise in "closed" speaking among presidents is not surprising in light of the corresponding increases in (media-based) political pressures faced by a modern chief executive. The incessant opinion polling to

Table 4.4   *"Closed" Speaking by Modern American Presidents*

	Period of Modern Presidency		
Audience*	N *Speeches* 1945–1957	N *Speeches* 1958–1970	N *Speeches* 1970–1982
Invited guests	114	497	566
Special interest group	350	836	1035

*U.S. locations only.

which he is subjected motivates the president to prove that he is loved. So, suddenly, a peculiar little group like the American Conservative Union will receive a presidential speech—if the speech is rock-ribbed and if the president is Ronald Reagan. In a booming economy the National Association of Realtors and the American Retail Federation will hear a Reagan speech; in an era of family values the Mount Vernon Ladies Association and St. Peter's Catholic Elementary School of Geneva, Illinois, will also be favored. Groups like these create what William Lammers has called "attention-focusing situations," situations that function not so much to get attention (the president always has that) but to insure that the audience in attendance sends the *correct* political signals to media representatives.[39]

Accordingly, presidents now wear such audiences on their sleeves, rhetorical chevrons for a rhetorical era: "Here's my medal of valor from the A.M.A. convention," "I got this one for the V.F.W. speech." The older notion of dialectic—facing down one's accusers, joining the political fray on the enemy's territory—is now largely passé. The mass media have caused presidents to seek security in discourse, not challenge, and have made the *perception of assent,* not assent itself, the valued commodity. What used to be a broad, bold line between argument and entertainment, between speechmaking and theater, now has no substance at all. Television viewers all too often fail to notice the political fabricating of a presidential speech event or to estimate how hard it was for the president to get the applause he did. Instead, they normally make the simpler discrimination—the president was liked or he was not.

One of the great ironies of this growing insulation of the presidency, an insulation almost wholly tied to a concern for favorable media attention, is that the traditional mode of exchange between reporters and the president— the formal press conference—has been downgraded in status. It is but one among many of the president's communicative opportunities. Print reporters especially decry this trend, but they seem not to penalize it, as we see in figure 4.3, which shows that when periods of heavy coverage in the *New York Times* were compared to periods of light coverage, an inverse relationship was found to exist between the number of press conferences held and the amount of coverage provided the president. To some extent, figure 4.3 is but an artifact of the personal habits of the presidents serving between 1945 and 1982. On the other hand, this figure is a useful reminder that the press avidly covers presidential encounters with special interest groups, White House ceremonies, party rallies, and the like.

Available though they were to the press, Harry Truman and Dwight Eisenhower received comparatively little coverage. The "revolution" of John Kennedy described in Chapter One largely involved the privatization of the presidency being discussed here. His press conferences were smash hits, but there were comparatively few of them. Likewise, the less Richard Nixon faced the press and the more he sought refuge in groups like the Billy Graham Crusade, the more coverage he received (much of which, of course, he could have done without). The lesson of figure 4.3 then is not that press conferences fail to garner attention for the president but *that they do not necessarily or exclusively do so*. Because of their volatility, press conferences tend to be either very good for a president or very bad. In contrast, the "pseudo event" tends to be more predictable—its highs are never as high, its lows never as low (or as frequent). The "closed" speech takes advantage of the media's susceptibility to reporting convivial interdependence between president and people. Thus, as one author observes, the "interest groups are in the wood-work, under the floors, in the hallways and in the rose garden."[40] This is too

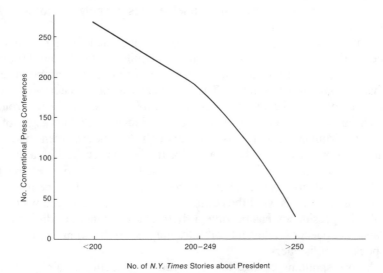

Figure 4.3. Presidential participation in conventional press conferences vis-à-vis news coverage. Press conferences held in Washington, D.C., and devoted to multiple topics.

clandestine a description. These groups are even more prominently located
in convention halls and at hotel banquets emceed by the president of the
United States.

The increases in closed speaking correspond to the more general processes of specialization and institutionalization of the past forty years. Politically, America has become a congeries of particularized groupings; now,
virtually any president can find an appreciative audience on virtually any
topic. With such possibilities, however, come rhetorical responsibilities. When
Harry Truman spoke to a civil rights group in January of 1947, for example,
he could afford to be direct and abrupt: "You have a vitally important job
. . . I want our Bill of Rights implemented in fact . . . We are making progress but we are not making progress fast enough . . . I don't want to see any
race discrimination . . . I hope that you will bring me something tangible
. . ."[41] Today's special interest groups, on the other hand, expect a more
complete and more polished performance, as do the mass media. Thus, when
he spoke to civil rights groups, Jimmy Carter began with a joke ("On the
way over here, I was trying to think of a story . . ."), gave a broad, sociological overview ("That was also a time of fragmentation—racial fragmentation, religious fragmentation . . ."), engaged in self-flattery ("When I was
sworn in as President, there was not a single U.S. attorney who was a woman
. . ."), generated appropriate metaphors ("We're not going to be satisfied
with blacks and Hispanics and women driving the bus—we want to see them
own the bus company . . ."), and ended with a soaring appeal to human
potential ("I want us to recommit ourselves this evening not to betray the
noble ideals . . .").[42]

Jimmy Carter's speech was also longer, included more personal references and anecdotes, and was far more artfully phrased than Truman's.
In Truman's day, the presidential speech was simply not as grand an event
as it has become in recent times. The president was not expected to preside
so completely over the proceedings, to combine so expertly the roles of
preacher and entertainer, or to reach so convincingly for the height of eloquence. In Truman's day, it was news enough that the president had taken
the time to comment publicly about a particular matter. Today, audiences'
expectations are more robust. They have come to expect a complete package
from their president—something chatty, something personal, something, well,
grand—because that is what the commentators on the evening news like. As
a result, the presidency has become a rhetorical machine, grinding out four,
five, and six speeches a day, all carefully tailored to the wants and whims of
little pockets of listeners.

A corresponding change has occurred in reelection strategy. In many
ways, Harry Truman's Pullman tour has become an anachronism. The "open"
rally (often held outdoors, all comers invited) is being made to share the

president's schedule with the planned gathering of the party's faithful. For example, although both were incumbents, Lyndon Johnson attended 124 of these closed rallies in 1964 whereas Jerry Ford presided over 200 when he sought reelection in 1976. Presidents Ford through Reagan have averaged 115 such rallies in their even-numbered years in office, twice as many as Presidents Kennedy through Nixon and four times more than Presidents Truman and Eisenhower.[43] Increasingly, "the people" are being left out in the cold, or more positively stated, they are being invited to join *formal* assemblages if they expect to hear their president.

Naturally, whenever a president speaks he is soliciting support from all quarters. But the partisan rally is a particularly attractive format because it televises so well. When he stumped through Illinois in 1964, for example, LBJ spoke at the county courthouse in Sangamon County and made the following polite request: "And I ask all of you, Democrats and Republicans, and whatnots—and, if you please, good Americans first of all—to realize that we are living in a critical era, in a difficult period, which will . . . "[44] Such courteous refrains were appropriate for an audience of mixed political parentage, but these remarks were unlikely to build a frenzy suitable for a ten-second "news bite" that evening. But sixteen years later in that same state, Jimmy Carter unleashed a kind of Democratic chauvinism perfectly suited to the news clip:

> Remember, 1980 is the year of a great Democratic victory. I want you to remember that we win elections from the precinct up. We defeat Republican candidates, despite all their money, up and down the ticket. But most of all, I want you to be able to tell your children and your grandchildren that you had confidence in yourself, confidence in the Democratic Party, confidence in this Nation, and in 1980 we began to rebuild America. I'll do my part, and what I'd like to ask is this: Will you do your part? [Cheers] We'll win together. We'll whip the Republicans from top to bottom on November the 4th.[45]

This rise in partisan speechmaking signals the burgeoning of formula politics, the growing of votes in hothouse environments. In his book recounting Richard Nixon's campaign in 1968, Joe McGinniss describes how even "town hall" audiences were carefully constructed through the use of ethnic and socioeconomic voting records in the communities Nixon visited.[46] (Reason: these events were televised.) When facing partisan audiences, a political candidate can practice a stock speech until its cadences can be depended upon to sweep up the emotions. It is not inconsequential that Ronald Reagan's deft campaign inquiry of 1980 ("Are you better off now than you were four years ago?") was delivered to a wildly partisan audience and later replayed—on the unpaid media—hundreds of times, *replete with audience reactions*.

A key element in the president's use of partisan audiences is, therefore, to have the event treated as news. This is especially possible during a re-election campaign, but recent presidents—notably Jerry Ford and, to a lesser extent, Jimmy Carter and Ronald Reagan—have used such rallies during nonelection years as well. Table 4.5 shows that this usage is fairly modest, but it does point up the essential logic of recent presidential rhetoric—have a camera pointed at you whenever an audience applauds. One way of getting media coverage of these transparently political outings is to schedule them alongside other, nonpartisan events. Thus, in September of 1977, Jimmy Carter traveled to Trenton, New Jersey, to give a major speech on energy resources (dutifully covered by all three networks), and thereafter addressed Democratic party workers in the Chambersburg neighborhood (covered by CBS). In October of 1979 Mr. Carter was even luckier, addressing the national Conference of Catholic Charities in Kansas City, after which he moved on to a fund-raiser in Chicago; all three networks covered *both* speeches. This same technique worked well in Iowa in May of that same year when Carter conducted a formal press conference, made a speech to the State Association of Counties, and later spoke before the State Democratic party. All three networks detailed the president's itinerary that day.[47]

It may seem a bit queer that presidents talk so often to persons whose minds and hearts have already been won over when there are so many other voters—the unsure, the skeptical—for whom presidential attention would be an attractive novelty. Most presidents, of course, address both kinds of groups, using partisan rallies early on in a campaign to generate momentum and open rallies later to reach a wider base of support. Table 4.6 illustrates how Jerry Ford did so in 1976 by comparing *when* he addressed "open" and "closed" rallies. Even as an incumbent, Mr. Ford was forced to give up the insulation of his party after the primary season in order to appeal to Democrats and Independents (e.g., via a boat trip on the S.S. *Natchez* down the Mississippi in September and by a train ride on the "Honest Abe" through Illinois in October). But even in the second phase of his campaign Ford spent nearly

Table 4.5   *Political Rallies by U.S. Presidents during Nonelection Years*

President	N Nonelection Years in Office	Average N Rallies/Year
Truman	3.7	0.5
Eisenhower	4	4.0
Kennedy	2	3.0
Johnson	2	5.0
Nixon	3	2.0
Ford	1	30.0
Carter	2	11.5
Reagan	3	10.0

Table 4.6   *Gerald Ford's Electoral Speaking during 1976*

Type of Rally	% Speeches: February–June (N = 162)	% Speeches: July–November (N = 101)
"Open"	51.2	70.5
Partisan	48.8	29.5

a third of his time talking to special interest groups. Typically, he intermixed these open and closed rallies each day, daring the media to sort out the partisan from the nonpartisan for their nightly reportage. Time pressures in the editing studios being what they are, Ford's mixing of speech events probably worked in his favor on many occasions.

During political campaigns, the mass media are often hard-pressed to determine just what sort of news is truly new and, of that, which really needs to be shared with a national audience. For instance, as the researcher Renee Meyers and her colleagues report, the concept of "momentum" is a slippery one but, equally, the sort of mellifluous construct the mass media adore.[48] After all, no matter how multicolored their graphics, the networks cannot make polling data dance or roll over. Black on white, or yellow on mauve, numbers just sit on the television screen. "Momentum," on the other hand, can be operationalized by media personnel—through talking to fellow reporters ("Do you seen any signs of it?") or to voters themselves ("Do you feel it inside of you?"). Momentum is also dynamic ("Is there as much today as there was yesterday?") and hence can be examined time after time without danger of repetition. Momentum lies just beyond empirical observation, close enough to seem substantial and yet still invitingly mythic. It appeals to the intuitive in us ("He's on a roll," "Things are turning around") and, therefore, is a construct ideally suited to television.

Momentum also feeds upon itself—if two persons speak of it, four will, and then eight. The partisan political rally is a perfect arena for talk of momentum. If a particular poll looks bleak, candidate-orchestrated pictures of listeners yelling themselves hoarse give it the lie. If another poll seems encouraging, that same sort of audience becomes visual confirmation—for the candidate and (potentially) the media—that that most precious of all political commodities, momentum, has been found. Fortunately for the politician, momentum is the sort of thing that can always be nudged into existence and whose presence can never be fully, concretely denied. Thus, presidents ask their partisan listeners to stand as collective evidence that their candidacy is strong, tempting reporters with rich visuals of political pandemonium. One senses in the following excerpts from Jerry Ford's campaign speeches that this is precisely the strategy he had in mind. By turning the campaign into a kind of metacampaign (Who's winning? Who's not?),

Ford shifted the ground to one on which he could stand just as comfortably as his Democratic rival. With public sentiment changing daily, Ford's speech-making enticed his listeners into becoming visible testaments to his candidacy's strength:

September 17, 1976 (Gallup approval = 36%)
> In the next couple of weeks after our convention the polls narrowed, and we ended up about 15 points behind. But some good news has been coming in from polls taken all over the country. We have narrowed that gap very significantly.
>
> And we have the momentum, as Betty said, and momentum is what counts. I would rather have the momentum going up than trying to be at the top and keep it from going down. I would much rather be a fast finisher than an early starter.[49]

September 23, 1976 (40%)
> . . . I haven't seen all of the polls, but from what I've heard we did all right in that debate. And when we get to the next one, which talks about national defense and foreign policy, we'll do even better.
>
> We have a turning point in this campaign. The polls are going our way, the momentum is on our side. The basic reason is that in the last 2 years, under most difficult circumstances, we have done a good job for America, and in the next 4 years we will do a better job.[50]

October 8, 1976 (42%)
> I go before you and the American people, proud of what we have done in the last 2 years and optimistic about what opportunities we have for progress in the next 4 years. We may still be behind by a narrow margin, but with your help and with the right programs and the fact that Mr. Carter makes mistake after mistake, we are going to win that election for the American people November 2.[51]

October 24, 1976 (44%)
> It's wonderful to be in California after a hard day yesterday in Virginia, where we got a wonderful reception; in North Carolina, where the enthusiasm was really spectacular; and where the results in South Carolina were far beyond our expectations . . .
>
> What I'm really saying is that we're making substantial inroads in those areas where my opponent thought he had a free ride. He doesn't and the net result is we're going to do very well in many parts of the country where a month ago it didn't look very optimistic.[52]

In a political world changed forever by the routines of the mass media, presidents are thus required to create their own kind of theater. They speak of such entities as momentum, windows of vulnerability, the Silent Majority, and the information age because these are exciting notions capable of stealing a headline or two. The presidency and the press are locked in a dramatic struggle for the allegiance of the American people. Presidents know they must match geography to topic, topic to ideology, and ideology to audience in order to receive publicity favorable to their administrations. The mass media refuse to provide such favors without recompense, so presidents have learned to think like broadcasters. Broadcasters, in turn, have learned to think like tragedians. Presidents and reporters are thus joined at the waist, conscious of each other's ambitions and, increasingly, conscious of each other's consciousness. The result of their interminglings is political life as modern Americans have come to know it.

Orchestrating the Presidency

In the previous section, we saw how a contemporary president uses the perquisites of scheduling to counteract what the mass media could do to his image if left to their own devices. In this section, we shall examine the presidential briefing closely to determine the kinds of pressures brought to bear on the presidency by the Fourth Estate. To do so, it is useful to compare the older terminology of "the press" with the newer parlance, "the mass media." The former term conjures up images of men, primarily, with haggard looks clothed in ill-fitting suits, hanging onto the presidents' words and then fighting over telephones as they attempt to call in their stories. "The mass media" is a different set of stories altogether. First, there is massness—instant, "live," nationwide communication directly to the voters. And there is medianess—comely male and female personalities seated amidst millions of dollars of expensive equipment used to amplify light and sound, haughtily selecting how much attention to give the president's speech and whether to follow that segment with a story about a trick animal or a commercial lionizing Post Toasties. Compared to his predecessors, the modern president is dogged by many more reporters when he makes his rounds; these reporters have a kind of swagger which would have been truly alarming for a premedia president; and they inject into the life of the chief executive an unprecedented sense of urgency and immediacy. Naturally, throughout American history presidents have been lampooned by print reporters and editorial cartoonists. But when reportage is *spoken* and when even the most casual or unguarded presidential remark becomes, potentially, a remark for the ages (e.g., Ronald Reagan's joke before an open microphone, "I've signed legislation that will outlaw Russia forever. We begin bombing in 5 minutes"), the native features of human speech—passion, spontaneity, and relationship—become influential.

    "Relationship" has now become especially important. One has to peruse only a very few transcripts of presidential press conferences to detect a subtle but important difference in how the president and representatives of the mass media relate to one another. Their former relationship resembled the stereotyped, traditional marriage, with the president reluctantly suffering the well-intentioned but somewhat addlebrained attempts at communication from his media spouse. One of Harry Truman's early press conferences exemplifies this tone:

> *Question:* Mr. President would you care to comment on the rumors that Attorney General Tom Clark is resigning, and that Senator Wheeler may succeed him? Likewise that Mr. Justice Jackson is resigning?
>
> *The president:* Both so absurd I have no comment to make.
>
> *Question:* Too absurd to comment on it?
>
> *The president:* Too absurd to comment on it.
>
> *Question:* When do you expect to take action on the resignation of Solicitor General McGrath?
>
> *The president:* That action has already been taken, I think.
>
> *Question:* You have accepted the resignation, sir?
>
> *The president:* Yes, I think it's accepted. He is going to be Senator from Rhode Island. He can't hold two jobs. [Laughter]
>
> *Question:* A little matter of election there, sir. [More laughter]
>
> *Question:* Mr. President, has the matter of John L. Lewis' latest statement on the coal contract come to you?
>
> *The president:* No, it has not.
>
> *Question:* Have you anything to say?
>
> *The president:* No comment. That is in the hands of Mr. Krug.
>
> *Question:* Mr. President, yesterday Mr. Churchill said, "It is not right for the United States, who are keen for immigration into Palestine, to take no share in the task and reproach us for our obvious incapacity to cope with the difficulties of the problem." Would you comment on that, sir?
>
> *The president:* I have no comment to make on that.
>
> *Question:* Mr. President, do you expect to issue the wage decontrol order before November 1?
>
> *The president:* That was covered in the meat speech completely. If you will read that, you will get your answer.
>
> *Question:* You say "Yes"—
>
> *The president:* I said read the meat speech and you will get your answer.
>
> *Question:* Mr. President, the Army and Navy Bulletin says this morning that the State Department has something in line for Mr. Forrestal, that he is leaving the Navy. Is there anything you might say about that?
>
> *The president:* That is in the same category with Tom Clark and Jackson.
>
> *Question:* Mr. President, time left in the campaign is running short. Are you going to make any speeches?

The president: I have no plans to make any speeches.

Question: Mr. President, does your meat speech mean that there may be no formal order decontrolling wages? Just pass out by lifting price control—

The president: I have answered that as definitely as I intend to answer it. You keep questioning me on it. I have no further comment to make on it. Read the meat speech. That will give you the answer.[53]

Mr. Truman's brusque approach contrasts sharply with that of Ronald Reagan. These differences are no doubt based in part upon facets of their personalities, but there is also little doubt that Mr. Reagan's easygoing style was mixed to perfection in the crucible of lifelong interactions with all of the mass media. Nothing of real importance is said by anyone in the following excerpt, but one clearly senses Reagan's willingness to go the extra length required in the modern marriage, fully prepared to enter into a bilateral, evolving, self-generating, open, introspective, role-transcendent relationship that acknowledges his/her freedom to just . . . be:

Ms. Thomas: Thank you, Mr. President.

The president: Oh, I just—Helen, did you—I think Mary [Mary McGrory, *Washington Post*] got up before you did, Helen, so I'll just take her question.

Ms. Thomas: Mary beat me to the—

Ms. McGrory: Mr. President, in New York last week, you called upon the rich to help the poor in this present economic difficulty. Are you planning to increase your own contributions to private charity to set an example to the rich people of this country to do more for the poor?

The president: Mary—[Laughter]—

Ms. Thomas: Now are you sorry? [Laughter]

The president: Helen, I just want you to know whenever you speak to me from now on, I'm shutting up and moving. [Laughter]

No, Mary, I'll tell you, you give me a chance to explain something that's been of great concern to me. I realize the publicity that is attended upon the tax returns of someone in my position. And I realize that some have noticed what seemed to be a small percentage of deductions for worthwhile causes, and that is true. And I'm afraid it will be true this year, because I haven't changed my habits. But I also happen to be someone who believes in tithing—the giving of a tenth. But I have for a number of years done some of that giving in ways that are not tax deductible with regard to individuals who are being helped.

And I'm afraid that to avoid future questions of this kind, maybe beginning this year, I'm going to have to start publicly doing some things. But my conscience is clear as to what I have been giving. And it has been for the reason that I've just told you, that the tax law doesn't say you help people, not organizations, that you can—or not by way of an organization—that you can deduct.

So, you can be watching. It'll be the same situation this year.

Next year, I'll try to be more public with what I'm doing.

Ms. Thomas: Thank you, Mr. President.

The president: I have to go now. Thank you.[54]

Perhaps the most characteristic feature of modern president/media relationships is their fickleness. Figures 4.4 and 4.5 point up the uncertain connection between rhetorical effort and media coverage. In figure 4.4, the Eisenhower/Kennedy change makes a certain kind of sense: hard work has its rewards. But that logic did not hold true for Lyndon Johnson despite his prodigious amount of talking, and Jerry Ford reaped no greater benefits from the mass media than JFK even though Ford doubled Kennedy's speechmaking. As we saw previously, Richard Nixon had to do comparatively little to attract the attention of the press, and this was just as true before the Watergate affair as during it. In 1972, for example, Nixon spoke four times

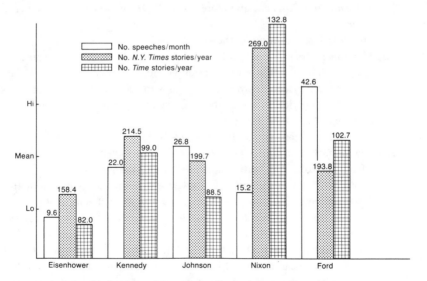

Figure 4.4. Comparison between presidential speechmaking and media coverage (1953–1976). Data re *New York Times* stories/year and *Time* stories/year adapted from M. B. Grossman and M. J. Kumar, *Portraying the President: The White House and the News Media* (Baltimore: Johns Hopkins, 1981), p. 260. Hi/Lo = ± 1 standard deviation.

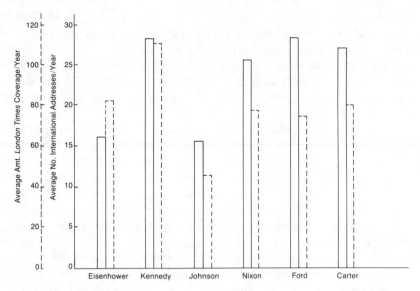

Figure 4.5. Comparison of international speechmaking by U.S. presidents to coverage in the *Times* (London). As measured in square centimeters of indexed coverage. Carter data through 1978 only.

less often than Gerald Ford did in 1976 (155 speeches vs. 682), but Mr. Nixon generated more stories in the *New York Times* than Ford (252 vs. 202) and more *Time* magazine profiles (110 vs. 80) as well. Later in his administration, of course, Richard Nixon no doubt began to think of his ability to obtain and hold the attention of the mass media as a mixed blessing.

Figure 4.5 continues this theme of fickleness, with Presidents Eisenhower and Johnson working equally hard on the international scene but with the former clearly outdistancing the latter in coverage by the *Times* (London).[55] In part, the difference here might be explained by the halo Dwight Eisenhower had earned via his wartime experiences in Europe. In part, the difference might be explained by Lyndon Johnson's virtual exclusion of Europe from his international travels (he concentrated on the Americas and Asia) or by his general discomfort when talking about matters lying outside his treasured bailiwick of domestic issues. (The most heartening praise he offered during one trip to the Philippines, for example, was that Filipinos had "retained an Asian identity without rejecting Western values.")[56] Figure 4.5 also shows that equivalent international efforts of Presidents Kennedy, Nixon, Ford, and Carter were rewarded disproportionately, no doubt because John Kennedy's élan ("Ich bin ein Berliner") was especially appealing on the Continent. The more substantive international contributions of Richard Nixon (and even Jimmy Carter) failed, in contrast, to excite the British media as had the more charismatic Kennedy. While press coverage (and perhaps press attitudes) can surely be manipulated by presidents, it is not yet clear what set of rules—if any—effectively guide such manipulations. One would like to think that the material accomplishments of a presidency best predict media reactions, but no data uncovered in this study confirms such a sanguine conclusion.

If one had to hazard a guess about these matters, one would probably be wise to choose style over substance. As we have seen in the first part of this chapter, the mass media in the United States are a people-centered institution. Their representatives are fascinated by human grandeur and human foibles and quite skilled in commenting upon them. The American press works to become familiar with both athletes and presidents because both are viewed as public performers. As a result, the American people probably know more about their politicians and less about their politics than do the citizens of most other industrialized nations. Figure 4.6 shows the dramatic contrast between the number of information-based briefings offered during the Eisenhower and Kennedy administrations and the amount of press cov-

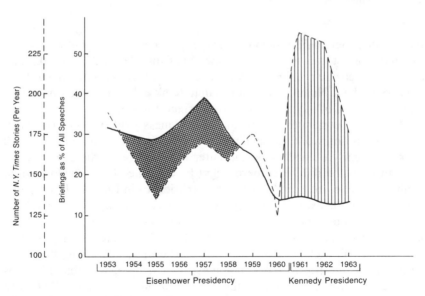

Figure 4.6. Comparison between presidential briefings and the *New York Times* coverage for Dwight Eisenhower and John Kennedy. *New York Times* data adapted from M. B. Grossman and M. J. Kumar, *Portraying the President: The White House and the News Media* (Baltimore: Johns Hopkins Press, 1981), p. 260.

erage they generated. Clearly, the relationship is inverse. To date, no publisher has yet had the temerity to issue a collection of Dwight Eisenhower's extensive press conferences, but several such volumes were produced in behalf of the Kennedy administration. (Twenty years after Kennedy's assassination, the Public Broadcasting System fashioned an assortment of JFK's press conferences into a show entitled "Thank you, Mr. President" that still had the power to entertain.) Because of his suasory abilities, John Kennedy was singled out for hagiography by much of the media of his time, and he was able to set a rhetorical standard not since equaled in the White House.

One need not look very far to discover why the press reacted differently to Kennedy and Eisenhower. Their last press conferences were particularly instructive. On these occasions both were lured by the press into commenting upon rather sensitive political matters, and their responses were revealing— of themselves and their presidencies:

Dwight Eisenhower, January 18, 1961

Question: Mr. President, have you come to a firm decision on the value of the third-term amendment–no third-term amendment?

The president: A funny thing, ever since this election the Republicans have been asking me this. [Laughter]

No, I think I told you that I had come or, I think at first way back even when I had no intention of ever going more than once that I was sort of against the third-term amendment because I thought the American people had the right to choose who they wanted. But we do know there are possibilities of building up great machines in a democracy and so on, and finally I came, on balance, and I think so said to this body, on balance to decide that I believe the two-term amendment was probably a pretty good thing.

Question: Mr. President, this is a question about the past and the future.

Could you tell us what you personally think were the major points which lost the Republicans the election; and do you have any counsel for the Republicans in '62 and '64 to avoid a repetition of November 8th?

The president: Well, I would think this: yes, of course I have ideas but here is one case where I think it would be better for me to keep still for the moment. I have to meet with these Republican leaders of the future and talk to them and give them the lessons I think I have learned, and where together we can point out what we believe are mistakes, and where together we can say what we believe is the best method to make sure that this country will have balanced government.[57]

John Kennedy, November 14, 1963

Question: Mr. President, as a possible candidate for President, would you
comment on the possible candidacy of Margaret Chase Smith, and
specifically what effect that would have on the New Hampshire
primary?

The president: I would think if I were a Republican candidate, I would not
look forward to campaigning against Margaret Chase Smith in New
Hampshire—[laughter]—or as a possible candidate for President. I
think she is very formidable, if that is the appropriate word to use
about a very fine lady. She is a very formidable political figure . . .

Question: You have been reported as saying you were very satisfied with the
vote in Philadelphia. Why were you satisfied?

The president: Because Mayor Tate was elected. As Joe Bailey said, the Republicans had the statistics and we, the offices. So that is why I was
satisfied . . .

Question: Mr. President, several months ago you nominated David Rabinovitz to be a Federal judge in western Wisconsin. Since that time the
American Bar Association has opposed this nomination and a majority
of lawyers polled by the State Bar Association said that he was unqualified. Do you still support this nomination, or in view of this opposition are you going to withdraw?

The president: No, I am for David Rabinovitz all the way. I know him very
well, in fact for a number of years. And the American Bar Association
has been very helpful in making the judgment, but I am sure they
would agree that they are not infallible. Mr. Brandeis was very much
opposed. There are a good many judges who have been opposed who
have been rather distinguished. And I am for David Rabinovitz.[58]

Where Eisenhower is, to put it kindly, elliptical, Kennedy is clear,
direct, penetrating. Where Eisenhower's syntax becomes convoluted, Kennedy's is unencumbered with excessive qualification or faulty parallelism.
Where Eisenhower reaches for abstractions ("great machines in a democracy"), Kennedy seizes the particular (Justice Brandeis), and where Eisenhower circumnavigates an issue ("finally, I came, on balance, and I think so
said to this body, on balance"), Kennedy states his position ("I am for David
Rabinovitz") and eagerly seeks the next question.

Eisenhower's press conferences challenged reporters to find the answers
within his answers. John Kennedy's mind, alternatively, traveled so swiftly
and so surely over conceptual territory that he often began answering a question before it had been fully asked. Above all, his answers were short, and he
made quick, associative jumps between different intellectual domains. When
combined with his handsome appearance and polished delivery, these answers
were both easy to listen to and, via the mass media, easy to listen to again.

But it is not altogether fair to compare Eisenhower and Kennedy in this way for this was Kennedy's way, not Eisenhower's. Dwight Eisenhower was an extraordinarily accomplished politician but one who never maximized the advantages of the mass media even though he surely took advantage of them. He was particularly adept at framing a public speech as if it were apolitical, a strategy no contemporary president would even attempt to suggest to a cynical press. But in October of 1958, Eisenhower could go to the National Corn Picking Contest in Cedar Rapids, Iowa, and begin his remarks by observing: "Now all of us know we are in the midst of a political campaign, but so far as I know, political speeches have never picked any corn. So I won't talk long, and as I stated before, in accepting this invitation, I certainly won't talk politics."[59] In less than two minutes after making this statement, Mr. Eisenhower made such observations as, "The free American farm worker out-produces the collectivized farmer of the Soviet Union by something like four or five to one," "Realized net farm income is up 20 percent over last year," and "We know that we face certain threats—and if we are going to speak about peace, we must do it from a position of strength and not of fear."[60] After describing "the great monolithic atheistic dictatorship that is centered in the Kremlin" and after reminding his listeners "that there are no guns shooting today," Ike concluded with a whispered request that "the Lord spare" him to maintain the peace in the days to come.[61] In the 1980s, no American president would even dream of using so transparent a strategy. He would know how unforgiving the rhetorical creatures in the media would be if they spotted a president being self-consciously rhetorical. Although it is difficult to specify exactly what *will* produce favorable and sufficient media coverage for a viable presidency, it is possible to specify what will not: disingenuousness. This is not to say that the mass media now require greater honesty from politicians, but it is to say that they demand subtlety.

One adaptation to media pressures made by recent presidents can be seen in table 4.7, which contrasts single-topic and multitopic briefings. The "smorgasbord" briefings, in which large numbers of assorted topics are discussed, is clearly being supplemented, in some cases supplanted, by encounters focused upon a single topic. This is an obvious case of *agenda control* on the parts of the presidents. Today's presidents, operating as they do under the klieg lights during press conferences, cannot opt for a response of "no comment" as often as Harry Truman and Dwight Eisenhower did in their day. The mass media punish verbal cowardice, and so presidents increasingly look for speech settings in which they can take a firm stand on issues they feel comfortable standing upon. Recent examples of such usages were Ronald Reagan's celebrated radio-only addresses, speeches delivered on weekends (to take advantage of the media's need-for-news during an otherwise dull time) and pitched toward those silent but stalwart middle-

Table 4.7   *Use of Presidential Briefings (1945–1985)*

President	Multitopic Briefings		Single-Topic Briefings	
	N	N *as % of* *All Speeches* *by This President*	N	N *as % of* *All Speeches* *by This President*
Truman	295	21.0	60	4.3
Eisenhower	206	22.3	44	4.8
Kennedy	70	9.0	37	4.8
Johnson	135	8.3	89	5.4
Nixon	54	5.2	128	12.4
Ford	100	8.0	132	10.7
Carter	213	16.1	198	15.0
Reagan	124	7.6	757	46.2
Total (average)	1197	(12.2)	1444	(13.0)

Americans who relish a sermonette style on topics as diverse as farm problems, tax legislation, Communist subversion abroad, and modern morality.

The single-topic briefing can also be taken on the road, allowing presidents to launch "minicampaigns" on a particular topic, slowly building momentum with each speech until some kind of rhetorical climax is reached (often taking the form of a national address). Prior to delivering his July 27, 1981, speech to the nation on federal spending, for example, Ronald Reagan tried out variations on his thinking at an editor's luncheon (July 22), before local and state officials (July 23), before the Republican House Conference (July 24), and before world trade representatives (earlier on July 27). Some six months later, Mr. Reagan used this same technique to talk about the nation's alleged economic recovery, beginning his tour with the state legislatures of Iowa and Indiana, then addressing a group of newspaper editors and media directors, next visiting with the National Association of Counties, and then facing the Conservative Political Action Conference. Reagan's seventeen-day tour (February 9, 1982, to February 26, 1982) was both single-minded enough and extensive enough to capture a goodly share of media attention.

In some ways, these data are merely the rhetorical counterparts to the "ideological" flavor of Reagan politics. Although Mr. Reagan largely steered clear of the social agenda of the New Right during his tenure in office, he was unrelentingly programmatic when it came to matters of conventional governance. This tenacity was shown by his extensive use of the radio addresses and also by his regional speaking, 24% of which dealt exclusively with economic matters (as opposed to 4.9% on this topic for all other presidents). Mr. Reagan ostensibly felt that a selective topic treated narrowly but forcefully provided his rhetoric with a succinctness and an intensity that would both motivate an audience and cause an efficient headline or two to be written. Thus, when traveling among the people, Mr. Reagan eschewed the all-purpose briefing favored by his predecessors (34%, on average, vs. less than 9% for Reagan), replacing it with highly specific speeches replete with unmistakable ideological overtones and, as a buffer, the usual Reagan panache. It was the Reagan panache that made us remember his ceremonial speaking so well even though, in fact, he conducted *twice as many briefings* as ceremonies during his first five years in office. In many ways, it was because of Ronald Reagan's charm that many Americans better remembered his soft rhetoric than his hard rhetoric. Yet, as could be seen in his judicial appointments, in his support for the contras in Nicaragua, and in his tax policies, Ronald Reagan never let up. Jimmy Carter's successor in office was the most persistent and insistent president heard by the American people since March 20, 1945, the day upon which Franklin Roosevelt gave his last formal public speech.

The single-topic briefing, then, is an out-flanking maneuver on the part of the president, and it poses a dilemma for the press. Because they depend so heavily on presidential news, representatives of the media can ill afford to ignore what the president says on any topic. But to report extensively on such controlled rhetoric is to disavow their complaints about presidential inaccessibility. Normally, the dilemma is begrudgingly resolved in favor of White House preferences because presidential copy is such good copy.

Although only 35% of Richard Nixon's speaking occurred during the second half of his administration, a full 52% of his single-topic briefings were presented during this time. His (multitopic) press conference of November 17, 1973, suggests why he avoided them. Of the twenty questions asked that day, nine dealt with Watergate, two with his personal finances, two with telephone taps of his brother, Donald, two with executive privilege, and one each with a milk fund scandal, his postretirement plans, and, ironically, the pressures of his job.[62] With such an agenda, it is little wonder that Mr. Nixon worked so diligently to avoid these exchanges. Some time earlier, Nixon had partaken of his first real press conference in five months, "deliberately throwing himself to the wolves" according to *Newsweek*,[63] but performing admirably. "I think the President outscored us on points" on this occasion, said Peter Lisagor of the *Chicago Daily News*.[64] What is interesting here is the use of hunting and sports metaphors, precisely the imagery Mr. Nixon probably had in mind when he chastised the press in the middle of this press conference, implicitly indicating to them why he so jealously controlled his rhetorical agenda:

> *Question:* Mr. President.
> *The president:* Just a moment.
>> We have had 30 minutes of this press conference. I have yet to
>> have, for example, one question on the business of the people, which

shows you how we are consumed with this. I am not criticizing the
members of the press, because you naturally are very interested in this
issue, but let me tell you, years from now people are going to perhaps
be interested in what happened in terms of the efforts of the United
States to build a structure of peace in the world. They are perhaps
going to be interested in the efforts of this Administration to have a
kind of prosperity that we have not had since 1955—that is, prosperity
without war and without inflation—because throughout the Kennedy
years and throughout the Johnson years, whatever prosperity we had
was at the cost of either inflation or war or both. I don't say that critically of them, I am simply saying we have got to do better than that.[65]

A final structural realignment occasioned in the presidency by the media is reported in figure 4.7, which reports *when* presidents made particularly
heavy use of briefings. On the face of it, most observers might assume that
the problems of governance would even themselves out across the president's years in office, thus calling for a fairly uniform number of briefings
from the chief executive. As we can see, however, there are general increases
in election-year briefings, with specific surges in March, April, and May as
well as October. It hardly needs to be said that these particular months are
crucial ones in a president's political calendar or that the chief executive's
need for publicity is greater then. Such speaking patterns demonstrate the
powers of incumbency since these so-called briefings are often scheduled
alongside political rallies.[66] Thus, Jimmy Carter's briefings shot up consid-

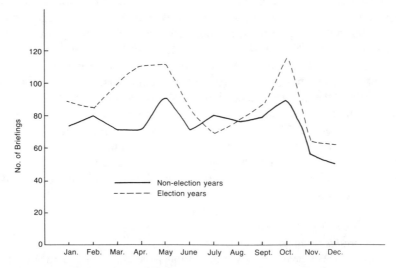

Figure 4.7. Use of presidential briefings in election and nonelection years.

Table 4.8   *Presidential Speaking in the Regional United States (Average N Speeches per Year)*

	Truman through Nixon		Ford and Carter	
	Ceremony	*Briefing*	*Ceremony*	*Briefing*
Northeast	3.9	0.6	7.2	4.8
Midwest	3.1	0.4	4.4	9.1
South	4.6	1.7	8.9	10.9
West	2.3	0.7	3.6	5.6

erably in October of 1980: he signed a proclamation declaring Italian-American Heritage Week, held a town meeting in St. Louis, spoke to the National Press Club on economic matters, agreed to an interview with John Chancellor of NBC news (and then another with RKO General Broadcasting), and also gave an unpaid radio address on foreign policy. Such briefings are an especially important cog in the electoral machine because they retain the image of nonpartisanship. The result is that reporters cover these events but are made to wade through a considerable number of campaign speeches as well.

Table 4.8 indicates that Gerald Ford and Jimmy Carter were particularly avid users of these forums. They spoke to their fellow citizens more often in election years than in nonelection years and, as we see, did so throughout the United States. Table 4.9 shows that Jimmy Carter used his briefings without regard to the political complexion of the states he visited. Carter especially liked the town-hall format. There, he could be filmed taking on a variety of questions from an even wider variety of people: "Mr. President, I'm Marlin Jackson from a small country town in Pargould, Arkansas . . . "; "Mr. President, I'm Sue Jankey, from Bartlett, Tennessee, and I'm very much concerned about America's natural resources . . . "; "Mr. President, I'm Caroline Graves, from Immaculate Conception High School here in Memphis. Seeing how ERA ratification is at a standstill right now, if you're reelected what would . . . ?"[67] For a president quick on his feet (and surely Jimmy Carter was that), settings like these are universally a good thing. Removed from Washington in a nonpartisan atmosphere and with real voters as interlocutors, a sitting president ought to be at his best. Regional, state, and local media are especially attracted to such exchanges, and the national media like the "color" they add. Jimmy Carter never looked better than he did during these encounters.

Gerald Ford used them heavily also. Ford's only really natural rhetorical gift was his sense of communication. His briefings brought this to the fore. During the second half of his administration he increased his use of public briefings by a factor of four, which allowed him to get out among the

Table 4.9   *Jimmy Carter's Use of Briefings in the Regional United States*

State's Political Significance*	Briefings as % All Speeches Delivered	
	Carter Only	*All Other Presidents*
Dense/neutral	22.9	8.7
Medium/neutral	17.9	6.4
Dense/partisan	23.3	10.7
Sparse/neutral	0.0	4.8
Sparse/partisan	32.1	9.6

*See Appendix for operational definitions of categories used.

people and still retain the image of a working president. Although presidents no longer go to the lengths that Richard Nixon did to orchestrate so completely these briefings during the campaign, it is normally the case that picking the locale and the sponsoring group will, ipso facto, narrow the range of questions being asked. Thus, scheduling a briefing at Southern Methodist University rather than the University of California at Berkeley insured Mr. Ford that he would be delivered a high fast ball when he came to the plate. One need examine only the *asking* of the questions to be in a position to estimate Mr. Ford's batting average that day in Dallas:

> What I would like to know is, do you have any workable plan on the boards right now in order to make our welfare system and the food stamp systems become more accountable?

> Mr. President, I would like to know your stand on the amendment to the Federal Election Act which, as it comes out of the House, would hamper corporate political action committees.

> And as a final question, I would like to ask, what specific steps has your administration taken to reduce Federal Government intervention, or whatever have you, in the life of the average American businessman?[68]

When examining how presidents schedule their briefings, two impressions become clear: (1) nothing that a politician does is devoid of politics, and (2) most of what a modern president does is done with a concern for its impact on the mass media. As stated, both propositions seem overly obvious, even truistic. These propositions would hardly surprise a contemporary citizen nor would these propositions disturb very many of them. The data reviewed here merely support the cynicism they feel when they resignedly sigh, "It's all politics." The interesting thing is that nobody—voters of the left, voters of the right, members of the press, or presidents themselves—

seems pleased with how American politics and the mass media relate to one another. Liberals decry how expensive it has become to run for the presidency; conservatives chafe at the restrictions placed upon them when buying media time; reporters detest the arbitrary decisions the president makes about who shall talk to him, where, when, about what, and for how long; and presidents feel besieged by the bewildering number of demands placed upon their time and their patience by reporters of every stripe. A conclusion worthy of Pollyanna suggests itself: perhaps a communication system in which all constituents feel discomfited, but discomfited equally, is the very best system modern minds can devise.

Conclusion

The presidency and the press have gotten themselves into a curious situation—they resent each other intensely but need each other now more than they have ever before. The mass media are addicted to grand persons doing grand things, and so the presidential beat has become their favorite beat. By basing much of their coverage in Washington, D.C., the networks and newspaper chains avail themselves of one of the nation's classiest stages, some of its most colorful scenery, and a full chorus of attractive, flamboyant actors. Combining these features with their own special abilities to tell a story visually, dramatically, the media make the American presidency an extraordinarily entertaining show replete with good and evil, agony and ecstasy.

In a penetrating analysis of contemporary politics, Paul Corcoran has argued that turning politics over to media moguls has undermined the very essence of political intercourse. He deplores the media packaging of "candidate images" and the increasing disuse in politics of "actual persons" sharing dialogue. Noting how "electronic" modern campaigning has become, Corcoran asks rhetorically, if despondently: " . . . why risk an awkward moment or a disastrous slip of the tongue in live appearances when these elements can be eliminated in the studio?"[69] Corcoran also observes that because of the media "political rhetoric has virtually lost its standing as a separate technique of communication, and that oral performance in its surviving manifestations is an archaic, subsidiary method in comparison with electronic technology."[70] Finally, Corcoran opines that politicians are now less orators than actors, that instead of facing "attentive masses, the image emerges of a speaker sitting in a bare cubicle, addressing not a throng, but merely a microphone and a camera lens."[71]

Corcoran may well be correct that eloquence in politics has declined because of the mass media, but he is quite wrong about the facts in the case. The last forty years have witnessed an unprecedented surge in the amount of presidential speaking—in television studios as well as in localities—precisely *because of* the corresponding rise of the electronic media. The speeches of presidents have become the raw materials of much political reportage, however these materials are reprocessed by the network studios prior to being shown in America's homes. Radio and television constantly intrude into the lives of presidents, goading them to find one more audience for one more speech in the hope that it will produce something important, or, if not important, at least something novel. A modern president now spends much of his time trying to outthink the media by outscheduling them. The result is the most plentiful and most skillfully choreographed speech the nation has known.

Media strategist David Garth has observed, "Most people believe what they see in the unpaid media."[72] Raymond Strother, another media guru, echoes him: "The messages in free media and paid media have to be the same. The free media has far greater impact in a presidential primary."[73] The "free media," for the uninitiated, is what used to be called the news. Perhaps the most distressing aspect of this "mediazation" of the presidency is how preoccupied with image reporters and presidents have become. And this self-absorption has consequences. What responsibility, for example, does the press have when voters are able to discourse knowingly about their president's golf handicap but unable to explain nuclear freeze legislation or trade import barriers? To whom must the president answer when he finds himself making a speech to steelworkers in Pittsburgh on a Tuesday night instead of investigating new ways to limit nuclear weaponry or to increase the fluidity of international markets? In the modern age, questions like this seem naive. "The people get what they ask for," responds the press. "The people need to touch their leaders," responds the president. These answers seem so right, so definitive, as to end discussion. But it is also worth asking what is *best* for the people, what might be the *highest* function served by political journalism, how the president could *most perfectly* meet his constitutional mandate to be the nation's leader, not its most canny follower. Were standards of this sort to be seriously invoked, contemporary American politics would be revised on a massive scale. Presidents and news commentators behave as they do because, on balance, it is convenient for them to do so. Only discerning voters, which now means discerning students of political communication, could cause them to behave otherwise.

FIVE

Speech and Choice:
The Presidential Election

WHEN *TIME* MAGAZINE PUBLISHED A STORY ON THE 1984 CAMPAIGN ENtitled "Facing the Fatigue Factor,"[1] it was a sign of the presidential times. Evermore, challengers as well as incumbents are finding it wise or necessary, expected or demanded, that they travel the length and breadth of the land and speak to the American people. If they are leading in the polls they must travel the rally circuit to insure that their campaign workers do not slacken their efforts. If they are running neck and neck with their opponents, the candidates must outtravel and outtalk each other to demonstrate that they have the stamina to fight the good fight. And if they trail their opponents, they must redouble their efforts by including two shopping malls in Joplin rather than one, three party fund-raisers in Kansas City instead of two. Somehow, candidates, reporters, and voters have come to equate electoral success with rhetorical energy, and no political mathematician dares question this postulate.

The irony, of course, is that this scurrying about has intensified during an era featuring the miracles of mass communication. Even though political remarks can now reach the ears of tens of millions of Americans simultaneously, their authors still insist on delivering the messages personally as well. Part of the explanation for these talkathons lies in tradition—the color and drama of a presidential campaign is a quadrennial expectation, a kind of political olympics. Another explanation lies in the psychodrama of American politics: long consecutive days spent on a heated campaign trail supposedly "harden" the candidates in the blast furnace of media scrutiny so that they are tranformed into tempered presidential steel. This latter explanation is reinforced by the *Time* article as it describes the Democratic candidate in the primaries as moving "at a ferocious pace, running an electoral marathon at sprinter's speeds."[2]

Such heroic (Spartan, not Athenian) imagery is a media favorite. *Time,* especially, enjoys featuring these stories as it has since the days of Henry Luce himself. Virtually no personal profile (of business executives, authors, athletes, or politicians) in its pages fails to mention the excessive workload of the profilee. There is some amount of artifice in the *Time* article, however, when, after detailing the Herculean labors of the 1984 candidates, it plaintively notes that "it is unclear whether surviving such a regimen is a measure of presidential mettle."[3] *Time's* concern for the rigors of campaigning is so pronounced that its editors even went to the trouble of including a chart comparing the candidates' ages, blood pressure levels, and serum cholesterol counts, and concluding, unsurprisingly, that Messrs. Hart, Jackson, Mondale, and Reagan were physiologically suited to the challenges of the political lists.

The great amount of press coverage offered to candidates by *Time* and the other media outlets are clearly sufficient to offset the physical and mental rigors of campaigning. Weekly interviews, full-color pictures from the campaign, occasional representations of the candidates' best remarks, and the media's own ability to provide enthusiastic descriptions of election-year hoopla are real allies to the candidates, especially if the candidates are comparatively bland (as they were in 1984). Moreover, as *Time* revealingly notes, " . . . a bushed candidate is more prone to mistakes and misstatements."[4] Because of this, the candidates are shadowed by the media as they travel their routes delivering their oratory. With campaign speeches being as formulaic as they are, the media are naturally attracted to the odd indiscretion, the misdelivered line, the inverted fact. Thus, it is a bit hard to tell whether candidates for the presidency are carrion for the media vultures or whether both are willing coparticipants in a kind of political symbiosis. Whatever their motivations, the effect of their mutual labors is clear: the modern presidential campaign has become a blizzard of political discourse, some of it repetitious, much of it acquiring the status of pseudo event, but all of it pursued with both vigor and intensity.

In this chapter we will focus on the rhetorical dimensions of the modern campaign. Throughout this book, we have seen political manifestations of incumbency, and we shall examine others here. We shall see that a president seeking reelection has special possibilities (regarding timing, information access, etc.) that his challenger does not have but also is somewhat constrained by his office in ways that his challenger is not (e.g., Jimmy Carter's electoral inaction during the Iranian hostage crisis). We shall see that elections often change both the content and the tone of presidential discourse and that, on balance, American elections serve as a kind of intellectual housecleaning for the nation. Finally, we shall see that there is both a rhetoric of geography as well as a geograhy of rhetoric in the United States and that both phenomena affect how presidents behave during a campaign.

To some readers, careful examination of campaign rhetoric may seem peculiarly profitless since so much of it is sterile, if not mendacious. But a recent study by Michael Krukones discovered that the campaign promises of American politicians served as surprisingly accurate predictors of what the politicians later did when serving in office.[5] My findings also suggest that some folk knowledge about presidential campaigns is quite wrong; other folklore is correct but for reasons previously unexamined. More than anything else, the presidential election reminds many Americans that they have a president, that what he feels affects how they feel, and that what he does affects what they are able to do. Every four years two prominent politicians ask voters to rewrite the story of the American presidency. Rhetoric is part of that story.

Talk as Solution

Table 5.1 is deceptively self-evident. It reveals that every recent American president spoke more frequently during election years than during nonelection years. As we saw previously, however, these increases involved not just campaign speeches but also ceremonies and briefings. Lately, international speaking has also increased during election years, signaling that the modern president becomes rhetorically omnivorous when votes are to be had. From the chief executive's standpoint the modern campaign is less political than presidential since he brings all of his office to bear on the election.

There is another way of looking at table 5.1 and that is to note how comparatively modest the nonelection/election year changes have been. Yes, presidents speak more frequently during elections, but they also speak a good deal all the time, as if the American people voted each day. In some senses, the voters do—via the Roper and Gallup polls, through telegrams to their representatives in Congress, and by saving or spending their money or by hoarding or flaunting their gasoline supplies (depending upon the presi-

Table 5.1   *Presidential Speaking in Nonelection vs. Election Years*

President	Average N Speeches (Nonelection Years)	Average N Speeches (Election Years)
Truman	122.2	244.8
Eisenhower	108.0	123.3
Kennedy	236.5	298.0
Johnson	280.0	347.1
Nixon	182.3	203.3
Ford	396.0	542.1
Carter	281.5	379.5
Reagan	293.7	382.0

dent's current request of them). The White House now houses a full-time rhetorical manufacturing plant. It is therefore not surprising that the president's best-known aides are often his most skilled communications' advisors—Ted Sorensen, Dick Goodwin, Ron Ziegler, Gerald Rafshoon, Michael Deaver. Modern presidents have become true rhetorical insurgents—grabbing at persuasive opportunities before others notice them, constructing the persuasive ground rules before their opponents have a chance to do so, injecting rhetorical solutions into situations that would have been previously dealt with privately. Thus, although presidents do increase their speechmaking during elections, they do so only by intensifying, not by redefining, their speaking schedules.

Given the pressures placed upon them by the mass media, it might seem surprising that presidents do not pursue their reelections even more vigorously than they do. One of the favorite games played by the media is speech baiting, an operation in which reporters play the role of White House booking agent. The game, of course, is played in public so that all participants know that an invitation to speak has been made. Sometimes, the matchmakers even go so far as to suggest the proper arrangements. During his September 18, 1980, news conference, for example, Jimmy Carter was confronted with the following question: "Mr. President, the big debate really concerns who will occupy this place next January 21. [Here, the reporter essentializes a complex political environment so that the president will not be tempted to wander when giving his answer.] And since presidential elections are now federally funded [Don't think you're going to escape our scrutiny, Mr. President], I was just wondering [Actually, I've planned this question very carefully, this is hardly a spontaneous thought on my part] whether you might consider [Note my qualifications; I'm being appropriately deferential in front of twenty million television viewers], as President [You *are* the president after all. You're not a coward, are you?], inviting your chief opponent, Ronald Reagan, to a debate here in the White House. [This place has nice lines. The paintings and the balustrades will photograph well]."[6] The presumptuousness of this particular brand of speech baiting is heightened when one recollects that, as of this date, Mr. Carter had already accepted three invitations to debate Ronald Reagan in other contexts. Essentially, the reporter's query dealt with staging and lighting.

In earlier days, the game was played less audaciously. When he inquired about Dwight Eisenhower's plans for electioneering, for instance, Robert Clark of the International News Service asked simply, "Can you tell us how much more speechmaking you now plan to do than you originally intended and whether you feel that your health places any limitation on the extent of your campaign activities?"[7] After commenting about the current state of his health, Mr. Eisenhower asserted in part: "I would say, yes, I am probably doing a little bit more than I originally planned in my own mind; but I will tell you one thing: I am not doing one-tenth of what a lot of people want me to do.'"[8] Eisenhower's full reply was 75% shorter than that supplied by Jimmy Carter to the inquiry posed above. By 1980, a president could not be cavalier about anything asked by the press, especially if it even remotely dealt with presidential valor. The press treats electoral speaking as akin to manhood since it and its readers like to think of politics as a form of civilized combat. If presidents fail to respond fully to such duels in behalf of Dame Politics, the press reminds them gently that nothing less than Honor itself is at stake.

Sometimes, not so gently. The October 14, 1976, transcript of Gerald Ford's news conference contains the following remarkable exchange:

> *Question:* Mr. President, a review of your travel logs from this fall and last
> fall shows that for a comparable period last fall you spent exactly as
> much time on the road—15 days last fall—when there was no cam-
> paign and no election than you have this fall when there is a hotly con-
> tested Presidential election. Doesn't this lend a little bit of credence to
> Governor Carter's charge that you've been kind of hiding in the White
> House for most of this campaign.
>
> *The president:* Tom [Tom De Frank, *Newsweek*], didn't you see that wonder-
> ful picture of me standing on top of the limousine with, I think, the
> caption "Is he hiding?" The truth is, we are campaigning when we feel
> that we can be away from the White House and not neglect the pri-
> mary responsibilities that I have as President of the United States. I
> think you are familiar with the vast number of bills that I've had to
> sign. We've done that. That's my prime responsibility, among other
> things.
>
> We do get out and campaign. We were in New York and New Jer-
> sey earlier this week. We're going to Iowa, Missouri, and Illinois be-
> tween now and Sunday. We will be traveling when we can. But my
> prime responsibility is to stay in the White House and get the job done
> here. And I will do that, and then we will campaign after that.[9]

This question was asked of Gerald Ford, a president who gave 682 speeches in 1976, over half of which were campaign speeches. On thirty-eight different days that year Ford gave between four and six speeches; on twenty-four other days he gave seven or more. Mr. Ford spoke in forty-four of the continental United States during his abbreviated presidency as well. What is truly remarkable about the exchange above is that Ford's election-year behavior was contrasted by reporter De Frank to the president's activities during 1975—the busiest nonelection year for any president since 1945 (and, presumably, since 1789) and the second busiest year *of any sort* during that time (only Lyndon Johnson's 1964 total of 471 speeches surpassed Mr. Ford's). In other words, as far as the press is concerned, a president can never speak often enough. If we are a "presidential nation," as some have claimed, we are so because the mass media now seem incapable of thinking beyond the occupant of the White House. With the chief executive providing copy for virtually every newspaper's front page everyday and visuals for the first three minutes of virtually every televised newscast, the president is nothing less than their Great Provider and his speeches their daily bread.

Whether stimulated directly by the press or not, a president's speaking patterns during his reelection year tell us much about that campaign as well as about that president. Figure 5.1 reveals the topical usages of the seven presidents studied during these years. Three different patterns appear. Harry Truman and Jerry Ford fought for reelection most vigorously and with the greatest sense of abandon. Neither had been placed into office directly by the voters, and so both took on all comers (and all topics) when they spoke. Whether talking for an hour or for five minutes, both Truman and Ford habitually ticked off a laundry list of political topics, briefly mentioning their stands on the issue and then diving headlong into the next area of discussion. How different this pattern is from Dwight Eisenhower, Jimmy Carter, and Ronald Reagan, who focused heavily on economic matters (particularly as they pertained to American industry) and on governmental operations (e.g., tax laws, the responsiveness of Congress, crime prevention, etc.). Naturally, their reasons for making these choices differed, with Messrs. Eisenhower and Reagan attempting to take credit for a burgeoning economy and Mr. Carter attempting to find appropriate scapegoats for the problems of his

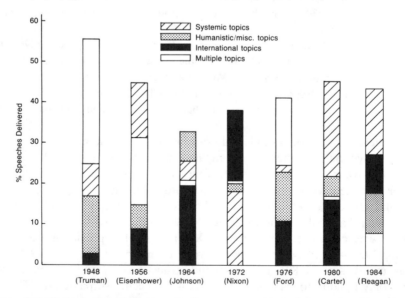

Figure 5.1. Topical alterations in reelection year speaking of recent presidents.

times. Most program specific (and, in retrospect, quite politically secure) were Lyndon Johnson and Richard Nixon. They could emphasize their pet projects—social issues for Johnson, international relations for Nixon—because the times were ripe for political specialization. (As we will see later, however, domestic economic issues were never forsaken by them or by any other president.) Although every election is a referendum on the president himself, this was especially true in Johnson's and Nixon's cases. How ironic this rhetorical boldness seems in light of the political fates to befall them later.

Although many have attempted the task, nobody has yet written the definitive treatise on how to be elected president of the United States. Every four years, presidential staffs try to write this book, but the advice they give is largely ad hoc. At times, of course, even such situational advice is bad advice. Of the last seven chief executives who sought reelection, four won by comfortable margins but used substantially different strategies, one barely managed to hold onto his job, and two lost despite the unprecedented amount of money spent on their campaigns. A quick retrospective of these campaigns points up the different (rhetorical) routes to the White House.

Table 5.2 reveals two of these routes by contrasting uses of "open" and "closed" rallies (i.e., rallies that welcomed all-comers and those that could be attended by invitation only). What appears to be a Democratic/Republican difference in audience preference is, in actuality, an artifact of two different campaigns—those of Harry Truman and Gerald Ford. Mr. Truman hit the open road, bringing his message of a recalcitrant, "do-nothing" Congress to the attention of every American within earshot of an engineer's whistle. He doubled the number of rallies Gerald Ford held in the twenty-four smallest states and spoke five times more often in such places than any of the other presidents seeking reelection. Only Harry Truman could have accomplished such an intensive, protracted rhetorical feat: almost 400 political rallies in less than six months without the benefit of either extensive air travel or a sympathetic press. Moreover, many local Democrats were understandably reticent about being associated with what appeared to have been a doomed candidacy. Circumstances like these prompted his open-ended campaign, and they also required him to become his own best press

Table 5.2   *Use of "Open" vs. "Closed" Rallies by Modern Presidents*

President's Political Affiliation	% Usage (with Truman and Ford)		% Usage (without Truman and Ford)	
	"Open" Rallies (N = 954)	*"Closed" Rallies (N = 385)*	*"Open" Rallies (N = 312)*	*"Closed" Rallies (N = 220)*
Republican	35.1	68.1	55.5	47.8
Democratic	64.9	31.9	45.5	52.2

agent. His speeches on the campaign trail had a raucous, at times bumptious, quality to them. The identifications he sought to build were more gemeinschaft than gesellschaft ("Providence—a great Democratic city in a great Democratic state. Rhode Island shows them the way!")[10] and they allowed Mr. Truman to reach out to potential supporters in almost primitive ways ("It certainly is a pleasure to be here tonight in your wonderful city of Vinitia [Oklahoma]. I have been here many a time. I was driving out here at one time and stopped here at 5 o'clock in the morning to get breakfast. And I got a good one, too").[11]

These "open" rallies permitted Truman to speak a political language that seems quaint by modern standards. He did not have to contend with the kind of strategy-sensitive press facing a contemporary chief executive. As a result, Truman could, without compunction, use the hoary ploy of contrasting the taste of his immediate audience with that of another, more removed grouping: "I can't tell you [citizens of Butte, Montana] how overwhelmed I am at the welcome you gave me this afternoon on the streets. In Kansas City, which is a suburb of my old hometown, I have never had such a welcome."[12] Used with some discretion, this strategy could be used profitably in virtually any locality: "I thought I had seen nearly all the people in New Mexico at Gallup. Then when I got to Albuquerque, it looked as if the people had come in from all the other States. The mayor of Albuquerque told me it was the biggest crowd that had ever been out in Albuquerque. And now it looks as if Las Vegas has shown them all how."[13]

The sounds of 1976 were distinctly different. Jerry Ford spoke often to specialized ("closed") groups of voters and toured the country on the other side of Truman's railroad tracks: the governor's mansion of South Carolina on October 23, 1976, the Huntington-Sheraton Hotel on October 24, the Grossmont Shopping Center later that day, Allstate Insurance Company Headquarters on the 26th, the New Jersey School Boards Association the day after. The presidential stopping places of 1948—Afton, Holdenville, Claremore, Marshfield—became more exclusive as well as more Republican in 1976: West Palm Beach, Ocean Ridge, Briney Breezes, Coral Springs. In contrast to 1948, the American people in 1976 did not wander into a presidential rally sociologically neutered. If geography was the key to Harry Truman's campaign, demography was the watchword to Gerald Ford's. One of Mr. Ford's speeches to the Veterans of Foreign Wars exemplified this. After making the obligatory introductory remarks ("As a proud member of Old Kent Post VFW 830, let me . . ."), Ford hastened to add: "Speaking of national unity, let me quickly point out that I am also a proud member of the American Legion and the AMVETS."[14] Later in the speech, Mr. Ford steered his vessel in the direction of other ports ("As a lawyer . . . ," "As a former naval reservist . . . ," "As a former Congressman . . ."), tacking in each case to particularized political winds.[15]

Mr. Ford's targeted campaign was born not just from Republican loins but from a more general sense that organized groupings of voters were far more dependable than the crowds that heard Harry Truman on a hit-or-miss basis three decades earlier. Truman traveled to forty states in 1948 and Ford to thirty-seven in 1976, but, while there, they talked to fundamentally different persons who had gathered for fundamentally different reasons. Their campaigns had different textures, and they evoked different kinds of emotions. On election eve, for example, Jerry Ford used his national address to recompartmentalize his campaign. His speech is a pastiche of the appeals he had made to the business community ("When I became President, inflation was over 12 percent"), to religious constituencies ("When I took the oath of office in August of 1974, I said I had not been elected by your ballots, but I asked that you confirm me by your prayers"), to the young people of America ("We have restored confidence and trust in the White House itself, and America is at peace"), to conservatives ("Some people have wanted to cut the defense budget. That would be a big gamble"), and to liberals ("We will do a better job in meeting some of the problems of our major metropolitan areas").[16]

Harry Truman's nationwide address on election eve was, in contrast, seamless because the Truman experience in 1948 had been more a social movement than a political campaign. His speech is less mechanistic than Ford's, more a statement of political philosophy than a listing of his stands on the issues. When he spoke he had little fear of crisscrossing his special interest groups because he had rarely faced them in his campaign. The result is a speech rich in bathos but also a speech reflecting the emotional unity of his protracted campaign:

> During the past 2 months the Senator and I have been going up and down the country, telling the people what the Democratic Party stands for in government. I have talked in great cities, in State capitals, in county seats, in crossroad villages and country towns.
>
> Everywhere the people showed great interest. They came out by the millions. They wanted to know what the issues were in this campaign, and I told them what was in my mind and heart.
>
> I explained the meaning of the Democratic Party platform. I told them that I intend to carry it out if they will give me a Democratic Congress to help.
>
> From the bottom of my heart I thank the people of the United States for their cordiality to me and for their interest in the affairs of this great Nation and of the world. I trust the people, because when they know the facts, they do the right thing. I have tried to tell them the facts and explain the issues.
>
> Now it is up to you, the people of this great Nation, to decide what kind of government you want—whether you want government for all the people or government for just the privileged few.

> Tonight I am at my home here in Independence—Independence, Mo.—
> with Mrs. Truman and Margaret. We are here to vote tomorrow as citizens of
> this Republic. I hope that all of you who are entitled to vote will exercise that
> great privilege. When you vote, you are in control of your Government.
>
> Tomorrow you will be deciding between the principles of the Democratic
> Party—the party of the people—and the principles of the Republican Party—
> the party of privilege.
>
> Your vote tomorrow is not just a vote for one man or another; it is a vote
> which will affect you and your families for years to come.[17]

When they ran for reelection, the other presidents also presented distinctive rhetorical profiles. Indeed, Dwight Eisenhower did not really run for reelection; he walked. With good reason, Eisenhower fancied himself as being above politics, and he nursed this image throughout his presidency. At some point early in 1956, Mr. Eisenhower and his advisors must have counted the votes and decided to wage their campaign by not waging one. Ike gave only thirty-one regional speeches that year (compared to Harry Truman's 336 eight years earlier), and virtually none of these occurred in Republican states. By husbanding his political energy in this way, Eisenhower provided few, if any, targets for Adlai Stevenson. In October of 1956, a month when other presidents would be busily fighting the political wars from coast to coast, Mr. Eisenhower did not speak at all on thirteen of those thirty-one days. He visited only eleven states (normally for one or two speeches per state). Such antipolitical politics is indeed rare from the vantage point of the 1980s and 1990s.

Lyndon Johnson's campaign in 1964 was certainly a busy one in contrast. His election-year October produced eighty-nine speeches even though LBJ enjoyed an Eisenhower-sized lead over his opponent, Barry Goldwater. But Lyndon Johnson loved politics, and he loved political oratory even more. In fact, as seen in figure 5.2, which compares, over time, speech frequency in large and small states, Mr. Johnson never really stopped running for the presidency even after he had been reelected to it. Presidents like Dwight Eisenhower and Richard Nixon abandoned the small states after achieving reelection, while Harry Truman, Gerald Ford, and Jimmy Carter largely ignored them until their electoral votes were needed. John Kennedy and Ronald Reagan (through 1982 only) visited such places only during the off-year elections. Lyndon Johnson, in contrast, toured the United States incessantly, and it seemed comparatively unimportant to him whether the states he visited had many or few electoral votes. Throughout his life, LBJ had run for some office or other, and he carried a campaigner's attitude into the White House. As we saw in Chapter Three, he sought out audiences favorable to his course in Vietnam just as avidly as he sought votes in 1964. For Johnson, politics was not something one did every four years but something one was—

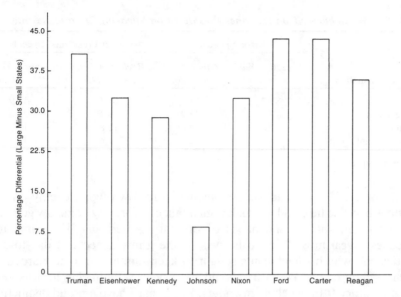

Figure 5.2. Variations in presidential speaking in large and small states (first half of administration vs. second half). High differential = wide variation in how frequently a president spoke in large vs. small states when the first half of his administration was contrasted to the second half.

always. His 1964 campaign for reelection required only minimal adjustments in a personal schedule and personal mindset which prized political opportunities over all other opportunities.

As one might suspect, Richard Nixon's reelection campaign was as tightly controlled and as given to expediency as Mr. Nixon was himself controlled and expedient. Table 5.3 indicates how carefully the Nixon campaign counted votes, with almost all of his speechmaking occurring in the twelve most populous states. No other president's rhetoric was nearly this "concentrated." Strategist that he was, Mr. Nixon did both politics and rhetoric by the numbers. Indeed, during one of the few token speeches he gave in one state of modest electoral value, Nixon justified his doing so neither philosophically nor politically but more as a way of settling a quantitative score he had intended to settle for some years: "As I stand here in Rhode Island, it just occurred to me that while in those elections to which I referred, in '60 and '68, I have at one time or another carried most of the States, Rhode Island is a State that I have never carried. Let me say, the third time will be a charm. This is the year when we take Rhode Island."[18]

Richard Nixon was an awkward man—awkward with people, awkward with his own emotions—and this came through most clearly in political set-

Table 5.3   *Richard Nixon vs. Other Presidents on Speaking in Various States*

	% Nixon Speeches		% Other Presidents' Speeches*	
State Population	*Reelection Year* *(N = 43)*	*Other Years* *(N = 207)*	*Reelection Year* *(N = 1142)*	*Other Years* *(N = 1354)*
Most populous states	83.7	55.5	63.5	51.9
Large states	7.0	22.2	19.1	23.6
Small states	7.0	14.4	12.8	13.3
Least populous states	4.7	7.7	4.6	11.2

*Through 1980 only.

tings. Some of Nixon's advisers thought him his own worst enemy on the hustings because he could not make small talk comfortably nor show genuine warmth when shaking the hands of ordinary Americans. His campaign speeches reveal how ill-suited he was to the grimy aspects of day-to-day politics and why his lieutenants sought to keep him in the Rose Garden as often as they could. When he should have been self-effacing he was self-congratulatory ("In checking my notes, I find that I have a proud distinction today: the first President of the United States ever to visit Prospect [Illinois]").[19] When he should have been subtle he was obvious ("I want you to know how very grateful I am for this enormous crowd . . . I think that all of you inside the hangar should know that there are at least twice as many outside the hangar . . .").[20] Instead of allowing the audience to draw its own conclusions and thereby persuade itself, Mr. Nixon heaped data upon them ("I want to thank the *San Jose Mercury* for their very nice editorial providing the red carpet treatment")[21] or mentioned items that would have been more impressive if left implicit ("I want to express appreciation for the fact that in hotel after hotel, there were signs out. 'Welcome President Nixon' ").[22] Naturally, the egos of all politicians are hardy, but Nixon had a special need to provide the color commentary and to evaluate the success of his game plan even as he executed it.

Although Richard Nixon's campaign rhetoric was hardly nuanced, he had little difficulty in determining the big picture strategically. Figure 5.3 presents an interesting contrast between American involvement in Vietnam and presidential discourse on international conflict (a great deal of which focused on Southeast Asia) between 1964 and 1973. During the 1972 elections, Mr. Nixon sharply increased his speaking on such matters (especially as the election drew near), in part to take credit for the winding down of the war and in part to exploit the dovish tendencies of his Democratic opponent, George McGovern. Although he was not normally given to legislative ceremony, Nixon made extended remarks on Vietnam when signing a bill increasing survivor benefits for military retirees on September 21, 1972. On

October 3 he presided over a ceremony marking the signing of a treaty on limiting ABM missiles. On October 16 he met with the National League of Families of American Prisoners of War and Missing in Action. On October 24 he signed another piece of legislation increasing veterans' benefits. And on October 29, the night before the election, he devoted his last campaign speech entirely to the Vietnam conflict. This flurry of activity contrasted sharply with the steady downturn in it Nixon had effected since taking office in January of 1969. But in 1972 Vietnam was more Richard Nixon's issue than it was George McGovern's, and it was an issue the president exploited. Normally, foreign affairs do not dominate a presidential campaign, but they did so in 1972 because George McGovern demanded it and because Richard Nixon happily obliged him. Mr. Nixon's majority was a silent majority in 1972 because it spent so much of its time listening to Richard Nixon speak and because it liked what it heard.

Jimmy Carter's reelection bid was hampered by the Iranian crisis (during which Mr. Carter retreated to the Rose Garden), but in September and October of 1980 the president came roaring back, delivering more speeches (118) during those months than any previous chief executive except Harry Truman. Moreover, as shown in figure 5.4 (which tracks Carter's speaking

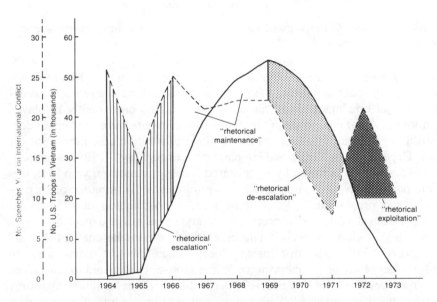

Figure 5.3. Presidential speechmaking on international conflict vs. *N* U.S. troops in Vietnam. Figures of U.S. troops in Vietnam adapted from H. M. Kritzer, "Federal Judges and Their Political Environments: The Influence of Public Opinion," *American Journal of Political Science* 23 (1979), pp. 194–207.

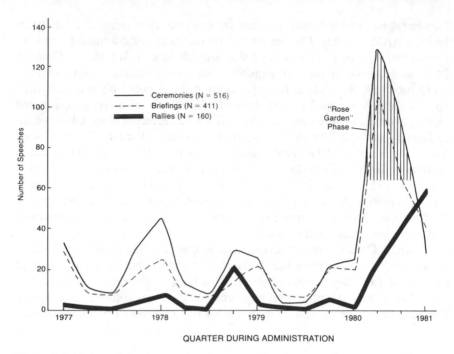

Figure 5.4. Jimmy Carter's use of various speaking formats during his presidency (recorded by quarter).

across his administration), Carter's days in the presidential Rose Garden were hardly spent cultivating the shrubbery. Instead, he utilized ceremonies and formal briefings to keep his face and thoughts prominently displayed before the American people. Oftentimes, these events were political in content if not in form. His remarks during the inauguration ceremonies for the new Department of Health and Human Services on May 14, 1980, were both tearstained ("I was raised by a registered nurse, my mother, who for a lifetime has devoted her talents and her commitments to caring for other people") and programmatic ("We must have a coordinated effort between government at all levels"), precisely the style one might expect during an election-year stump speech.[23] The ceremonial ribbons he cut that day did not prevent Mr. Carter from using either political jabs ("Compared to the last budget of my predecessor in the White House, Federal aid to education, for instance, in our 1981 request is 73 percent higher") or an almost unseemly kind of political preening ("We've increased aid to mass transit programs by two-thirds; doubled economic development aid grants; increased spending for subsidized housing").[24] His conclusion also employed the motifs one might expect to hear on the campaign trail: "We still have a long way to go, and we face more years of hard work . . . I both congratulate you on this day and pledge that together you and I will redouble our efforts to meet that noble challenge."[25]

In this and in many other of his speeches during 1980, Carter camouflaged his partisan rhetoric with the trappings of ceremony, thereby experiencing some of the pleasures of campaigning without the strictures of a campaign regimen. No doubt, this restraint produced some amount of frustration for an aggressive politician like Jimmy Carter. Still, Carter's approach reveals how everything a president touches turns to politics during a reelection year. For Jimmy Carter, as well as for his predecessors, speech often becomes a solution when the fall elections roll around. The forms they choose will vary—badgering for Truman, pontificating for Johnson, ritualizing for Carter—but most presidents find the voice that suits them, and they use it when their job is threatened. In doing so, they are responding to instincts both political and primordial.

What Do Elections Do?

With the rise of the professional politician in the United States has come the rise of the political professional. For each individual running for public office there are thousands of other support personnel—pollsters, speechwriters, campaign advisers, media economists, and the like—and each of them knows what elections are for: getting their candidate a job. Understandably, after an election each of these experts "lobbies" for his or her own interpretation of why the campaign turned out as it did ("They made the wrong media buys at the wrong times," "His demographics were all wrong," "She needed to drop the abortion argument"), because their continued employment depends upon others accepting their epistemological assumptions about political life. Viewed from a strictly scientific vantage point, the predictive abilities of any one of these "lobbies" is abysmally low; their most eloquent explanations of November election results appear in December, not in October. Nevertheless, the political professional is now something of a shaman in campaign circles. Because politics is more art than science, candidates sense that they need to be surrounded by several versions of each of these experts; thus, campaign staffs (and campaign budgets) have swelled at the national as well as at the local levels. These individuals employ their own arcane vocabularies when discussing political phenomena (e.g., counterspots, voice-overs, Q/A techniques, tight vs. loose screens, issue salience, etc.), and after the elections, when the bunting has been placed in storage, each writes knowingly about how politics works.

Virtually none of these specialists, however, asks the more basic question of what elections *do*. Besides placing a particular individual in office on a particular occasion, how does a federal election affect the life of the average American citizen? Does a campaign make any special demands—socially,

psychologically, philosophically—on the voter? Is governance well-served
or ill-served by the roadside oratory heard every four years? And what of
the chief executive himself? How must he change, if at all? Does he alter
either the level or the direction of the nation's dialogue? Do elections—on
balance and when viewed from a distance—contribute to or detract from the
nation's understanding of itself? Or are the pundits correct? Are questions
such as these needlessly academic? Should political elections be treated as
isolated events containing meaning no grander than the ambitions of the
candidates seeking office? Is political history a history devoid of
generalization?

When examined in the large, the federal election contests waged between 1948 and 1984 tell an interesting story. Generally speaking, these campaigns have returned the American political process to its essentials. They
have served as a means of reconnoitering, a way of determining what is truly
native to the political terrain in the United States. They have also broadened
the perspectives of presidents. Figure 5.5 makes this point especially clear
by reporting topical foci in election and nonelection years. Clearly, elections
encourage not only more discussion but also more discussion about all matters. With the exception of the topic of international cooperation, presidents
increased their rhetorical efforts across the board during elections. As we
saw in Chapter One, the topical *proportions* do not change from election
year to nonelection year, but the absolute numbers clearly do. American
elections appear to reward the centrist, the candidate who can address the
full range of issues affecting the nation's constituencies. These topical pat-

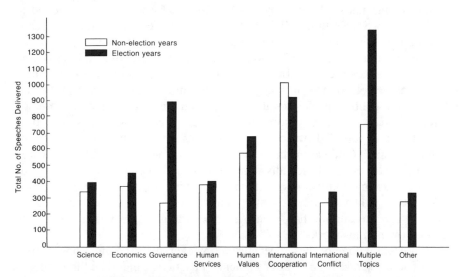

Figure 5.5. Topical distribution of presidential speaking in nonelection vs. election
years.

terns probably point up institutional forces at work. During elections, both progressives and conservatives become Americans above all else, the former bowing to industry, the latter to the blue-collar worker. Elections shape presidential discourse by suggesting appropriate, traditional themes, and it is the sounding of these themes, more than their specific manifestations, that is important.

Presidents thus pay homage to all of the nation's deities even if they do so more from a sense of obligation than from one of personal conviction. Dwight Eisenhower's genuflections were particularly noteworthy in 1956:

> Take labor. The opposition say that they alone truly care for the working men and women of America and that the Republican Party is really a vague kind of political conspiracy by big business to destroy organized labor and to bring hunger and torment to every worker in America.
>
> This is more than political bunk. It is willful nonsense. It is wicked nonsense.
>
> Let's see what the record shows about this:
>
> The record shows: organized labor is larger in numbers and greater in strength today—after these years of Republican Administration—than ever in our Nation's history.
>
> The record shows: Not under the opposition's leadership, but under the leadership of this Administration, the workers of America have received the greatest rise in real wages—the kind of wages that buys groceries and cars and homes—the greatest rise in 30 years.
>
> The record shows: We—not they—have made the most successful fight to stop inflation's robbery of every paycheck.
>
> The record shows that this check upon inflation is most vital—not for the few who are rich—but for the millions who depend upon salaries or pensions, those who are old, those who are sick, those who are needy.[26]

Eight years later, Lyndon Johnson, he of the Great Society, visited Mr. Eisenhower's home state of Kansas to establish his responsibility in fiduciary matters:

> This tax cut that I put into effect when I signed the bill this year giving back $12 billion to American taxpayers—this tax cut put money into Kansas pocketbooks, $22 million more in the State of Kansas alone. That tax cut is helping to create more jobs. It is helping to put more Americans to work.
>
> Here in Wichita where we meet today, there are 13,000 more jobs than there were 3 years ago. The unemployment rate was 4.6 percent 3 years ago. Today it is down to 3 percent, well below the national average for the other States. When the tax cut is fully effective it will mean 22,000 more jobs for Kansas workers. Yes, responsibility is serving America, and I think and I hope, and I believe that you people in Kansas want it to continue next Tuesday.[27]

Democrats as Republicans, Republicans as Democrats. The presidential election brings a variety of political instincts to the fore, probably justifying the Marxists' charges that institutional politics in the United States is a unity of economic interests. Presidents of both political parties become especially aware during election years that every political topic, each piece of proposed legislation, attracts the (oftentimes) frenzied interest of large and powerful groups. Thus, elections cause presidents to stretch, to reach out for every issue they can possibly embrace and to pull it to their political bosoms.

When examining presidential speeches during election years, one senses a Returning, a returning of the presidency to its essential purpose (preservation of the common-wealth); a returning from the chief executive's complex political agenda to the simpler concerns of the everyday voter; a returning of the federal government to localized issues, localized control. There is a literal returning too. In the average president's first year in office, less than 17% of his speeches were delivered in regional contexts. That number jumps to 28.8% in the second year, to 37.2% in the third year. If the president's fourth year in office was a "normal" (i.e., electoral) fourth year (as it was for Eisenhower, Nixon, and Carter), regional speaking often increased even more. A national election makes any American byway a powerful political magnet, slowly drawing the president and his speeches toward it. In this limited sense at least, the presidential election serves exactly the purpose the Founding Fathers intended for federal governance—keeping the president the nation's first citizen, not its lord.

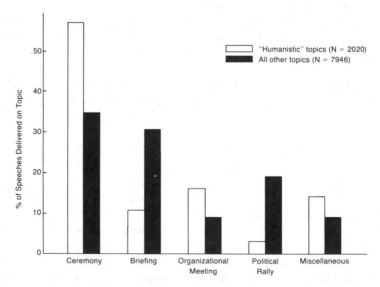

Figure 5.6. Distribution by setting of "humanistic" vs. all other topics.

Table 5.4   *Presidential Speaking on "Systemic" vs. "Humanistic" Topics during Election and Nonelection Years*

Topic	*N* Nonelection Year Speeches	*N* Election Year Speeches	% Increase
All speaking:			
Systemic	990	1736	75.3
Humanistic	954	1066	11.7
Regional Speaking Only:			
Systemic	228	899	294.3
Humanistic	196	301	53.6

Figure 5.6 offers a useful reminder that American politics combines the empirical and the transcendent, that a good deal of presidential speechmaking is devoted to matters of value (ethics, destiny, goodness, bravery) which even presidents of the United States cannot control or, at times, even understand. Since colonial times, Americans have seen themselves as a people scrounging out an existence in God's wilderness, free persons freely pursuing their fortunes but beholden to spiritual values as well. As I have suggested in *The Political Pulpit,*[28] this civil-religious theme has punctuated the rhetoric of American presidents since the time of George Washington. I have also suggested that a contract between church and state has been effected in America. It specifies that politicians will set aside ample time to revere the nation's values (largely through ceremonial functions, as we see in figure 5.6) but that these powerful, yet potentially divisive religious themes will be largely omitted from the practical business of either establishing governance (e.g., during political rallies) or maintaining governance (e.g., in formal briefings). Many nations, of course, find it useful to separate these social/political/ rhetorical functions, but *The Political Pulpit* suggests that the American political establishment has found a special need to do so.

Elections are apt times to renew this unique covenant, to affirm that no matter how vigorously Americans may disagree about certain social or philosophical matters, they still appreciate their heritage: the freedom to strive for material comfort. Largely, then, presidents blow the economic/ technological trumpet during their political rallies. They emphasize the importance of family farms, mass transportation, scientific research and development, small business initiatives, lower interest rates for housing. About these things Americans have often agreed, no matter how they have argued about prayer in the schools, racial integration, or affirmative action. Naturally, these latter topics are discussed during elections, but they are clearly relegated to secondary status by the president *especially when he tours the nation,* as can be seen in table 5.4, which reports regional/topical variations in election and nonelection years.

As we observed in Chapter One, the pragmatic themes found in American presidential elections are essential to maintaining some level of interdependence for several hundred million Americans who are variously skilled, variously educated, variously churched, and varied, too, in ethnic composition. Thus, it is not surprising that this effect is increased threefold when the president tours the hinterlands, there where the bottom-liners dwell. No matter what the watchwords of the president's previous three years might have been (the Peace Corps, Medicare, détente), the watchwords of American elections—jobs, profits, prosperity—do not change. Residents of the Third World may call it crass materialism or economic imperialism, but presidents call it Basic Americanism when they are among basic Americans. It is revealing that, no matter how hard Walter Mondale tried in 1984 to accuse Ronald Reagan of militaristic jingoism, the American people had difficulty seeing beyond Mr. Reagan's "economic recovery." And it is also revealing that even though the Republican platform's social agenda was radical by many standards (strong philosophical opposition to busing, abortion, and women's rights), Mr. Reagan himself largely ignored these themes when campaigning.

Although it would be reductionistic to suggest that American elections are solely pragmatic, that is certainly their direction. Lyndon Johnson's case is an interesting one. Although he spoke about "humanistic" matters more often than other presidents, Johnson's systemic speaking still dominated his agenda in 1964 (roughly 60% of his speeches were of this sort), was reduced during the off-year elections of 1966 (50%), and reduced even further during his last year in office (40%). That is, the gross national product, not his projected social programs, became the focus of a great many of his campaign speeches when he sought reelection. But as he approached the end of his administration, as he became more and more committed to Vietnam and more enamored of his Great Society, and as he became less and less encumbered by thoughts of another reelection campaign, Mr. Johnson slipped further and further away from the earnest, albeit pedestrian, macroeconomic theories he espoused when running for reelection. During the 1964 campaign, however, he spoke of debits and credits, especially credits. He talked of cooperation and understanding between the company and the workers with greater profits for both. "If business puts everything that it has and all it can muster into the pot, and you put, as workers, everything you have into that pot, and then you take a spoon and scoop it up and make a big pie out of it, the bigger that pie is the more you will get and the more they get if we divide it reasonably equitably . . . then Uncle Sam, the Government, I come in and I take my knife, and the bigger the pie is the more I get for Government because I get 52 percent of all that is left."[29]

The call of the economy is a siren call, even for a socially progressive

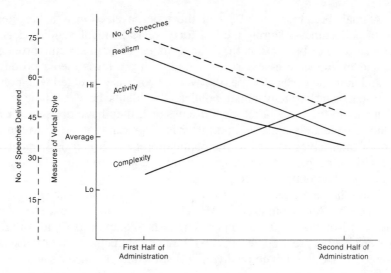

Figure 5.7. Jimmy Carter's alterations in speech frequency and verbal style (on the topic of human services). Measures of verbal style based on a selected sample of all speeches delivered, as reported in R. P. Hart, *Verbal Style and the Presidency: A Computer-based Analysis* (New York: Academic Press, 1984).

thinker like Jimmy Carter. Figure 5.7 traces his speaking on human services across his administration and contrasts it to the kind of *language* he used in such speeches. Not only did he avoid such issues as election day loomed ahead but he also changed the way he talked about these problems in the few speeches he did give. The clear, crisp diction of his earlier administration gave way to a kind of sociological jargon later on: ". . . our people are more mobile . . . People are uprooted . . . Television . . . affects families in ways that we are only now beginning to understand . . . Some laws, some government policies, tend to disrupt family structures."[30] The concreteness he showed when he first took office lapsed into a kind of moralizing that caused blacks and women, among others, to doubt his commitment to domestic human rights: "[The family is] the first place that we learn to care and nurture the child, and to recognize its centrality in society. That has always been the special responsibility of the family."[31]

In his own defense, no doubt, Mr. Carter would argue that political circumstances—rising unemployment, a stagnant economy, international tensions, and the like—forced him to soft-peddle his call for social responsibility in order to be reelected. But Jimmy Carter would not have to resort to special pleading in this case. By concentrating as he did on practicality, he followed the electoral trail blazed by his predecessors in office.[32]

A final, broad-gauged effect of the modern election is a heightened sense of politicalness. During the last forty years political punditry has become a land-office business in the United States. With presidents producing more and more election-year rhetoric and with the mass media producing more and more analyses of same, the average voter is inundated with politics and strategy and strategy about politics. Presidents have become willing participants in these metarhetorical discussions, they have done so for reasons not immediately apparent, and they have probably done so to the detriment of themselves as well as the political process. It is little wonder that the American people opt in ever-greater numbers not to vote at all since so much political activity now seems so game-like.

The following question was addressed to Gerald Ford during a press conference by Ann Compton of ABC News. The question seems simple enough but is actually quite complex since Ms. Compton is (1) asking President Ford in (2) a press conference to (3) make comments about (4) a speech delivered (5) about a debate relative to (6) something he never said:

> Mr. President, in a recent speech—I'm afraid I don't recall where—you cut a line from your text in which you said something about the campaign should not be just a quiz show to see who gets to live in the White House for the next 4 years. And I assume you stand by that advance text. Were you trying to suggest that the debates have not been as effective as they should have been and they have not kept up the level of the campaign?[33]

Questions of this sort have several effects. They tend to heighten the importance of political intention versus political action. They provide a public opportunity for a reporter to uncover a strategic president. They throw light on rhetorical aspects of the campaign rather than on policy aspects. They reinforce the idea that politics is a world of seeming rather than a world in which tangible goods are distributed and redistributed. They place the canny media strategist and the canny politician on the same canny level, thereby justifying the kind of horse-race coverage the mass media devote to presidential elections. And, ultimately, the asking of such questions and, more important, the willing answering of such questions insure their reappearance four years hence:

> *Question:* I'd like to return to a portion of Miss Santini's question. There are people who say that in political campaigns you get mean; that you attempt to savage your opponents. They cite Hubert Humphrey, Edward Kennedy, and now Ronald Reagan. Will you tell us why you think this is not correct, and will you discuss your campaign style from that standpoint?

> ***The president [Jimmy Carter]:*** I have not raised these issues today in the
> press conference; it's been raised twice out of three questions. And
> obviously in the heat of a campaign there is give and take on both
> sides. An incumbent Governor or a President is almost always the sub-
> ject of the most enthusiastic attacks by those who seek his office, and
> quite often those kinds of political verbal exchanges from those who
> seek to replace someone are either accepted as a normal course in a
> political campaign or ignored. If an incumbent, a Governor or a Con-
> gressman or a Senator or a President responds, that's immediately
> given the highest possible notice as an attack on one's challengers.
>
> So, I try to keep a moderate tone; I try to discuss the issues. And
> I do not indulge in attacking personally the integrity of my opponents,
> and I hope that I never shall.[34]

Presidential elections do more than get presidents elected. They do, in
fact, broaden the national dialectic. They do, in fact, lure the president out
among the people. They do, in fact, cause the chief executive to abandon
many of his particular, philosophical notions in favor of the more general and
more practical concerns for nationwide prosperity. They do, it seems, throw
as much light on the how of politics as on the what. Viewed collectively, this
breadth, this sociability, this pragmatism, and this strategizing contribute to
what has come to be known as modern politics. Elections, those special
choosing times, remove from politics all but its politicalness. Perhaps that is
what was always intended.

Rhetoric and Geography

As anyone who has traveled in the United States knows, Americans have a
sense of place or, perhaps, a sense of places. Vast though the land mass is,
Americans have grouped themselves into various localities, and these localities have taken on political features—conservative Mormons building a nation within a nation beside their great Salt Lake; ruddy-faced Irish in South
Boston instinctively pulling the Democratic lever; well-to-do Evanston, Illinois, banking executives taking the scenic lake route to the Loop; Mexican-
Americans laboring next to rutted roads in the South Texas valley. These
Americans distinctively flavor the places they inhabit. When would-be presidents run for office, they must reckon carefully with these subcultural facts
and find a rhetoric capable of reaching Americans where they live.

Table 5.5 is altogether unremarkable, which is itself remarkable. No
matter how one looks at the regional speaking patterns of presidents the
totals are virtually isomorphic with population figures (trends that continued
to be true through 1985 as well). Table 5.6 also reveals an almost perfect

Table 5.5   *Regional Speechmaking by American Presidents (1945–1982)*

	Population* (in thousands)	% U.S. Population ($N = 192,039,000$)	% Presidential Speaking ($N = 2746$)
State's location:			
Northeast	51,550	26.8	24.6
Midwest	56,495	29.4	29.8
South	52,739	27.4	26.5
West	31,255	16.3	19.1
State's population:			
Most populous	115,579	60.2	57.5
Large	44,370	23.1	21.3
Small	24,044	12.5	13.0
Least populous	8,046	4.2	8.1
State's politics:			
Partisan Democratic	58,650	30.5	27.2
Partisan Republican	23,291	12.1	16.1
Neutral	110,098	57.3	56.7
State's significance:			
Dense/neutral	89,881	46.8	43.0
Medium/neutral	17,977	9.4	10.9
Dense/partisan	53,980	28.1	26.7
Sparse/neutral	2,240	1.7	2.6
Sparse/partisan	27,961	14.6	16.8

*Based on 1967 figures (roughly the midpoint of this study). Alaska and Hawaii not included.

"democratization" of rhetoric—one person, one vote, one speech.[35] No matter where one looks—at region, at population, at party affiliation, or at a combination of these variables—it is clear that voter density drives presidential speechmaking.

It must be kept in mind, of course, that this is a forty-year picture of regional speaking and that it somewhat blurs the twists, turns, and personalities of recent presidential history. In some ways, however, that history makes these parallel trends all the more interesting. We have been led to believe that American politics has been completely nationalized by the mass media, that speech-as-regional-flattery has thereby been rendered passé. We have also been led to believe that political power is distributed unequally in the United States—that, for example, the Northeast's money, education, and media outlets make it the nation's political soul and that the other sections of the country need be attended to only when expediency (i.e., electioneering) dictates.

But Table 5.7 shows that all four regions in the United States play an important role in presidential politics, during election year and nonelection

Table 5.6 *Regional Speaking by Presidents and State Population Contrasted*

State	Population Rank	Speech Frequency Rank
California	1	2
New York	2	1
Illinois	3	3
Pennsylvania	4	6
Texas	5	4
Ohio	6	5
Michigan	7	8
New Jersey	8	9
Florida	9	7
Massachusetts	10	19

year alike. The Northeast clearly does not dominate, and the other areas of the country are obviously visited with great frequency even when the polling booths are empty.

All of these data tell a similar story. Political oratory is no *affaire de coeur,* no sudden, uncontrolled moment of passion with the audience assembled. The political orator is a strategist above all else, one who knows that the Midwest may not have the physical endowments of the mountain states but that its many millions of inhabitants make campaign visits there rewarding nonetheless. Politics is a studied courtship and speechmaking a carefully selected dowry (since presidents have little else to offer. Members of Congress, after all, are more prone to regional pork barreling than is the president). So the president travels and speaks, and his speech often becomes a major local event whose sectional impact both precedes and follows it. Such a speech is a spectacle for the townspeople. The president becomes a potential source of exciting disclosures; he travels in an imposing and slightly mysterious entourage; and he impresses even the cynical because he has risen to a station grander than that of the audience.

From the president's standpoint, such speaking is also attractive because it allows him—especially during an election year—to depend upon certain stock themes having virtually automatic regional appeal. Often, these themes are so rich in tradition, so rhetorically suggestive, that the president can speak for a considerable period of time without once entering into politically dangerous territory. Consider, for example, Richard Nixon's campaign speaking in 1974. In a speech in Atlanta on October 12, 1972, he made the following "safe" declaration:

> I do not believe in dividing this Nation—region against region, young versus old, black versus white, race versus race, religion versus religion. I believe this is one country. I believe this is one Nation. And I believe that while we are all proud of our backgrounds—some are westerners, some are southerners, some

Table 5.7   *Regional Speaking by Presidents in Nonelection vs. Election Years*
             (Reported in Percentages through 1985)

Location	Nonelection Year Speeches (N = 779)	Election Year Speeches (N = 2242)
Northeast	28.1	23.2
Midwest	18.7	32.6
South	31.5	24.8
West	25.9	19.4

are northerners, some are black, some are white, some are Italian background, some are of American stock, as they call it—but whatever we may be and whatever our backgrounds may be, we are Americans first, and that is what we must always remember.[36]

Immediately after making this statement, Nixon denounced those who had charged him with having a Southern Strategy for the campaign. "It is not a Southern strategy; it is an American strategy," Mr. Nixon declared.[37] Then, he went on to talk of his training at Duke University ("a fine law school"), the exploits of Robert E. Lee ("the best general produced on either side"), the cultural hallmark of the South ("a deep religious faith"), and then ended his speech by quoting the views of a Southern southerner (Richard Russell) and a Northern southerner (Woodrow Wilson).[38]

Mr. Nixon carried his regionless rhetoric to other areas of the country that year. In the East, he was pleased to be in a place "with so much history, with so much character, with so much to offer America," and he spoke with a fondness for the region ("My wife's father was born in Connecticut," "Our two girls went to camp in Vermont"), a fondness seemingly unmatched anywhere in the nation.[39] Except in Oklahoma. There he noted "that out here in the middle of this country there are a people—a people who are strong, a people who have backbone, a people who will stand up for America."[40] And except in New Mexico, a state with "a great tradition, a background of Spanish-speaking Americans" who especially had impressed this president-of-all-the-people-but-you-in-particular early in life: "When we, in English, say we want to welcome somebody someplace, we say, 'Make yourself at home.' But those who speak Spanish . . . say, 'Estan ustedes en su casa'—you are in your own home—and that's the way we feel today."[41]

Although Richard Nixon's rhetoric was unusually transparent (and his social self unusually contrived), his expediency seems fairly typical of presidential politics. Using other research techniques, researchers have found similar regional trends. Whether they called it "coalition building" and based their results on the 1980 race,[42] or whether they studied campaign logs from

1932 to 1976,[43] researchers agree that population, not ideology or personal preference or geographic proximity, is the single best predictor of where presidents campaign. This becomes even clearer in figure 5.8 which shows how shifts in population bring about shifts in communicative focus (at least in the six states contrasted). This rhetorical census taking often has interesting consequences. When concluding a 1982 campaign speech in job-needy Pennsylvania, for example, Ronald Reagan concluded with a quotation from James Russell Lowell's poem, "Columbus." Mr. Reagan set up the poem exquisitely:

> Lowell wrote of that momentous voyage across the Atlantic. The crew had been told again and again that they would soon see land on the horizon, and they saw only water. They were tired, hungry, lonely, desperate, and ready to mutiny. But as Lowell wrote, "Endurance is the crowning quality and patience all the passion of great hearts."[44]

It is hard to determine how comforting Reagan/Lowell were for Pennsylvanians in May of 1982 since that state was experiencing extraordinary

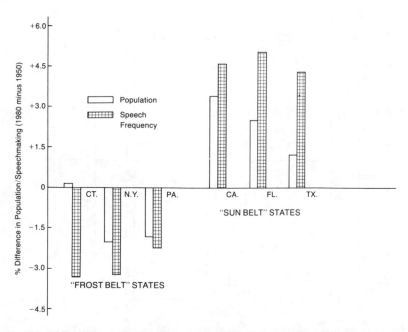

Figure 5.8. Differences in population and presidential speaking for selected states (1950s vs. 1970s). Population figures = 1950 census vs. 1980 census; speechmaking figures = 1945–1957 vs. 1970–1982.

economic distress at the time. How different Mr. Reagan spoke when he ventured into Texas the next month, a state whose then-booming population and then-booming economy removed the constrictions from his voice and allowed him to conclude on a booming rhetorical note: "What you've created here has captured the imagination of the world. Entrepreneurs, laborers, and men and women looking for opportunity are flocking here not expecting a handout, but knowing that with hard work they can improve their lives. That's what Texas is and, I hope, will always be about."[45]

Figure 5.9 further refines our understanding of presidential campaigning and shows that, through 1982 at least, *population plus voter directionality* predicts most precisely who the chief executive talks to when the chips are down. Harry Truman badgered New Yorkers in 1948; Lyndon Johnson did the same to Pennsylvanians in 1964; Jimmy Carter dramatically increased his speaking to Floridians in 1980. In other words, *electoral diffidence* best assures the attention of the president of the United States. In contrast, the political loyalty found in such states as Maryland, Massachusetts, Georgia, and Kansas may be appreciated by presidents but does not result in very many election-year speeches. Such data accent the expediency of politics but make it a double expediency since we are talking here about human

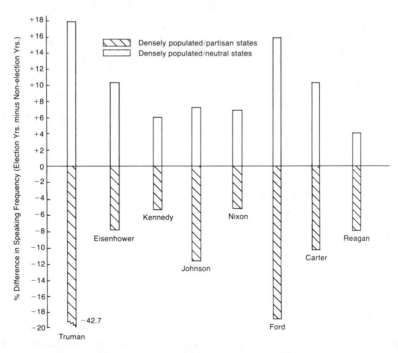

Figure 5.9. Differences in regional speaking during nonelection vs. election years by recent presidents.

Table 5.8   *Presidential Speaking in Ohio vs. Other States*

State	N Nonelection Year Speeches	N Election Year Speeches	% Increase
All other states	764	2103	175.0
Ohio only	15	139	827.0

speech, normally thought of as a gift freely given to another. Political speech is thus not speech at all but a kind of mechanical interfacing between machine parts resulting in a political widget carefully adapted to market forces. This is a metaphor for the times because this is speech for the times.

Nowhere is this love-'em-and-leave-'em attitude better shown than in the state of Ohio, a state bulging with electoral votes but one in which the upstate, urban Democratic voters are counterbalanced by downstate, rural Republicans. There is an eloquence of brevity to table 5.8, with Ohio being virtually ignored by the presidents during nonelection years but avidly pursued when votes were being cast. Harry Truman spoke there only when campaigning. Lyndon Johnson spoke there fourteen times during election years but only twice otherwise. Neighbor Jerry Ford spoke in Ohio only three times in 1975 but twenty-eight times in 1974 and 1976. Apparently, Ohio is the sort of state that only an acquisitive politician can love.

Perhaps even more interesting than this crass politicalness is what the presidents actually said when they arrived in Ohio. They spoke not as if they were long-lost relatives looking for a political handout but as if they knew the people of Ohio down to the sinews of their beings. Said Dwight Eisenhower in 1956:

> When they [the naysayers] visit a city like Cleveland, let them look around at the hustle and bustle; talk to, and especially listen to, the people here. Let these politicians absorb some of the spirit that animates Clevelanders, all of them—whether they work in banks, in factories, in orchards and fields or in kitchens. Their worries and fears of the future of America should begin to sound foolish—even to them.[46]

Said Lyndon Johnson in 1964:

> I think I know something about the people of Ohio. I think they are good, patriotic Americans. Some of them are Republicans and some of them are Democrats and some of them are Independents. Nearly all of them are pretty independent. But I believe when the chips are down, whether it is when the draft calls them or Uncle Sam summons them, I believe that most of them do what they think is best for their country, regardless of their party, and that is what I want you to do.[47]

Said Jerry Ford in 1976:

> If I might add a special observation and comment—us Michiganders look at
> people from Ohio and, you know, we have nothing but great, great respect for
> you . . .
> The thing that impresses me about the many people I see here and what
> I saw on each side of the street is that you have so many wonderful traditions,
> such distinctive and delicious food, a uniquely spirited way of life, a very special
> place in this great American family. Through your support for people [like]
> Frank Lausche, Jim Rhodes, Bob Taft, myself, we want to make certain that
> what we do politically preserves these unique things that each and every one
> of you represent.[48]

Ohio, it seems, brings out the sociologist in a president. Ostensibly, it is a
state presidents know so well that they need visit it only when the spirit
moves them. That spirit has moved powerfully during election years.

Table 5.9 records the workings of a kindred spirit, one that brings
presidents home differentially. For a politician, a home state is not just an
emotional haven but also a political launching pad. A speech there is virtually
guaranteed to produce colorful banners, smiling faces, an enthusiastic band,
and an ocean's roar of applause. Thus, presidents returned home twice as
often during election years as during nonelection years, an imbalance repeated by all of the presidents except John Kennedy (who, of course, was
assassinated before a possible reelection bid). The rhetorical advantages of
such speeches are prodigious, especially in a mediated age. These talks
abruptly remove the president from the lockstep formulas of the typical
campaign address. They also extend an invitation to an unusual visitor in a
campaign—genuine emotion. They discourage use of election-year clichés in
favor of plain, highly specific language adapted to local surroundings. They
encourage a president to feel like the human being he perhaps rarely feels

Table 5.9 *Presidential Speaking in Home States in Election
and Nonelection Years*

	N Speeches	Average N Speeches per Nonelection Year	Average N Speeches per Election Year
Truman	40	2.1	8.0
Eisenhower	22	2.0	3.5
Kennedy	8	4.2	0.0
Johnson	90	15.0	19.4
Nixon	39	6.3	7.4
Ford	34	5.0	20.7
Carter	23	5.5	6.0
Reagan	64	10.3	16.5

like, to speak in a neighborhood sort of way. Gerald Ford's return to Michigan just before election day in 1976 possessed all of these features. The timing of his address, the presence of the national media, and his own, earnest style made for a vignette Charles Kuralt would have been proud of:

> I have made a lot of speeches, and this is the hardest one to make, because as I look out in this audience and as I saw so many people as we came down Monroe Avenue—Democrats, Independents, Republicans—people that Betty and I lived with, that Betty and I love, that I tried to help over the years when I had the honor of representing this great congressional district, I could tell you some stories about how the tough problems came to our office. And we never asked the person that walked in that office whether he or she was a Democrat or a Republican. We said, what can we do to help you, and that is the way I want to be your President.
>
> You know, those wonderful experiences over a period of time, of taking that trailer down through Ottawa County, Ionia County, Kent County, and sitting and listening to wonderful people who had a problem, who wanted to give me a little trouble, give me a hard time—and they did—but also we had a couple of friends that might come in and say nice things about us. But the wonderful experience of representing the Fifth Congressional District will be something that I will never forget, and I thank you for the opportunity.
>
> You know, I had a speech I was going to make, but I threw it away . . .
>
> As we came off the expressway, we went down College Avenue and Betty said, "I went to Fountain School." We went right by it. Then we went by Central High School, but then, you know, I said to her, "Well, South High, that was a great school, too."
>
> But anyhow, Grand Rapids, Kent County, Ottawa County, Ionia, well, all of them—western Michigan can make the difference and this is what I want you to know and what I think it is all about tomorrow.[49]

To examine such regional speaking patterns is an invitation to cynicism. Hometown becomes photo opportunity. Voters become audiences, if there are enough of them. Place becomes scene. Nowhere are these patterns better noted than in the American South, a region that has grown steadily in importance during the forty years examined in this study. Table 5.10 shows how presidential speaking has increased considerably in what might be thought of as the "industrialized" South (as opposed to the more rural South of Alabama, Mississippi, Kentucky, South Carolina, and Arkansas which also experienced similar, but less dramatic, increases). The political partisanship and cultural provincialism earmarking that region for so many years has given way to manufacturing plants, financial centers, and, inevitably, to presidential speeches. Jerry Ford averaged almost ninety speeches a year in the South, an area in which Harry Truman and Dwight Eisenhower rarely spoke. Ford's

Table 5.10   *Alterations in Presidential Speaking in Selected Southern States*

State	N Speeches 1945–1957	N Speeches 1958–1970	N Speeches 1970–1982
Florida	15	28	84
Georgia	1	13	39
Louisiana	3	8	19
North Carolina	6	12	34
Tennessee	2	12	29
Texas	28	104	95
Virginia	6	16	35

average was three times higher than that of native son Lyndon Johnson. During his first year in office, Ronald Reagan spoke in the South more often than in any other region of the United States. Because the favor of a presidential speech carries both cultural as well as political significance, these trends may signal a permanent deregionalization of the American South.

Figure 5.10 plots these changes for all Southern states during election years. The trend lines indicate just how marked, and how politically motivated, these alterations have been. One set of researchers describes the South as having experienced "sectional volatility" since 1944, and they see no fundamental reason why this volatility should not continue to characterize it in the foreseeable future.[50] Although many observers have proposed an assortment of explanations for these changes, Raymond Wolfinger and Robert Arseneau largely reject all but socioeconomic ones: "The most consequential outside influence is the northern migration. Newcomers keep streaming into the South, the fastest growing, most economically dynamic part of the country. Younger, better educated, and more prosperous than the natives, they are also more Republican and more active in politics."[51] This Yuppies-in-Dixie argument seems incontrovertible. These are the sorts of persons most likely to attend a political rally and to believe that they have profited by so doing. Thus, when Jerry Ford spoke in Biloxi, Mississippi in September of 1976, he tipped his hat in the direction of traditional Southern values ("All right-believing people who are law-abiding ought to have the traditional right under the Constitution to retain firearms for their own national protection, period"), and he acknowledged Southern institutions as well ("But let me talk for just a minute about the military. I'm mighty proud of the people out at Kessler Air Force Base. You're a very vital part of this great national defense team that we have").[52] But Mr. Ford saved the majority of his speech for those whose emotional residence was the New South. In doing so, he appropriated the pragmatic themes characterizing political rhetoric throughout the United States in the latter twentieth century: trust in the White House, inflation, the economic recession, and Vietnam, and a better future for all ("We're making all kinds of progress to get this economy healthy again . . . there's a new spirit in America").[53]

Jerry Ford's speech in Biloxi is distinguished by how little distinguishes it. The modern campaign is surfeited with such tired oratory, no doubt because presidential candidates themselves are exhausted from racing about the nation's landscape. Mr. Ford's speech in Biloxi is plain indeed. The old rhetorical monsters he exhumes fail to frighten—recession is still at its accustomed brink, people are being once again divided, and trust, alas, is still lost. The grand new forces on the American scene seem neither grand nor new; waters that are calm, jobs that are meaningful, and lives high in quality always seem desirable, although neither voter nor candidate knows what such phrases mean. But campaigns and speechmaking and prodigious amounts of traveling continue, in part because they emerge from traditions continuing to work themselves out and in part because even the nation-spanning, nation-shrinking mass media cannot completely remove sectional tribalism. But increasingly, only the introductions and conclusions of campaign speeches bear geographical markings, perhaps signaling that America is growing up, if not growing together.

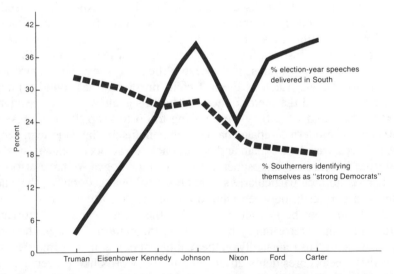

Figure 5.10. Relationship between election-year speaking in the South and voters' political affiliations (1952–1978). Figures of Southerners identifying themselves as "strong Democrats" adapted from W. E. Miller et al., *American National Election Studies Data Sourcebook:* 1950–1978 (Cambridge, Mass.: Harvard University Press, 1980), p. 91.

Conclusion

The importance of speech in the modern presidential campaign cannot be gainsaid even though many observers would have us believe that the mass media have so homogenized electoral politics that factors of space, time, and personality no longer obtrude. My findings suggest the contrary: who an incumbent president decides to talk to and how he decides to talk to them are every bit as distinctive today as they were prior to the advent of the mass media. This is not to say, of course, that the mass media have failed to *accelerate* these normal political processes. But it is to say that modern campaigns still develop distinctive profiles resulting from an amalgamation of sociodemographic variables, political calculations, and the rhetorical mindsets of the persons running for office. Even more intriguing is that these profiles are revealed at the primitive level of the speech act itself, suggesting perhaps that nobody—neither pauper nor prince nor president—can hide when they speak. Such a conclusion might be faintly heartening to us as citizens for it suggests that even in an era of daily political polling, saturation advertising, focus-group testing, automated mailings, and PAC-controlled fundraising much of a political campaign consists of people talking to people, just as it always has.

In this chapter, we have seen that a presidential election strips the presidency bare of all but its essential, political soul. Rhetoric is used to reclothe the presidency, to make it seem that even the crassest form of campaigning is nothing less than an institutional mandate. During election years presidents barnstorm the country, trying on a new hat in each locale and extending their coattails, if they have them, to those who share their political worldviews. Each of the last eight presidents has found a unique campaign style, and the rhetoric they produced signals what the presidency meant to them and what they were willing to do to keep their jobs. As we have seen, the modern campaign has certain benefits for the American people since it forces presidents, again and again, back to socioeconomic basics and away from the rarefied atmosphere of political ideology. We have also seen that there is nothing particularly subtle about political geography, that there is almost a perfect fit between what a particular constituency can do for a president and what he is willing to do for them (or to them) rhetorically. There is something refreshingly honest about the patterns observed here, for they have focused us repeatedly on the realities of power in the United States. When they speak, presidents do not like to use words like power, but it is the only concept available to explain why they speak when they speak.

Although each presidential campaign since 1948 has had its distinctive features, its managers have all been deadly serious about achieving political dominance. As we saw in Chapter One, however, modern presidential politics also has a soft side, a ceremonial side; presidential campaigns are now

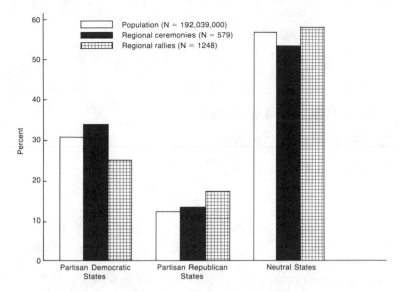

Figure 5.11. Proportional comparison between states' populations and presidential ceremonies and rallies. Population figures shown are 1967 figures (the midpoint of the presidential era examined; excludes Alaska and Hawaii).

four-year propositions, not just autumnal rites of passage. Thus, figure 5.11 shows that presidential ceremonies are linked more closely to population (and hence to power) than are even the transparently political rallies themselves. The president now runs a continuing campaign for reelection, and if not for that, then for political immortality. Most of us tend to think of ceremony as seasonal rather than geographic, emotional rather than cognitive, spontaneous rather than plotted. Ceremony is, after all, a special time for remembering special people, a way of building social solidarity for its own sake, a time to reach out to others and have them share our happiness or sadness and we theirs. But the heights of the bars in figure 5.11 are too precise and too similar to sustain these myths about political ceremony. This figure captures the broad view of modern presidential politics. It suggests that, in politics, phenomena like seasons, emotions, spontaneity, memories, solidarity, happiness, sadness, and all else serve political masters. Therein lies the essential strength and the fundamental problematic of a presidential form of government.

SIX

Speech and Wisdom:
Whither Presidents?
Whither Leadership?

Reporter: Mr. President, do you have any New Year's wishes?

The president: Well, I certainly want all Americans and all people throughout the world to have a happy, healthy, and prosperous New Year, and I believe the opportunities are there that they will. And if we all pray and work, I think we can have that health and happiness and prosperity.

Question: Mr. President, did you make any personal resolutions for the New Year?

The president: Yes, but I don't reveal them. Well, I think I have said what I really hope, that not only the people here in the United States but people throughout the world will have a wonderful New Year, and I think they will.

Question: Do you think the snow is an omen for a good New Year?

The president: Well, every time I ski with Russ Ward we get good snow.

Question: Thank you, Mr. President.

The president: Good. It's nice to see you all.[1]

Thus spoke Gerald R. Ford, the thirty-eighth president of the United States of America—at chairlift 6 in Vail, Colorado, during his Christmas vacation. Presumably, the president had on his skis when he spoke, and he probably gestured vigorously when guaranteeing that all Americans would have health, happiness, and prosperity in 1977. Throughout this book, we have seen that Jerry Ford's ever-ready speechifying made him a typical modern president. We have seen that presidents often have precious little to say but that there are precious few moments when they are unwilling to say it. We have seen that the majesty of Mr. Ford's mountaintop declarations (". . . all Americans and all people throughout the world")[2] stoutly echoed the splendor of his surroundings and of the presidential oratory that had preceded his during the previous half-century. Even when schussing presidents take themselves seriously.

It is unlikely that Mr. Ford thought very hard about what he was going to say when he saw members of the press corps coming toward him on that New Year's eve, just as it is unlikely that the reporter who questioned him did so because of a felt need burning deeply within him. Both probably merely played habitual, unthinking parts in what has become The Drama of Presidential Communication. It would seem that neither reporter nor president exercised their intellects when speaking and neither listened very hard to what the other had to say. Our reporter surely could not have cared about Mr. Ford's personal resolutions for 1977 nor about his attitude toward the fresh snow at Vail. The very asking of questions like these signals the reporter's personal resignation to the ritual of presidential exchange but the need to cling to it nonetheless. Maybe presidents answer such questions in part because they are polite, in part because such questions cannot hurt them, and in part because they would rather speak than think. When speaking, Mr. Ford knew quite well that Americans unable to afford essential medical services would hardly enjoy good health in 1977, that Americans fearing an unprecedented nuclear buildup would experience little happiness, and that Americans who numbered among the fifteen million unemployed would be bypassed by the prosperity he twice promised that day. In short, the exchange at chairlift 6 did little for the cause of freedom, little for the national dialectic, little for journalistic excellence. But this exchange did accomplish one thing: it promised a continuation of the Rhetorical Presidency into the New Year.

In 1977, just as in 1976 and in the years preceding, the president of the United States continued to speak with only the slightest provocation; he continued to purport to control realities he could not control; he continued to be cheerful when he was sad, and knowing when he was not. He did these things because he believed that public communication, with anyone, about anything, constituted both his best chance for political salvation as well as the essential duty of the government office he held. In 1977 and thereafter, presidents appeared to question neither of these assumptions, nor did the nation's mass media, nor did the American people themselves. Many of them would agree (unthinkingly, I argue) that a president performs one of his most important services to the nation when he stands and speaks to them. Presidents can no longer imagine what their jobs would be like if opportunities for public communication were denied them. Members of the electronic media would be horrified at the thought of issuing a presidential news story unaccompanied by visuals depicting a chatty chief executive. The nation's citizens would also think it odd if presidents did not run about the country saying the splendid things presidents allegedly say. So the Rhetorical Presidency continues, producing almost ten thousand major communicative events in forty years. Interestingly, the countless minor events like those at chairlift 6 are not even included in this total, indicating how widespread and how entrenched presidental communication has become in the modern age.

Many, of course, would argue that the revolution begun by John Kennedy in the executive branch of government is a matter of small moment. They might claim that American politics has always been a shallow enterprise run by quite ordinary people and that the publicity communication events provide for the presidency merely makes this more obvious. Optimists, on the other hand, might argue that presidential oratory ultimately does little harm and that presidential ribbon cuttings and Rose Garden crownings provide psychic benefit to a nation deprived of monarchical trappings. Pragmatists would defend the Rhetorical Presidency on other grounds, asserting that communication performs necessary and important functions for a beleaguered president. We have seen these functions at work throughout this book: rally speeches sustaining a Truman presidency, legislative rituals insuring LBJ's greater society, televised addresses maintaining the Vietnam war until Richard Nixon could effect his peace with honor. Political revisionists might be outright heartened by these increases in presidential communication, arguing that John Kennedy's ceremonial trips and Jerry Ford's local press conferences and Jimmy Carter's town meetings dramatically improved citizens' understanding of their political options.

Other observers, I among them, are less impressed by the trends observed in this volume. Presidential communication, after all, should teach, and yet no greater number of Americans could find Nicaragua on a map in the 1980s than could find Pakistan in the 1950s. This is hardly to say that presidential communication is alone responsible for political ignorance and cultural provincialism. But it is to say that the themes developed previously in this book must be examined in light of what presidential communication can do and what it has failed to do.

My own examination of presidential discourse has left me conflicted. The political cynic in me wants to argue that what presidents say makes little difference—few listeners take presidents' speeches seriously since so much political action occurs behind closed doors and since presidents must share political power with Congress and the lobbies. The political realist in me knows, however, that most political deals made in private ultimately must be remade in public in a democracy, that the president is the nation's designated salesperson, and that his remarks cannot, therefore, be discounted no matter how richly they may sometimes deserve it. The political idealist in me senses how challenging and instructive and uplifting and healing communication can be—especially communication authored by a president—and is thus doubly dismayed to find so little that could be called heroic, not to mention honest, about presidential speaking. Because of these conflicting

humors, this book will not end on an optimistic note. Examining the implications of the data reported throughout this book provides little reason for
the American people to cheer, no matter how ardently and how frequently
presidents urge them to do so when speaking to them.

Whither Presidents?

In previous chapters, we have seen how central speechmaking has become
to modern chief executives and how White House routines have been altered
dramatically as a result. But it is also worth considering the impact of this
rhetorical worldview on the president himself. What difference does it make
to a president—emotionally, psychologically, intellectually—that he has chosen to speak for a living? For one thing, it means that a president becomes
a special kind of person—a public person—and therefore one who forfeits a
private self. It might be argued that politicians have always risked exposure
of their innermost selves, but in an era supersaturated by mass communications presidents are now allowed no hiding places at all. This is an eventuality that would have appalled John Kennedy and that might have caused
him to draw back from his public persona had he been able to foresee its
consequences. But it was left to Kennedy's successors to bear the brunt of
his burden. Now, they must, if they are Ronald Reagan or Jimmy Carter or
Gerald Ford, discuss with the American people why they sleep as often as
they do, why they converse with their adolescent children about foreign
policy, and what they say to their wives when settling down for the evening.

   The American people and the national press have always been interested in such tidbits about celebrities, but increasingly presidents are expected to provide both the objects of scrutiny *as well as to comment upon
them*. This seems to be the price exacted from anyone seeking a public
audience in contemporary times. And this bargain goes well beyond the
simple disclosing of personal habits. Presidents are increasingly expected to
experience private thoughts in public, not just to report on them after-the-
fact. The delay between a political event and a president's reaction to that
event is also vitiated by a news-hungry mass media and an emotion-hungry
populace. The omnipresent minicameras and the reporters who cover the
president like a blanket all but insure that the natural human gap between
intellection and utterance is all but erased. Even more important, that "gap"
itself is now declared immoral by an imperious mass media as they make the
constant demand that feeling and saying occur simultaneously in a public
official.

   Because presidents now speak so often it is all but impossible to conceive of a single presidential emotion that has not been caught on videotape.
After all, simply because one lives in the public eye does not mean that one's

normal emotional experiencing ceases. To the contrary: the living and the experiencing, as well as the talking, must be done simultaneously. By the time he spoke to a conference on physical fitness in 1971, for example, Richard Nixon had already learned that *a president* does not have the luxury of bifurcating his private and public selves. Mr. Nixon's speech reflects the thoughts of one who had little conception of what he wanted to say but knew only that an audience awaited him. By 1971, Richard Nixon had been a public person for some thirty years, and by then he had long since lost the ability to distinguish between things worth thinking and things worth saying:

> Let's face it. This is a sports-minded country. That isn't bad. It has a lot to do with the spirit of a country, the fact that people are interested in how a golf match or a football game or a baseball game or, for that matter, a tennis game, any kind of sport that you might figure that people who may not participate, who never will be champions, like to watch.
>
> But now we come to the key point with television and those marvelous closeups they have and the reruns and everything else, with television these days the tendency is for people just to sit there, feet up, eating pretzels and drinking—well, drinking, in any event—and that is their participation in sports. I do not think that is bad. As a matter of fact, that can do something for the spirit, as well—in both ways.
>
> But what I am suggesting is this: that we need to alert the people of this country, and particularly the young people of this country, that they can do something about their future to make them develop the health patterns which will avoid physical illness and very serious physical illness in the years ahead.
>
> I am not the best one to speak on this subject. As a matter of fact, as I have said, I really hate exercise for exercise's sake. Bud Wilkinson has constantly told me I must jog every day. I do a little, but about a minute is enough.
>
> But the point is that I feel that the emphasis on exercise, the fact that some exercise—call it what you will, jogging, walking, participation in competitive sports—some of this is so essential for the physical well-being of the people of this country.[3]

Mr. Nixon evidences here the clear signs of the rhetorically punch-drunk: constant self-interruptions, starting down one conceptual path and then veering off, convoluted syntax, interspersing descriptive and evaluative statements, random searching for a laugh. Perhaps the more revealing feature of Nixon's speech is the odd confederation of personal experience and athletic philosophizing. Mr. Nixon seemed to sense that he was supposed to say something about the value of sweating and that sharing his private experiences was also required in an open, disclosive presidential era. The fact that his personal testimony logically confuted his remarks probably seemed to him a price worth paying for an opportunity to share the national spotlight with sports' celebrities. The steady rhetorical schedule a modern president follows ultimately tempts him with the notion that all his thoughts are worth sharing. As a result, a great many presidential speeches amount to little more than pontification cum anecdotalism.

Because so many rhetorical demands are placed upon a modern president and because his own psychological needs are no less pronounced than those of any other citizen, presidents often use their speaking opportunities for catharsis, for a kind of public auto-therapy. Certainly this was true of Lyndon Johnson, one who felt much and spoke much. On one occasion Mr. Johnson was asked to address the International Platform Association, a non-descript organization promoting no particular political cause. Mr. Johnson used the IPA engagement to get things off his chest, and how he did so is interesting. He began by recounting the things for which the IPA stood (freedom of speech, etc.), then told a long-winded joke that had been a Dwight Eisenhower favorite, next launched into a kind of political free-associating focused on the Bill of Rights, and then suddenly threw himself into the following remarkable transition:

> Now I don't hear any people worrying much about this word aggression. They talk about the bombs. They talk about intervention. They talk about fighting a war in rice paddies. They talk about what sacrifices we are required to make. But during all of our history we have died in order to keep our contracts, in order to protect human beings.[4]

What followed was Mr. Johnson's standard litany on Vietnam—traditional commitments to be honored, the domino theory, America's ability to fight successful wars, etc. Then, just as suddenly as he had begun his diatribe, LBJ lurched into a new discussion of his domestic programs and of future national possibilities. The oddly placed Vietnam segment served no particular thematic purpose and had little relevance to the aims and goals of the International Platform Association. But the speech provided Mr. Johnson purgation in the manner suited to a modern president—public purgation.

From the president's standpoint, public speaking can therefore be an enormous emotional ally. By choosing his audiences carefully, a chief executive can receive social reinforcement for virtually any sentiment dear to him. The natural inclination of one who speaks for a living is to become audience driven, to become less and less inclined to examine one's own thoughts analytically and more and more attentive to the often uncritical reactions of popular assemblages. As we have seen earlier in this book, presidents are increasingly speaking in closed settings to special interest groups, audiences whose prejudices can be assessed beforehand and whose reactions to a presidential speech can therefore be anticipated. If a president speaks frequently to such groups, the challenges confronting him become less intellectual than performance based. Presidents polish their acts before such groups, often becoming seduced by the applause they and their staffs have prearranged. Such speechmaking thus has a self-reflexive impact on a president, insulating him from contrary viewpoints and rewarding him for feeling the emotions he is currently feeling.

Consider, for example, some of the comments Ronald Reagan made about the lot of American women early in his administration. On one occasion he observed that "we've appointed more women to substantive jobs than any other administration in history. And let me assure you this is only the beginning."[5] One month later he noted that "some critics have expressed concern that we're not addressing women's issues. So let's set the record straight right now: That charge is a bum rap."[6] Yet another time he pronounced himself delighted "to be here today, Women's Equality Day, the 63rd anniversary of women's suffrage and the date on which, in 1920, the 19th amendment was finally added to the Constitution."[7] Mr. Reagan's remarks were delivered, respectively, to the National Federation of Republican Women, to a White House luncheon for the Fifty States Project for Women, and to the Republican Women's Leadership Forum. Needless to say, none of these groups actively disabused Mr. Reagan of his view that women had been well treated under his administration. Reagan spoke about women's issues on less cozy occasions also—to the National Press Club, to the American Bar Association, and during several news conferences—which brings up a second point: extensive public speaking by a president begets repetition since there are only a limited number of topics confronting any given president and because so many different audiences wish to hear him speak. Repetition, in turn, begets (1) a dulling of the intellect, (2) a growing sense that one's views are correct, and (3) the feeling that rhetorical action is equivalent to empirical action.

Mr. Reagan's speeches on women's rights bore the marking of all three effects. He spoke in clichés about the progress women had ostensibly made, quoting liberally from standard Republican documents and, not infrequently, from himself. One heard no new analysis of the problem, no fresh directives, but merely the resaying of thoughts previously thought and then put away. Repeating oneself over time, especially when done so publicly, also gives one a growing sense of rectitude. Any public setting introduces some element of personal risk for the speaker, and so each speech becomes a kind of battle star earned in the heat of combat. To disavow such hard-earned statements is therefore not easy for a president. Often, then, repetition breeds further repetition.

Finally, because the rhetorical dimensions of the presidency are now so pronounced, and because each speech requires emotional and physical stamina from the chief executive, many presidents come to feel that *to have spoken about a matter is to have done something* about that matter. For example, Ronald Reagan made extended remarks on women's rights on over two dozen occasions during his first two years in office. Regardless of how his audiences responded, his efforts on their behalf—rhetorically based though they were—may have convinced him that action had been taken on the matter. To a nonpresident such a notion seems absurd. Any day laborer knows that no pavement can be broken without a jackhammer, despite the eloquence of one's street-corner exhortations. Presidents, in contrast, live in a world of words. Their proudest victories are often rhetorical victories ("You handled that question beautifully, Mr. President") and their greatest challenges often rhetorical challenges ("Be careful not to say anything that will alienate the farmers"). Such a world often has no more substance than that of Alice's Cheshire. But like Alice's Cheshire, a president can sometimes smile and make us forget what is missing.

In other words, the distinction made by the average person between saying and doing becomes no distinction at all in the White House. Ronald Reagan's speechmaking about womens' rights may have made him feel that he was a reincarnation of Elizabeth Cady Stanton, even though his actions in that arena mostly consisted of appointing several dozen traditional Republican women to largely ceremonial posts in his administration. In his first term in office, he did not push affirmative action programs, antidiscriminatory legislation, or federal prosecution of cases involving sex bias. But his *talk* was upbeat and available, giving him and others the feeling that he was president of all the people, women as well as men. He confidently addressed groups like the International Federation of Business and Professional Women's Clubs because they were willing to accept sweet words sweetly spoken. In a completely rhetorical world gaffes occur occasionally, but even remarks like the following can be laughed off by a president because they are, after all, just words: "And we have been doing a number of things here with regard to the thing of great interest to you, and that is the recognition of women's place. I want you to know I've always recognized it, because I happen to be one who believes if it weren't for women, us men would still be walking around in skin suits carrying clubs."[8]

Even the most casual student of presidential discoursing will discover just how many silly things like this a president says. They will also come to realize the incredible amount of time devoted to public speaking by a modern chief executive. Even a speech of, say, twenty minutes in duration will require some rehearsal by the president, travel to and from the event, visiting with members of the audience, after-speech processing with his aides, and, inevitably, reacting to the press's reactions to his remarks. Since the average modern president gives more than one such speech during each working day, his time on the job has increasingly become rhetorical time. All of this leaves few moments for the other sorts of things we expect a president to do—namely, to think.

Speaking in public is concentrative. A fidgeting audience rivets the mind of a speaker like nothing else can as he or she strives to discover what will satisfy the assembled listeners. Speechmaking also makes one self-conscious in the extreme. That is, it makes one conscious that one has a self that must cope with the mental, social, and even physiological tensions generated by public display of that self. When a president stands alone on stage addressing hundreds or thousands of people, he can't think about how he will cut the budget deficit when he returns to the White House or how he will deal with the Russians when next meeting them. Such a president also has reduced time for sharp, private dialectic with experts, for imaginative political forecasting, for listening thoughtfully to others.

For their part, reporters expect the president's reactions to the events of the day to be virtually "on line" as they press him to begin speaking even before his brain is fully engaged. Harry Truman's crisp and plentiful "no comments" have virtually disappeared from the political scene. During his first term in office, Ronald Reagan answered questions from reporters while on horseback, when at the beach, while climbing into a helicopter, and during physical workouts. Rarely did clear, cogent thinking inform these hurried exchanges, but Ronald Reagan was, in the media etiquette of his times, intensely obliging.

It is axiomatic that the more one speaks, the less time one has to reflect. Examining the *Public Papers of the Presidents* can be disheartening indeed. Such reading is not recommended to a reader already harboring significant doubts about the essential soundness of American governance. Like all independent Americans, presidents should perhaps be allowed to speak to whomever they please. But it is unclear to me why a tolerably good mind like that of Richard Nixon should have applied itself to the passing thoughts of a group of senior citizens who were on a thirty-five-day bus tour of the United States in October of 1973 and who dropped in at the White House to pay their respects to their commander-in-chief. This is not to say that the elderly are undeserving of presidential words. But it is to say that all Americans deserve better than the pap Mr. Nixon delivered that day. He randomly strings his locutions together, interrupting his semantic processing constantly with useless asides. He appears to do so out of habit or social pressure or sentimentality and not out of a searing passion to share an important conceptualization with his guests. The passage below reveals a president who has nothing to say:

> Let me say, too, that when I noted senior citizens on a bus trip of this length, I just think, who thought up the idea? Well, it is just a wonderful idea. I can remember when I was in Whittier—and to go to Washington, of course, to even think of the possibility, but here you are traveling the whole country and seeing the great parks, and you are going south next, I understand. It will be beautiful. Have you seen the fall leaves?

I remember my mother—of course, my mother, as you know, was born in Indiana. Most Californians are from some other State, but the thing that she and my father, who was also born in the Midwest, in Ohio—and they were both from farms—they always missed was the fall colors.

I took a little ride yesterday with General Haig down through Virginia. We didn't have much time for this, because we just go in the car and work a bit, and already while going south, the colors aren't as brilliant as they will be a month from now. If you go further north, they are pretty good right now, but you will find the colors very beautiful and something we don't have in California. We have almost everything else, though.

Let me say finally that Mrs. Nixon, as you know, Pat—as a matter of fact, this is one of the few crowds that comes in here and you call me Dick; my mother used to call me Richard, and I appreciate that, too—but Pat will be over in the White House, and she is going to have you for coffee in a very famous room. It is called the Yellow Oval Room. In fact, the mark of the White House is oval rooms. This is an oval office, and the Yellow Oval Room is a room that the visitors do not get to see, that is, the regular tourists, because it is on the second floor of the family rooms, and it is one of the most beautiful rooms in the whole White House. It is where the state visitors come and are received by the President before going down to the big state dinners. So when you are up there, just remember that coming as you do from Whittier, you are all going to be either a king or a queen.[9]

Defenders of the Rhetorical Presidency might well argue that there is nothing particularly worrisome about Mr. Nixon's meanderings on that October morning. They would claim that this little welcoming speech cost the president less than thirty minutes of his time and that forty Americans felt better about themselves and about their nation as a result of visiting with their president. They might argue further that a chief executive needs this kind of rhetorical recreation occasionally, given the weighty matters that press upon him. But it seems to me that such defenders must also acknowledge that modern presidents spend more and more of their hours saying less and less of substance to more and more audiences clamoring for just-a-few-remarks from their president. Such defenders would have to reckon with what meetings were *not* held and what decisions *not* made in the White House during the half-hour spent with the senior citizens and what problems remained problems because the head of state had directed his mind so completely to the fall colors. Such defenders would have to explain why it was so necessary for *the president of the United States,* of all people, to welcome this particular caravan to a city employing several million federal employees, many of whom could have performed the honors with aplomb.

Such defenders would have to reckon with an even more important consequence of this seemingly innocent exchange. If a president speaks off the top of his head in this fashion, does so with great frequency, and is socially rewarded for doing so (for surely the senior citizens applauded him heartily), why would he not be thus reinforced in half-thinking all of the thoughts he had that day? As we have seen, presidents speak in just such prepackaged, no-lose formats constantly. They almost never address audiences harboring substantial disagreements with them, and they do all in their power (via timing strategies, through format control, and by extending selective invitations for attendance) to seal themselves off from public exchange with the press and/or their critics.

It is not only important to consider how well presidents think but also to consider what they think about. A rhetorically minded president often gives less scrutiny to the conceptual heft of the ideas he peddles and more to who will buy what he has to sell. Even worse, he often tries to discover what is selling so that he will know what to manufacture. Naturally, no democratic system can function without attention being given to the needs and aspirations of the electorate. But it is a far different matter to gear all of one's decisions to changing audience fashions, a tendency quite naturally and quite powerfully reinforced in one who constantly confronts large audiences and who constantly searches for things that will inspire them or placate them or make them laugh. Presidents have become so audience driven that they unself-consciously use polling data to substantiate the essential wisdom of the positions they champion. The old notion of leadership—that is, leading—seems out-of-date as presidents and their advisors try to outsmart, rather than to outthink, the American electorate. They increasingly ask each other what can be told about an issue rather than what is known about it.

Each day, presidents are instructed by their staffs to think of how audience predispositions can be exploited rather than of how citizens' needs can be met. Presidents have thus become rhetorically enterprising, transmuting every social situation into one that can be potentially dominated by them and their messages. Newsworthy though his speech at the Johns Hopkins graduation exercises may have been in 1965, and powerful though Lyndon Johnson's rhetoric may have been that day, the 1965 graduates of that university did not attend a normal commencement, the spotlight was not placed upon them and their scholastic achievements, and their campus became an attractive piece of presidential scenery rather than one with its own personality and traditions. But rhetorical successes like this feed on themselves. When Vietnam became more frustrating and when Watergate became intertwining, Presidents Johnson and Nixon searched increasingly for supportive listeners. In both cases, the audiences who applauded their remarks prevented the presidents from rethinking the basic correctness of the stances they took. In a mottled nation like the United States, there is an available, appreciative audience for virtually any political position one might adopt.

As a result, there is always potential reinforcement for whatever a president is currently thinking.

In ancient Greece and Rome, the art of rhetoric was taught to all school-boys on the assumption that they might someday be called to statecraft. When they studied such matters they did so within the context of what would now be recognized as a full liberal education—philosophy, politics, mathematics, art. In such a curriculum, rhetorical training was meant to help the schoolboy energize his thoughts, not to substitute for them; rhetoric was to be used to announce, not to supplicate. Many thousands of years later, Gerald Ford hired a joke writer. This was a reasonable decision on Mr. Ford's part because one uses up material quickly when one speaks for a living. When he assumed the presidency in late 1974, Ford began to speak in behalf of an entire administration, and, in some sense thereby, he became self-alienated. Like many public persons he came to regard himself as a conduit for the words of others. He would speak constantly during the next thirty months even though he only half-owned the words he spoke since he virtually never participated in their construction. (As Francis Bacon has said, only writing makes a man exact.)[10] For Gerald Ford and for many of his contemporaries in the Oval Office, speech and mind were no longer fused nor was speech and self. Presidential speech has become so plentiful and so strategic that it has become almost pure performance. The self-checking process of public argument envisioned by the ancients is now a parody of dialectical give-and-take. Gerald Ford once told the citizens of New Hampshire that theirs was "more than a State; it is a state of mind,"[11] and he probably didn't have the faintest idea of what he meant when he said so. But he also knew that nobody would really press him on the matter.

It is more than a bit ironic that an era that has made public discussion so technologically feasible has also produced so little of communicative excellence. Presidents are now inundated by their rhetorical duties, but they all too often shrink from rhetoric that challenges or stimulates or questions or educates. White House aides become preoccupied with the correct sociological superstructure for the president's speaking events but give scant attention to what the nation's leader ought to *say*. For their part, modern presidents seem to view public speech as their most dependable political ally and, increasingly, as the very essence of the office they hold. Be that as it may, it is still possible to ask: Who speaks for America? What is being said? Is there nothing better?

Whither Leadership?

Thus far, I have argued that the speech habits of presidents signal changes in how they conceive of their jobs and in how they perform them. Moving away from the president-as-person, we can view the data reported in this book as telling a larger story about the presidency itself. That is, because rhetorical skills have been highlighted so often during the last forty years, they have changed how people view the executive branch of government itself. A particularly chilling manifestation of these changes is the criteria people use when selecting a president. While the personal attractiveness of a candidate has always been part of the electoral scene, voters now match up prospective leaders to standards suspiciously resembling those employed by media talent scouts. There is a certain strategic logic to such an approach, but it is nevertheless unnerving when one hears these criteria being applied not by political insiders but by ordinary citizens.

For example, during the Democrats' midterm convention held in June of 1982, a variety of would-be candidates strode across the stage attempting, in serial fashion, to woo the delegates with their oratory. Standard political fare. When commenting on the candidates, the *Washington Post* spent no time talking about their respective political philosophies but focused solely on their salesmanship. As we saw in Chapter Four, this is also standard political fare. The *Post's* evaluations were cast in the language of the theater, as they described one candidate as "lacking a flair for the dramatic," another as having "smooth undulating delivery," and a third as "never equaled for pure drawing power."[12] The *Post* article solemnly observed that "favorable impressions are the principal instruments of this prepresidential season and conversions are the coin of the realm."[13] This, too, is standard political fare.

What is especially disconcerting, however, is how pervasive such language was among the *delegates* and, presumably, among the voters they represented. Thoedis Gay, chairman of the District of Columbia delegation, noted that Gary Hart's speech was "excellent, but a lot of its power was lost because of the lack of luster in delivery."[14] John Glenn did not find an advocate in Jan Gray of Los Angeles because, "He [Glenn] comes off as pretty much of a loud ho-hum."[15] David Manley of Mason City, Iowa, on the other hand responded positively to Walter Mondale, observing that "boy, he's hot today. He really is hot."[16] Melvina Scott of Waterloo concurred: "It was wonderful, spectacular, beautiful—all those words."[17] Of the dozen or so comments by delegates reported in the *Post,* none dealt with the issue positions of the candidates, and only a few used the language of traditional power politics (e.g., "Teddy will always have his piece of the party [machinery]").[18] In other words, these potential presidents of the United States were being asked to audition for a part in a political morality play and were judged by criteria appropriate to such an enterprise.

From this perspective, the presidency of Ronald Reagan was inevitable for he, more than any other contemporary politician, perfectly met the criteria for this new American presidency. Mr. Reagan was born under the klieg lights, a perfect environment for incubating a New President. He knew cadence, he knew timing, he knew dramatic pauses, and he knew the seductiveness of allusion. He may not have known price support policies, or oil deregulation legislation, or international monetary funds, but there was no topic that he could not reduce to an anecdote and no concept he could not fashion into a political slogan. Thus, when the delegates at the midterm convention reacted as they did they reasoned, perhaps correctly, that these were the very measures the people themselves would use come election time.

There is, therefore, an indigenous, metarhetorical dimension to presidential politics in the contemporary United States, with politicians, media personnel, delegates, and voters themselves discussing not who is right in a campaign but who is appealing, not which candidate is most dangerous but which is least boring. With rhetorical skill having become such a primary filtering device during an election, many potential leaders never enter the political lists at all since, in the language of the midterm conventioneers, they do not "project" well. Business leaders, educators, military heroes, and jurists—the sorts of persons who might have turned to politics in another age—now are often counted out at the start. Those skilled in the verbal arts— religious spellbinders, trial attorneys, former newscasters, literate athletes, and, yes, cinema personalities—may well provide more and more of our presidents in the future. Such an eventuality should not overly concern us since a president is but one variable in a complex political equation. But we should at least ask ourselves whether it is wise to use such selection processes. We should ask what we gain and what we forfeit when employing persons like these as our leaders and why we increasingly feel the need to be diverted as well as to be led. And we should surely ask why, when entertainment is called for, Americans send in their presidents and not the clowns.

We should also ask why, in such a complex political society, Americans spend so many of their emotional chips on their presidents. Political offices in the United States are plentiful, with each precinct, district, town, county, state, and region containing many persons wielding political power, persons who may, if the truth be told, affect our lives a good deal more than he (perhaps someday she) who sits in the Oval Office. But the presidency clearly dominates American politics psychologically. Because of the president's high profile (maintained via his public communications), most Americans know more about his suit size or his daughter's dating patterns than they do about why their local utility rates have been raised or who they can turn to if their social security check is delayed in the mail. The eyes of most Americans are constantly fixed on the White House, dazzled by the show jointly produced by the president and the mass media. Meanwhile, local politicians go about the business of local politics, comparatively undisturbed by the glare of the public spotlight.

The psychological dominance of the president is not, as we have seen often in this book, a product of happenstance. Presidents jealously guard all of their political roles and co-opt a good many social roles as well. For example, when speaking to the student body of Rio Grande High School in Texas, Richard Nixon ran the full gamut of available personae. He played "Happy Birthday" on the piano (for a local congressman), gave a fairly detailed history of Mexican-American progress, philosophized about theories of religious integration, gave a quick upbeat summary of his own political history, spoke of a teacher he had known long ago and of a border guard he had met more recently, gave a short homily on being dutiful ("A few of your parents are here. Always respect them. Always remember what they did . . ."),[19] and then ended on a teary note: "I remember my father. He wasn't very well educated, because he came from a very poor family, quit school in the fifth grade, but he worked hard. And he earned the respect of his sons . . ."[20] The logic of such a speech is apparent: in whatever direction one turns, Richard Nixon is there. He is convivial, informative, humorous, responsible, relevant, touching. Presidents use such aggrandizing techniques constantly, overpowering listeners with their all-around fittingness. A speaker who is equally comfortable discussing God's special plans for America as well as missile launch placements, whose reach extends from the sacred to the profane, can occupy our attention at will, if not preoccupy it.

Much of the rhetorical escalation occurring in the White House can be accounted for by the sharp upturn in ritual over the last half-century. While a British prime minister may be free to say, as one is alleged to have said, "If you're looking for meaning, look not to me. Go see your archbishop," American presidents are more than willing to provide whatever brand of meaning is needed. Ceremonies are an enormous political asset to a president because they obviate unseemly dialogue with detractors and because they encourage, rather than inhibit, pontificating. From the president's standpoint, ceremonial speaking is self-consuming and self-reinforcing as well—it leads nowhere in particular, but it allows the president to do the leading. His remarks in such settings are exempted from normal scrutiny by the press, and even the most somber ceremonies have a nice feeling to them. Although several commentators have urged badly pressured chief executives to abandon their ritualistic duties, relegating them, say, to the vice-president, few presidents agree. They argue that ceremonial speaking actually improves presidential functioning by providing a respite from the stresses and strains of concrete decision making. Still others argue that citizens themselves need their president to perform these functions since he is for them a "priest, a prophet, and a king."[21]

The most recent presidents would heartily endorse this latter characterization of their jobs. Richard Nixon, for example, had marine buglers play a fanfare with banner-draped horns during formal occasions at the White

House and temporarily even costumed three other marines and had them stand in full-dress uniform as an honor guard outside the West Wing.[22] His ceremonial speechmaking was often no less grand. But it is well worth asking whether we actually want our presidents to spend so much of their time intoning the special language of ceremony. All of this takes an extraordinary amount of effort on the chief executive's part, and yet virtually none of it has been proven to have political, moral, or legislative value (despite the protestations to the contrary of the many who like the socioaesthetics of the events). Moreover, every such ceremonial speech reinforces the notion that the American president is lord of all he surveys, surely an unsavory notion in a republic. As the political scientist Bruce Buchanan argues, "Deference can foster overidentification by encouraging a president to incorporate the trappings, power, and prerogatives of office into his self-definition."[23] In other words, ceremonial events encourage the people to, temporarily at least, diminish their surveillance of the nation's leader. The president, in turn, becomes accustomed to standing away from, and slightly above, the people he serves. Granted, these are subtle dangers but, then too, politics is a damned subtle business.

Not only does the staging of ceremony bring to the surface latent imperialism, so does its content. Rituals elevate the tone of political discussion as presidents share thoughts fit for the ages. This can be good. But rituals also cause the president to speak abstractly as he tries to transcend the day-to-day pettiness (and obstreperousness) of political life. Modern chief executives like to think of the presidency as, in FDR's terms, "pre-eminently a place of moral leadership" because such a description excuses them from being unable to fix broken politics—"I don't do tax legislation; I'm a moral leader." Presidents speak confidently about "health care systems," "pockets of poverty," "nuclear stalemates," "balances of trade," "windows of opportunity," and the other benumbing abstractions of modern politics, but the use of such phrases presents the constant danger that the chief executive will fail to remember the empirical problems of the empirical people being discussed. Indigent women living in substandard housing must wrestle each day with a sometimes degrading "health care system." Unemployed factory workers sometimes drink themselves to death because of an unstable "balance of trade." In a removed sense, a president knows about these human referents of the abstractions he treats in his speeches, but the more he lives in a world of words the less he is able to see the various tragedies etched into the faces of those he governs.

Each time the president uses a phrase like "the Soviet Union" rather than "the Russian people," he is reinforced in thinking of "nuclear stalemating" as some sort of chess match between fictional opponents rather than a flesh-and-blood struggle between flesh-and-blood people having flesh-and-blood consequences. Presidential rhetoric, then, seduces both speaker and

listener. All too often presidents come to believe that by speaking of a problem—by promising to solve it—they have indeed solved it. The American
people listen to these pretty words, often believing them even if they do not
understand them. Over time, this grand rhetoric builds grand expectations
in voters. Their president, after all, has told them that their values are decent,
their paths true, their futures assured. Yet life rarely cooperates. Oil shortages spring up because of embroglios in the Middle East. U.S. ambassadors
are kidnapped and held hostage. A major automobile manufacturer moves
to the brink of bankruptcy. Life is not as the president has promised. Voters
become disillusioned at first, intensely cynical later. In response to such
difficulties, presidents speak once again, seeking to assure with newer, richer
abstractions. The cycle is repeated.

But almost never is this rhetoric of assurance candid, complete, concrete, or devoid of political shibboleth. The rhetorical worlds in which
presidents live convince them that all problems are essentially attitudinal.
Behind-the-scenes discussions in the White House are devoted evermore to
rhetorical fixes rather than to substantive ones. Even though behavioral research shows time and again that the decline of confidence in American
institutions is tied to inadequate *performances* of governance and not just to
people's perceptions of governmental leadership,[24] few presidents believe
such research findings. Instead, they fill their ceremonial calendars, hoping
in an almost primitive fashion to please the political gods with their
incantations.

The more frequently presidents retreat to political ceremonies, to closed
rallies, and to carefully staged media events, the less they use communication
to promote understanding among all people, to challenge the minds and wills
and hearts of citizens, to solve immediate human problems. It is ironic that
presidents reach for the grandest of abstractions precisely because they are
unable to solve the least abstract of problems—hunger, sickness, anger, des-
peration, violence. Presidents often speak to their constituents as if their
constituents could not think, which only encourages their constituents not
to try. During the 1984 presidential campaign, Ronald Reagan asked the
American people to dream old dreams anew while Walter Mondale told them
he would raise their taxes. Mr. Mondale's approach was largely unprecedented in modern politics; Mr. Reagan, on the other hand, spoke like an
orthodox president.

In making the choice they made in 1984, the American people showed
how responsive they were to the soothing abstractions of presidential oratory
and how little interested they were in being told that they spend too much
money, share too little of their wealth, and often live fairly ignoble lives.
When he spoke to the American people, Ronald Reagan demanded nothing
of them. He did not check their various antipathies for undocumented workers, homosexuals, or nonChristians. He did not admonish them for their

unkindnesses to blacks, pacifists, or the unemployed. Instead, he told them that they were right in reacting instinctually to the Soviet Union and that they need not refurbish traditional visions even though they were being thrown headlong into an untraditional age. This is not to quibble with Mr. Reagan's politics. But it is to say that he used communication to flatter rather than to challenge, to placate rather than to activate. When the American people chose Ronald Reagan over Walter Mondale they embraced a certain style of presidential communication as well as a certain brand of politics. The communication they opted for soothed them by trotting out old answers to new questions. But did it ennoble them in the way only real eloquence can? No, clearly no.

The 1984 campaign also pointed up another unsettling aspect of the Rhetorical Presidency—namely, the tendency of excessive speechmaking and of excessive scrutiny of excessive speechmaking to undermine the presidential form of governance. Throughout this book we have seen presidents rely on speech to solve their social, political, and even emotional problems, thus contributing to an unprecedented rise in personality politics. Throughout the 1984 campaign, attention was devoted again and again to Mr. Reagan's affability and to Mr. Mondale's lethargy. Mass media coverage of the campaign centered on these psychodramatic aspects, with ordinary citizens becoming fixated by the contrasts in personality between the two candidates. Naturally, presidential politics has always involved such considerations, but the intensive brandishing of a politician's personality through never-ending speechmaking makes it seem as if the president-as-person were all that was important to the executive branch of government and as if the executive branch were all that was important to American politics.

When voters sense that they know the essential person of a political person they have little need to attend carefully to what he says or does. With the president speaking so often, this sense of understanding is heightened in voters' minds. When they are pleased with political events, they lionize their president. When their political world runs amok, they crucify him and him alone. And this is to say more than simply that the buck stops on the president's desk as it always had. It is to say that a citizenry that cannot see past a political *person* is often blind to political consequence. During 1984, for instance, one cab driver explained to this author how he could never vote for a "nerd" like Walter Mondale. It was not immediately apparent to me how the socioeconomic life of a unionized cab driver in a Northeastern city would be enhanced by another four years of Reaganomics, but I had little doubt that my interlocutor knew what he knew and that he could know no more. He felt that he understood Ronald Reagan as an individual and hence as a president and hence as his benefactor. He had gotten to know Mr. Reagan by listening to him and by listening to others listen to him. End of discussion.

This superpersonalization of the American presidency has obvious rhetorical roots and considerable political consequence. Presidents now appeal directly to the voters rather than to the Congress when pursuing a course of action central to their administration. Cabinet government has all but disappeared, in part because only the president's profile is allowed to loom above the political horizon. Press conferences are held infrequently and only when the president deems it absolutely necessary. "The news" in even a sober journal like the *Washington Post* looks increasingly like a political version of the *National Inquirer* as it features the comings and goings of the president and the cast of characters surrounding him in the White House. At the height of the 1984 campaign, for example, even a distinguished writer like Meg Greenfield was moved to interview the Democratic candidate relative to what she called "the Mondale issue." Ms. Greenfield asked Mr. Mondale if he thought he was wishy-washy, how he assessed his own "political projection," whether ridicule bothered him, and if he dyed his hair.[25]

Attention of this sort to the personalities of presidents and would-be presidents obviously makes the office less dependent upon traditional political forces. Formerly, for example, the president needed the other institutions of governance in part because they controlled the rhetorical forums. He needed a political party for his convention speech, the Congress for his budget messages, state caucuses for his campaign speeches, the press for his news conferences. With the rise of television and, more important, with the president's growing sense that he is in control of what he says *as well as of why, when, and where he says it,* the chief executive has become considerably less interdependent. The networks give only scant attention now to the major political conventions, implicitly acknowledging the diminishing role party plays relative to personality. Congress seems increasingly docile vis-à-vis the president, perhaps because its members know how powerful a bludgeon a modern president has who has rhetorical prowess and who is not inhibited at the thought of using it.

There are signs that even the press has become deferential in the modern, rhetorical era. Reporters doggedly follow the chief executive looking for a handout; they record his every utterance, film his every handshake, and then share his largess with viewers on the six-o'clock news. The media's agenda now seems isomorphic with the president's. Reporters often cover presidential performances without asking themselves why. This is not to say that political reportage is neither bold nor penetrating. It is often both. But it is to say that a presidency-dominated medium has great potential for undermining intelligent and, above all, independent news coverage. It is also to say that as presidents become more and more familiar with the sorts of "communicative packages" the media prefer, they will make their remarks even more irresistible to the media personnel who follow them about. All too often, even hard-nosed reporters are caught up in the dramaturgy of politics by focusing heavily on the strategic—how the president achieved the effects he achieved—and not on the moral worth of the policies the president endorsed when speaking.

With the president's aides generously directing reporters' eyes toward their boss's prearranged activities, it is also easy for reporters to become lazy or to think it presumptuous or unseemly to look behind the presidential staging. Moreover, by focusing its attention squarely on what the president has said, the press runs the risk of ignoring those topics and audiences the president avoided completely. The Rhetorical Presidency has emerged because the electronic inventions of the mass media have permitted it. Accordingly, guardians of the mass media have a greater obligation than ever not to be seduced by the seductions they have implicitly and explicitly encouraged.

But it is hardly enough to depend upon the Fourth Estate to help us sort out the sense from the nonsense in presidential politics. Presidents speak as often as they do because they know that a good many someones are listening to them. Presidential staffs scrutinize the hoopla surrounding a presidential speech-act more than they work on the president's text because they believe that the sizzle sells better than the bacon. Pollsters report that voters are bored with conventional politics, and so America's thirty-ninth president conducted a national call-in show and wore a cardigan sweater during a fireside chat. Media specialists explain that American adults are child-like and that they wish to hear only short bursts of political discourse, discourse that is simplistic, dramatic, occasionally passionate, always entertaining. Political psychologists tell us that the more often a voter is asked to listen the less carefully he or she will listen, and yet presidents speak constantly, hoping to beat the odds by overwhelming the voter. But it cannot be forgotten that when presidents, presidential staffs, pollsters, media specialists, and political psychologists offer the advice they offer, they are making direct commentary about the American people. All of these speeches, all of this strategizing, is designed to meet the demands that you and I are said to place on our national leaders. But you and I are also said to have an unexalted conception of political leadership and to not demand very much from a president when he speaks to us. Henry Fairlie argues that it is you and I, not our presidents, who are ultimately responsible for governance; we have this responsibility, I would add, because we live in a rhetorical age:

> It is *we* who drive the politician to use jargon, words that evade and obscure the truth. It is *we* who make them say that troops are "advisors," that war plans are "scenarios," that invasions are "incursions," that bombing is "air support." It is *we* who are afraid of the truth that politicians would tell us. We do not wish to be confronted. We do not wish to be challenged. We do not wish to be inspired. We do not wish to act.

The purpose of oratory is to persuade men and women to act or (which is the same thing) not to act with a joint will and purpose. But a nation with its ears in a Sony Walkman does not wish to act, or even to face the moral difficulties in the choice not to act . . .

Oratory will return when people look to their politicians for leadership. It is not the politicians who are now failing to give that leadership; it is we who do not wish to receive it from our politicians, or indeed from anyone else.[26]

Conclusion

In the 1980s, it may seem quaint, if not eccentric, to end a book of this sort with a cry for political eloquence. But that is precisely what is needed, and it is precisely what Henry Fairlie called for without saying so. Eloquence—not glibness or deftness or even greater clarity—is needed from our presidents. Eloquence is more than communication. It is communication that reaches deep into the emotional sinews of voters and motivates them to be grander than they are by nature. Eloquence is the blending of the practical with the imaginative so that old thoughts are given fresh life and so that new truths can be passionately embraced. Thus, when he spoke about voting rights in March of 1965, Lyndon Johnson was eloquent. He was eloquent despite his homespun imagery and ordinary language. He was eloquent because on this occasion he shook loose the cobwebs of his highly political mind and thereby risked audience disfavor. He linked his intellect with his words and then with his feelings and urged his suspicious, sometimes hostile, listeners to throw off their old ways and to reach for something new and better. Mr. Johnson's speech was a long one and that too was risky because even by 1965 Americans had become accustomed to receiving "political communications" in scattergun fashion.

In his speech, LBJ found new ways of linking familiar nationalistic myths with untried domestic policies, thereby allowing his listeners some comfort as they contemplated doing uncomfortable things. One senses in his remarks a special kind of rhetorical sensitivity because he knew how difficult it would be for many of his listeners to accept what he had to say. But his eloquence also derived from his willingness to make a public investment in the rights of the disadvantaged. Mr. Johnson was, in many ways, a conventional Southern politician. Thus, when he marshaled the courage to embrace the policies he did—*no matter what his personal reasons may have been*—he became a beacon to others in government that the political tides had changed. While serving as chief executive, Lyndon Johnson delivered 1,636 speeches. Virtually none of these speeches is worth remembering, and virtually all of them are shot through with political expediency. But on one of these occasions Lyndon Johnson chose to speak like a leader. And eloquence followed:

So I ask you to join me in working long hours and nights and weekends, if necessary, to pass this bill.

And I don't make that request lightly, for from the window where I sit with the problems of our country I recognize that from outside this chamber is the outraged conscience of a nation, the grave concern of many nations and the harsh judgment of history on our acts.

But even if we pass this bill the battle will not be over.

What happened in Selma is part of a far larger movement which reaches into every section and state of America. It is the effort of American negroes to secure for themselves the full blessings of American life.

Their cause must be our cause too. Because it's not just Negros, but really it's all of us, who must overcome the crippling legacy of bigotry and injustice.

And we shall overcome.

As a man whose roots go deeply into Southern soil, I know how agonizing racial feelings are. I know how difficult it is to reshape the attitude and the structure of our society. But a century has passed—more than 100 years—since the Negro was freed.

And he is not fully free tonight.

It was more than 100 years ago that Abraham Lincoln—a great President of another party—signed the Emancipation Proclamation. But emancipation is a proclamation and not a fact.

A century has passed—more than 100 years—since equality was promised, and yet the Negro is not equal.

A century has passed since the day of promise, and the promise is unkept. The time of justice has now come, and I tell you that I believe sincerely that no force can hold it back. It is right in the eyes of man and God that it should come, and when it does, I think that day will brighten the lives of every American.

For Negroes are not the only victims. How many white children have gone uneducated? How many white families have lived in stark poverty? How many white lives have been scarred by fear, because we wasted energy and our substance to maintain the barriers of hatred and terror?

And so I say to all of you here and to all in the nation tonight that those who appeal to you to hold on to the past do so at the cost of denying you your future. This great rich, restless country can offer opportunity and education and hope to all—all, black and white, all, North and South, sharecropper and city dweller.

These are the enemies: poverty, ignorance, disease. They are our enemies, not our fellow man, not our neighbor. And these enemies too—poverty, disease and ignorance—we shall overcome.[27]

A careful analysis of presidential speechmaking since 1945 finds few such brave moments. Most of the speeches analyzed in this book were the products of ad hoc thinking, not careful deliberation. They were delivered by persons who had no time to write their own speeches and hence who could never fully embrace the thoughts they spoke, thereby producing the mechanical speech-for-hire often observed here. These speeches rarely bore the marks of thoughts newly thought or of passions recently felt because they were produced according to a formula and adjusted to a political calender. There is an interminable sameness to them, a lack of what the ancient rhetoricians called "invention." The setting of a speech now dictates what a president will say. Or presidential staffs do. Or audience composition does. Or political traditions do. Or media coverage does. The thoughts and feelings *of presidents themselves* rarely do.

Presidential speechmaking—perhaps presidential communication in general—has now become a tool of barter rather than a means of informing and challenging the citizenry. "Scene" is now more important than message, a perception reinforced daily during newscasts about presidential activities. The press seems to have lost respect for presidential words, no doubt because too many words are spoken, a condition created, ironically, by the press's own imprecations. The people have lost respect for presidential words, no doubt because anything discursive seems old-fashioned in a nonverbal, symbol-filled age. Presidents have lost respect for presidential words and that is perhaps the saddest fact of all. They regard the speech act as a political favor to others or an opportunity for personal aggrandizement, not a chance to stretch their minds and the minds of their listeners. For them, eloquence is something one does, or tries to do, not something one is. As Harry McPherson has said "There is a kind of Gresham's Law of all of Presidential Rhetoric, that too much of it spoils the effect of all of it."[28]

With the rise of the mass media, opportunities for presidential speechmaking have increased enormously, but eloquence itself has become a faintly antiquarian term, if not a term of total disuse. It is a term fit for a less sophisticated age, an age in which time seemed less precious than it does today, an age prizing formal argument over casual conversation, an age in which speech occurred subsequent to thought, not simultaneously with it. Eloquence makes no sense in a political era dominated by thirty-second political spots or in an era placing a premium on the quickness of a political reaction rather than on its depth. Today, White House advisors worry about presidential audiences, speechwriters worry about presidential words, and the media worry about presidential performances. Presidents, presumably, are left to worry about presidential ideas. But all too often they do not seem worried.

The Liberal view of these matters holds that handwringing about the modern presidency is not justified. Such Liberals argue that the president is hemmed in by such a panoply of political and economic forces that his ultimate influence on the affairs of state is comparatively benign. The Rhetorical Presidency, they might contend, is but a harmless affectation reflecting certain media realities, realities that need not concern modern Americans. The Conservative view, in contrast, holds that major structural changes must be made in the presidency: less freedom for the president to go over the heads of the Congress to the voters; more attention by the president to actual problem solving and less to regional politicking; a deritualization of the president's speaking schedule and more required, sharper exchanges between the chief executive and representatives of the press.

To my way of thinking, the events of the last forty years give the lie to the Liberal view of presidential communication. Throughout this book we have seen the considerable use modern chief executives have made of public persuasion—how they have moved legislation forward, prolonged war, built personal reputations, altered party fortunes, and, in general, caused the American people to be more conscious of their head of government and, presumably, more greatly influenced by his thoughts and wishes. Because the president of the United States can now assault both the eyes and the ears (and hence the hearts and minds) of the American people whenever he chooses to do so, the political and economic forces that supposedly keep him in check are themselves confronted by a powerful social force in the person of the president. The age of the mass media, in short, has substantially altered traditional political compacts, and the president of the United States has been the primary beneficiary of such alterations.

The institutional changes proposed by the Conservatives dovetail with the structuralist mentality characteristic of American pragmatism. But such changes seem patently unrealistic. Rhetoric, after all, defies all masters but itself. No amount of structural tinkering is likely to force a wily president into communicative forums unfavorable to him. No preset agenda for discussion will ever constrain a chief executive intent on sharing his particular view of the world. No changes in White House scheduling will deny a media-savvy president (which is to say, all modern presidents) the chance of reaping political capital during each and every social encounter in which he participates. Presidents are rhetorical animals, kings of the political jungle they inhabit.

No. Only you and I, as voters and hence as listeners, can set the standards for public discussion, even if it means that in doing so we hear things that make us feel, dare I say it, uncomfortable. It is enticing to think of listening, especially political listening, as a comparatively inert activity. Politicians talk so often that it is tempting to disregard them completely or to depend upon the mass media to do our reacting for us. It is easy to listen to the conventional wisdom of politicians and to conceive of conventional wisdom as the only sort of wisdom available. It is easy to resign ourselves to what seems to be the inevitable mendacity of spoken politics and to presume that all political thinking is shallow, all political values corrupt, all political leadership flawed. It is hard to become genuinely informed about

complex policy options. It is impolite to demand real thoughtfulness from
elected officials during public hearings. It is vaguely unpatriotic to view presidents as persuaders or to insist that they deliver goods to us that have not
been politically sanitized. It is strange and uncomfortable to regard media
personnel as manipulators of information. And it is hard to listen critically—
to watch for the reductionisms embedded in political slogans, to spot the
careful choreography of a political event, to ask constantly what has *not* been
said in a political speech, to see how politicians pit one of our emotions
against another in order to influence us, to examine the linkages between the
data and the claims of a political platform, and to gauge how far a politician
has strayed from our own standards of political eloquence. These tasks are
not easy to perform, and we naturally resist them on the assumption that
citizenship should be effortless. But listening and speaking have always been
connected, and thus it is we as individuals, not our fellow citizens, not our
presidents, not the political parties, and not the mass media, who ultimately
determine what will be regarded as the sound of leadership in the modern
age.

Appendix: Methods and Overall Data

The bare facts of presidential speaking were gathered in this study. Who said what to whom, when, where, and under what circumstances were the sorts of data retrieved from archival records. Admittedly, these are humble data. They are the sorts of unobtrusive facts prized by the anthropologist or sociologist, persons trained to discover the extraordinary within the ordinary. Elementary though these data are, their suggestive power increases substantially when they are gathered for ten thousand cases across four decades. Since each speech event was coded in some twenty different ways, over 200 thousand data points were introduced into the data base. The sheer size of such a pool of information is valuable because it forces the researcher to look at the "mass" of the American presidency. Admittedly, one must stand at some distance to properly view such an assemblage of data; in standing thusly, one risks missing the subtle insight or appreciating the pregnant instance. Equally, however, such procedures offer the researcher *perspective,* thereby turning distance into something of a scholarly virtue by turning the researcher away from the fascinations of particularities. Moreover, such a large (computerized) data base helps one discover *patterns of co-occurrence* in presidential behavior that would probably remain hidden if other methods of inquiry were used.

This latter methodological advantage cannot be underestimated since so many previous studies of the executive branch of government have been president-specific at best or instance-specific at worst. The data gathering attempted here, in contrast, required me to focus upon *institutional* facts since, even though the data assembled were modest in both scope and significance when viewed in isolation, they additively pointed up broader realities. In short, if one assumes as I have (1) that any sort of speech behavior is revealing of human circumstance, (2) that *patterns* of speech behavior are

215

especially suggestive, (3) that some of the most important aspects of national governance come together during presidential exchanges with citizens, and (4) that the essential, skeletal structure of a presidential speaking event (speaker, audience, topic, time, place, etc.) can be as significant as the actual message spoken, then the methodological approach of this study will be seen as sensible.

Coding Procedures

The data reported in this volume derive from an exhaustive investigation of some 9,969 public speaking events featuring the president of the United States. The speeches in question were delivered between 1945 and 1985 by Presidents Truman through Reagan (although some of my analyses extend through 1982 only). All speeches were reprinted in either *Public Papers of the Presidents* or in *Weekly Compilations of Presidential Documents,* both of which are published by the Government Printing Office in Washington, D.C. These documents typically contain essential, historical information about the speaking events in question, including (brief) designations of audience, setting, timing, etc. When necessary, supplementary information about the speaking events was drawn from other government publications or from periodical literature.

Initially, some ambiguity existed over what did or did not constitute a "public speaking event" for the president. When deciding what to include in the data base, several operational rules were therefore employed: (1) Nothing labeled a "Statement" was included since these were, in every case, written documents taking an oral form. (2) Nothing labeled "Informal Remarks to Reporters" was included. (3) Finally, all oral remarks by the president were introduced into the data base if they met either of the following conditions: (a) The president's remarks were discursive (i.e., not interrupted); remarks of any length were included if they met this criterion. (b) When the president's remarks were interrupted by others (as, e.g., during a press conference or public interview), they were included if the president's total verbal output amounted to at least 150 words. This latter criterion effectively eliminated all casual and spontaneous exchanges between the president and a variety of other persons (often, reporters), exchanges that have been recorded with fidelity by government archivists in recent years.

Each speech event meeting the criteria just listed were coded in a number of ways—some simple, some more subtle, none nuanced. Listed below are the types of discriminations made and the operational rules employed when doing the coding:

Elementary Coding

1. *Timing* (early vs. later administration). A simple measure by which the date of the speech was judged to fall prior to or subsequent to the middle-most month of the presidential administration under consideration.
2. *Type of Year.* Election years included all even-numbered years, nonelection years all odd-numbered years. In addition to these gross designations, the presidential election years of 1948, 1952, 1956, 1960, 1964, 1968, 1972, 1976, 1980, and 1984 were given special consideration at various points in this study.
3. *Party.* Speeches emanating from Democratic or Republican presidents were separately analyzed.
4. *Season.* The *political* seasons of the year were designated thusly: Winter (December, January, February); Spring (March, April, May); Summer (June, July, August); Fall (September, October, November). Conceiving of the calendar in this way permitted discriminations to be made between speeches delivered during "primary seasons" and "election seasons."
5. *Speech Activity.* A simple measure of the "rhetorical density" of a given presidential day. (Was it a single speech? The fourth that day? etc.)
6. *Era.* Recent presidential history was evenly demarcated as follows: Early Modern presidency (1945–1957); Later Modern presidency (1958–1969); and Recent Modern presidency (1970–1982). These delineations made possible rapid inspection of temporal trends and of institutional (as opposed to personality-based) factors affecting the presidency.
7. *General Location*
    a) *Washington, D.C.* Includes all White House speeches, those delivered in Washington-area hotels, meeting halls, and government offices as well as those presented to audiences in Maryland and Virginia communities contiguous to the District of Columbia (e.g., Mount Vernon).
    b) *Domestic city.* All other locations in the continental United States. (Alaska and Hawaii were excluded because they had not reached statehood in 1945, the beginning point of this study.)
    c) *International city.* Any site not included in nos. 1 or 2 above. Also included speeches delivered aboard ships at sea.

Primary Coding

1. *General Topic.* The broadest possible designation of a speech's primary subject matter. Speeches were coded as *Systemic* if they focused primarily on legal or technological solutions to human problems. This category included such matters as science and agriculture, labor disputes, economic fluctuations, governmental bureaucracies, and formalized institutions and statutes. *Humanistic* topics, in contrast, were centered in

speeches discussing patriotic values, moral or spiritual attitudes toward problems of the day, health and human services, the delivery of public welfare, and educational goals and achievement.

Because the purpose of the "General Topic" coding was to obtain a close look at how the various chief executives treated *domestic* matters, all international speeches and all speeches dealing with multiple topics were excluded from this analysis.

2. *Specific Topic.* If 25% or more of the printed content of a given speech could not be easily assigned to one of the following categories, it was designated *Other.* If 75% or more of such content dealt with two or more of the following categories, it was designated *Multiple.* In all other cases, one of the following topical designations was used:

a) *Science.* Speeches focusing on the political ramifications of understanding the fundamental laws of nature and on preserving or exploiting natural phenomena. Includes environmental concerns, space exploration, agricultural production, energy resources, transportation advances, wildlife protection, new technologies, and medical *research* opportunities.

b) *Economy.* Speeches dealing with budgetary operations at the federal level and with broad-scale economic fluctuations on the domestic scene. Includes unemployment trends, labor-management disputes, spending policy, interstate banking, industrial development, and supplies of goods and commodities.

c) *Government.* Speeches commenting upon the regulatory function of government, primarily as that function is institutionalized in the executive, judicial, and congressional branches of the federal bureaucracy. Includes criminal prosecution, law and its implementation, judicial appointments, intergovernmental relations, the two-party system, federal election procedures, etc.

d) *Human services.* Speeches describing immediate social problems, the political remedies available to solve those problems, and the implications for society of meeting these human needs. Includes discussions of educational standards, school busing, public welfare, medical care, social security, urban decay, public housing, etc.

e) *Human values.* Speeches heralding the overarching importance of philosophical commitments, ethical responsibility, and creative genius. Included such topics as religious freedom, historical truths and events, patriotic duties, charitable institutions, moral obligations, and aesthetic achievement.

f) *International cooperation.* Speeches focusing on the obligations of the United States government and its people to participate with other countries in scientific, educational, and cultural projects and to provide medical and other assistance when needed. Includes such matters as the Peace Corps, historical commemorations, cultural exchanges, international trade, Voice of Democracy, detente, UNESCO, etc.

    g) *International conflict*. Speeches dealing with major ruptures in the international community and with the relative advisability of using military action to resolve those disputes. Includes topics like international terrorism, major police actions, arms control, military embargos, weapons systems, and such major conflagrations as Korea, Vietnam, the Middle East, etc.

3. *Audience*. To the extent that the specific members of a given audience could be isolated for the presidential speech in question, the group was assigned to one of the following categories:

    a) *Governmental employees*. Any duly authorized assemblage of federal employees, most of whom were either members of the military, cabinet officers and/or White House staffers, or civil service workers in the various departments of government (Department of State, the Pentagon, National Parks employees, etc.).

    b) *Local and/or press*. By far the most common audience, consisting typically of undifferentiated persons in local communities gathered together spontaneously for a presidential address. Presidential remarks made exclusively to members of the press had to conform to the criteria (of duration) described above to be included in the data bank.

    c) *National*. Included all mediated presidential addresses before live audiences, those delivered in real time to a television or radio audience exclusively, or those presented on a tape-delayed basis.

    d) *Invited guests*. Persons specially selected for attendance at a presidential event who represent no discernible group or organization but who have gathered together for some formal purpose (e.g., a state dinner).

    e) *Special interest group*. Includes members of any formally constituted group or organization who assembled for a special presidential speech or who were being visited by the president as part of their normal schedule of meetings (e.g., such groups as the United Steel Workers, International Press Association, Republican party, etc.).

4. *Setting*. Refers to the social/spatial environment surrounding the presidential speech in question, including its interpersonal circumstances as well as its comparative formality. Specifically includes the following:

    a) *Ceremony*. Any speech event whose purpose is to certify formally some existing relationship or condition or to formally (often legally) commence some new relationship or condition. Further subdivided as follows:

        (1) *Initiating ceremony*. Includes the public signing of a newly created piece of legislation, the formal enactment of a compact or treaty, or the swearing-in of a government official or some other newly designated person of authority.

    (2) *Honorific ceremony.* Includes remarks at testimonial dinners, at Medal of Honor ceremonies, at college or university commencement exercises, or at some other event designed to bestow formal recognition of achievement on some group or individual.

    (3) *Celebrative ceremony.* Includes presidential eulogies, patriotic remembrances, anniversary celebrations, building dedications, formal dinners for visiting heads of state and other events designed to herald important values, historical truths, and interpersonal relations.

    (4) *Greeting/departure ceremony.* Includes all presidential speeches in which the president formally welcomes a visiting dignitary to the United States (often at either the airport or the White House) or when the president himself arrives at some new locale for (largely) diplomatic purposes. Many such greetings were followed within a day or two by departure ceremonies.

  b) *Briefing.* Consisted of all formal (i.e., regularly scheduled or specially arranged) interactions between the president and members of the press or ordinary citizens or both. Includes official announcements from the Oval Office, press conferences with national, regional, or local journalists, major policy statements to the nation, etc.

  c) *Organizational meeting.* Typically consisted of the president meeting with members of fraternal, educational, corporate, or social organizations as part of their normal schedule of meetings. Occasionally, such encounters took place at the White House, but convention halls and hotel ballrooms were the more common locations. Often, the president's speech served to introduce or keynote the proceedings, and, not uncommonly, the president's remarks bore only tangential relevance to the stated purposes and goals of the organization in question.

  d) *Political rally.* Speeches by the president given in avowedly political surroundings. Included convention keynote addresses, brief airport visits, annual political remembrances, standard stump speeches, fundraising dinners, etc. Occasionally, such remarks were presented in ceremonial surroundings; in such "mottled" cases, the designation of "political rally" was used if the speech made repeated reference to campaign activities or occurred adjacent in time to other election-based events.

  e) *Miscellaneous remarks.* Consisted of a wide variety of communicative events which could not be expressly assigned to one of the foregoing settings. Included spontaneous remarks during foreign and domestic travel, introductions of dignitaries or artists visiting the White House, miscellaneous commentaries on events of the day (e.g., at the site of a natural disaster), etc.

5. *Specialized Settings.* A variety of unique speech events distinguished by location, topic, or by audience composition. These categories proved useful for examining the individual speech habits of the presidents and consisted of the following special types:

   a) *Traditional press conferences (national).* Nationally telecast (or radio-only) briefings by the president for the press. This category included only those briefings that focused on a *variety* of topics.

   b) *Traditional press conferences (D.C.).* Multitopic encounters between the press and the president taking place in the Nation's capital.

   c) *Traditional press conferences (local).* That is, those multitopic press conferences held in one of the continental United States.

   d) *Traditional ceremonies (D.C.).* Formal commemorations or celebrations during which the president spoke *exclusively* about human values; included those in the District of Columbia proper as well as those at the national shrines contiguous to the District (e.g., Mount Vernon).

   e) *Traditional ceremonies (local).* Regional variations on (*d*) above.

   f) *Open rallies.* Political gatherings explicitly featuring a candidate for political office and attended by self-selected audience members. Typically, such gatherings were held on public grounds, in public buildings, or in private, large-space facilities rented for the event.

   g) *Partisan rallies.* Political gatherings explicitly featuring a candidate for political office and attended by audience members especially invited for the event or by persons united by some sort of formal, organizational tie. Typically, such gatherings were held in private dining or meeting facilities.

   h) *Local foreign policy speeches.* Any set of public remarks by the president devoted exclusively to international matters and presented to an audience in one of the continental United States. Although not terribly common, such speeches proved to be interesting markers of a chief executive's willingness to "campaign" for specific foreign policy initiatives.

It should be noted that the press conferences referred to here consisted exclusively of the traditional, multitopic conference. Excluded were the single-subject press conferences that have found special favor with chief executives lately. Also, the ceremonies mentioned here accounted for fewer than 20% of all rituals conducted by the presidents. These more specialized ceremonies were highly traditional in that they dealt solely with the topic of human values. Clearly, presidents have also found it possible to ceremonialize about many other subjects in many other locations.

Collateral Coding

A useful way of examining any set of behaviors (such as presidential speaking) is to examine those behaviors in light of other, standardized measures. Thus, to better appreciate the political, social, and economic environments of presidential speechmaking, I compared my speech data through time with certain geographical and temporal measures derived by other researchers. These collateral observations provided a richer context for examining presidential behavior but were not used here in a probative fashion. (Indeed, in some cases, these measures were used in ways unintended by those who originally assembled the data.) Nevertheless, the rough picture they helped to sketch of the presidential times allowed me to examine a number of orthodox assumptions about political behavior and, on occasion, to call them into question.

1. *Presidential Popularity.* A gross measure of the president's annual standing in the eyes of the American people (or, at least, in the eyes of those sampled by the directors of the Gallup poll) between 1953 and 1978. Three plateaus of presidential popularity were established for use in this study: (1) 50% or less popularity, (2) 51%–64%, and (3) over 65%. The annual averages used were those calculated from the Gallup data by Harvey G. Zeidenstein, "Presidential Popularity and Presidential Support in Congress: Eisenhower to Carter," *Presidential Studies Quarterly* 10 (1980), pp. 224–233.
2. *Unemployment Rate.* Another gross measure of the "climate of the times" in which the presidents spoke. After calculating the mean rate of unemployment for 1948–1982, annual unemployment levels were assigned to the following plateaus: (1) low (0%–4.5%), (2) medium (4.6%–5.9%), and (3) high (over 6.0%). Additional data can be found in *The Economic Report of the President* (Washington, D.C.: Government Printing Office, 1983), p. 199.
3. *Congressional Control.* Used in this study as a rough estimate of comparative political difficulty. Each calendar year (from 1945 through 1982) was assigned to one of two conditions: (1) president's party controlled both houses of congress or (2) one or neither house. These data are readily available in the *Statistical Abstract of the United States: 1982–3,* 103d ed. (Washington, D.C.: Government Printing Office, 1982).
4. *Congressional Initiative.* Between 1953 and 1982, an average of 257 separate pieces of legislation per year were proposed by the chief executive. Variations around this mean were used to provide a general indication of how legislatively active a president was (as distinguished from his *rhetorical* activity). One of three levels of activity was assigned to each year studied: (1) low initiative (less than 200 bills initiated), (2) medium (201–

300 bills), (3) high (over 300). See *Congressional Quarterly Almanac: 2nd Session, 1982,* vol. 38 (Washington, D.C.: Congressional Quarterly Inc., 1983).

5. *Congressional Success.* The president's ability to have legislation adopted was calculated on a per-annum basis for the years 1953–1982 and rendered as a simple percentage: (1) low success (less than 69% of bills passed), (2) medium (70%–79% successful), (3) high (over 80%). As with all other collateral measures, these data were used in conjunction with speaking rates on a correlative, not causal, basis. Presidential success rates can be found in *Congressional Quarterly Almanac: 2nd Session, 1982,* vol. 38 (Washington, D.C.: Congressional Quarterly Inc., 1983).

6. *Newspaper Coverage.* The frequency with which a president of the United States is covered in the popular press was seen to be potentially related, in part at least, to the types, frequency, and comparative success of that president's speaking activities. It was expected, however, that any such relationship would be complex. Thus, rough and somewhat arbitrary measures of the "mediated environment" were used. Data assembled by Michael Grossman and Martha J. Kumar for the *New York Times* coverage of the presidency were assigned, by year, to one of three levels: (1) low coverage (less than 200 stories per year), (2) medium coverage (201–250 stories), and (3) high coverage (over 250 stores). For additional information see their *Portraying the President: The White House and the News Media* (Baltimore: John Hopkins University Press, 1981), pp. 260 ff.

7. *Magazine Coverage.* A similar rationale was used when comparing presidential speaking to coverage of the president in the popular press. Grossman and Kumar's assessment of *Time* magazine's coverage was again used, with each calendar year being assigned to one of two conditions: (1) low (less than 100 stories about the president) or (2) high (100 or more stories). Between 1953 and 1977 (the years sampled by Grossman and Kumar), an average of 100 stories/year appeared in *Time* about the chief executive.

8. *Specific Location.* To better understand the logic underlying presidents' regional speaking patterns, data about the forty-eight contiguous states were compared to the frequency and type of presidential speaking performed in such locations. When these comparisons were examined across time, a "geography of speech" could be described based on the following collateral measures:

   a) *Regional location.* Standard groupings of the continental United States: (1) Northeast, (2) South, (3) Midwest, (4) West.

   b) *State population.* The states were rank-ordered by population and then segmented into quartiles: (1) twelve most populous states, (2) large states (next twelve), (3) small states, (4) twelve least populous states.

   c) *Political partisanship.* Based on the results of state-by-state balloting for the presidency between 1948 and 1976, the various states were designated thusly: (1) Democratic—provided 51% or more of the vote to the Democratic candidate in five or more of the eight presidential elections, (2) Republican—provided 51% or more of the vote to the Republican candidate five or more times, (3) Neutral—neither party received 51% or more of the vote on five or more occasions. (In all cases, third-party candidacies were assigned to their party of origin.)

d) *Political significance.* This was a composite measure of the comparative political influence exerted by the forty-eight contiguous states. By combining measures of population density and voting behavior, five logical types resulted: (1) dense/neutral (consisted of the ten most populous states having neither a consistent Republican nor Democratic voting record, (2) medium populated/neutral (five large states with inconsistent voting patterns), (3) dense/partisan (the ten states ranking within the top half of the states by population and having a history of political partisanship), (4) sparse/neutral (three comparatively small states having neither a consistent Democratic nor Republican allegiance); (5) sparse/partisan (the remaining twenty states in the continental United States).

Listed on page 225 are the specific designations made for each state relative to the categories just described. (The numbers correspond to those used above.)

Media Coding

The early portion of Chapter Four of this study presents in highly abbreviated form some of the results from an earlier, detailed study of network news stories about the presidency. With the assistance of the Vanderbilt University News Archive, a sample of forty-five different newscasts presented between 1969 and 1978 was assembled. Each of these newscasts had been presented in response to a major (televised) presidential address. In almost all cases, the early evening news programs were broadcast by the networks less than twenty-four hours after the president spoke.

Each of the stories was subdivided into major thematic units (MTUs) which were operationally defined as news sequences uninterrupted by (*a*) a commercial break or (*b*) the studio-bound anchor correspondent. The average newscast in the sample contained 3.8 major thematic units, each of which lasted for roughly two minutes. Of the eighteen "stimulus" speeches used, eleven were covered by all three networks, five by two networks, and two by one network. The resulting sample is fairly evenly divided among responses made to the three presidents (Nixon through Carter) by the three networks (ABC, NBC, CBS).

State	Regional Location	State Population	Political Partisanship	Political Significance
Alabama	2	2	1	3
Arizona	4	3	2	5
Arkansas	2	3	1	5
California	4	1	3	1
Colorado	4	3	2	5
Connecticut	1	2	3	1
Delaware	1	4	3	4
Florida	2	1	3	1
Georgia	2	2	1	3
Idaho	4	4	2	5
Illinois	3	1	3	1
Indiana	3	1	2	3
Iowa	3	3	2	5
Kansas	3	3	2	5
Kentucky	2	2	1	3
Louisiana	2	2	1	3
Maine	1	4	2	5
Maryland	1	2	3	1
Massachusetts	1	1	1	3
Michigan	3	1	3	1
Minnesota	3	2	1	3
Mississippi	2	3	1	5
Missouri	3	2	3	2
Montana	4	4	3	4
Nebraska	3	3	2	5
Nevada	4	4	2	5
New Hampshire	1	4	2	5
New Jersey	1	1	3	1
New Mexico	4	4	3	4
New York	1	1	3	1
North Carolina	2	1	1	3
North Dakota	3	4	2	5
Ohio	3	1	3	1
Oklahoma	3	3	2	5
Oregon	4	3	3	2
Pennsylvania	1	1	3	1
Rhode Island	1	4	1	5
South Carolina	2	3	1	5
South Dakota	3	4	2	5
Tennessee	2	2	2	3
Texas	2	1	1	3
Utah	4	3	2	5
Vermont	1	4	2	5
Virginia	2	2	3	2
Washington	4	2	3	2
West Virginia	2	3	1	5
Wisconsin	3	2	3	2
Wyoming	4	4	2	5

Each newscast was coded for *president, network,* and *topic*—International Affairs, Domestic Policy, and State of the Union (typically, a hybrid of the former two topics). In addition, durational measures of presidents' *speaking length* were obtained (i.e., the extent to which the president's "stimulus" speech was excerpted during the newscast). Durational and frequency counts were also made for the *domestic locations* (Washington, D.C.; urban North; South/West; and Mixed) presented in the newscasts, as well as for the *general locations* depicted—(1) network studio, (2) White House, (3) United States Capitol, (4) elsewhere in the United States, (5) international location, and (6) miscellaneous (nondescript settings).

In addition to these general markers, each of the 173 major thematic units was analyzed for relative emphasis on the following, non–mutually-exclusive categories:

1. *Reporter Categories*
   a) *Reportorial type.* Each MTU was designated as either (1) simple (only one reporter shown) or (2) complex (two or more reporters depicted).
   b) *Reporter purpose.* If the major thematic unit exclusively contained descriptive statements of what the president had said and done, it was labeled "Explanation"; if the unit reported citizens' reactions (either those of laypersons or leaders of special interest groups) or the reactions of elected officials, it was labeled "General Evaluation"; finally, if the unit consisted of reporters' own reactions (typically, these were highlighted as such by the networks), it was labeled "Official Commentary."
   c) *Reporter activity.* For each MTU, reporters' verbal comments were coded as "Summarizing" if they primarily quoted from or paraphrased what the president had said, "Extrapolating" if they stressed the social and political implications of the president's speech, "Introducing" if their sole purpose was to set up either the president's remarks or some other person's responses to those remarks, and "General Discussion" if the reporter touched upon two or more of the foregoing purposes (or upon some miscellaneous purpose).
   d) *Reporter focus.* When a given major thematic unit was devoted *exclusively* to a discussion of the substance of a presidential speech, it was recorded as being centered on "Presidential Policy"; "Presidential Style" was used when the focus was exclusively upon *how* the president had prepared or delivered his remarks; and "Presidential Action" became the label for reports of official steps taken by the president subsequent to his presenting the remarks in question. If instead of having a presidential focus the unit dealt exclusively with "Congressional Reaction" or "Lay Reaction" (by definition, any noncongressional or nonpresidential reaction), it was so designated. Finally, if a

given report dealt with information, events, or opinions existing *prior* to the president's speech, it was designated a "Background" unit (or, if none of the foregoing applied, "Miscellaneous").

2. *Nonreporter Categories*
    a) *Lay response.* Those thematic units containing the verbalized comments of the nation's citizens were categorized as "Individual" or "Multiple" depending upon the number of reactions presented in the unit.
    b) *Republican response.* Included reactions to the president's speech by elected officials or official spokespersons of the Republican party. (Also subdivided as "Individual" or "Multiple").
    c) *Democratic response.* Obverse designations of the above.

3. *Visual Categories*
    a) *Visual background.* For each MTU, the *primary* visual background (i.e., the background depicted for the greatest duration) was designated as "Natural" if the ground behind the focal figure consisted of people, identifiable buildings, or aspects of nature (e.g., a running stream), or as "Artificial" if it contained a *projected* visual, an emblem, or a blank wall.
    b) *Visual focus on citizens.* In those units *primarily* centered upon laypersons, simple distinctions were made between segments containing verbalized "Reactions to President" and those in which the nonvocalized "Everyday Behaviors" of people were depicted (e.g., jogging, waiting in gas lines, protesting, etc.).
    c) *Visual focus on president.* Whenever the chief executive was shown *speaking* (as opposed to walking, playing golf, etc.), the president's behavior was classified as "Public Speaking," "Ceremonial Exchange" (e.g., shaking hands with a head of state), or "Casual Conversation."

For additional information on the methods and results of this study, see R. P. Hart et al., "Rhetorical Features of Newscasts about the Presidency," *Critical Studies in Mass Communication* 1 (1984), pp. 260–286.

Overall Data

The following tables present in the broadest possible fashion the essential data gathered in this study. (The various figures and tables presented in the body of this volume contain more specific information.) Clearly, given the size of the data base generated for this study, still other data could have been reported. But I have chosen to paint the picture of the modern presidency in boldest relief here, realizing full well that other researchers would array these facts differently and would be intrigued by patterns of data ignored by me in this investigation.

Table A.1   *Presidential Speaking in Various Contexts (1945–1985)*
(Reported in Percentages)

	N Speeches	% All Presidential Speeches
President (years in office):		
Truman (8)	1407	14.1
Eisenhower (8)	925	9.3
Kennedy (3)	771	7.7
Johnson (5)	1636	16.4
Nixon (5+)	1035	10.4
Ford (2+)	1236	12.4
Carter (4)	1322	13.3
Reagan (5)	1637	16.4
General location:		
Washington, D.C.	6235	62.6
Domestic city	3006	30.2
International city	725	7.3
General topic:		
Systemic	2728	57.5
Humanistic	2020	42.5
Specific topic:		
Science	733	7.4
Economics	814	8.2
Governance	1181	11.8
Human services	785	7.9
Human values	1235	12.4
International cooperation	1917	19.2
International conflict	617	6.2
Multiple	2068	20.7
Other	617	6.2
Audience:		
Government employees	142	1.4
Local and/or press	5116	51.3
National	783	7.9
Invited guests	1556	15.6
Special interest group	2369	23.8
Timing:		
First half of administration	4430	44.4
Second half of administration	5539	55.6
Type of year:		
Nonelection	4272	42.9
Election	5696	57.1
Party:		
Democratic	5136	51.5
Republican	4833	48.5

Table A.1　(*continued*)

	N Speeches	% All Presidential Speeches
Season:		
Winter	1836	18.4
Spring	2597	26.1
Summer	2282	22.9
Fall	3251	32.6
Speech activity:		
Single speech	5883	59.0
2–3 speeches	3105	31.1
4–6 speeches	701	7.0
7 or more speeches	280	2.8
Setting:		
Ceremony	3740	37.5
Briefing	2642	26.5
Organizational meeting	1023	10.3
Political rally	1497	15.0
Miscellaneous	1066	10.7
*Presidential popularity:**		
Low (0–50%)	2144	34.5
Medium (51–64%)	2447	39.4
High (Over 65%)	1620	26.1
*Unemployment rate:**		
Low (0–4.5%)	2637	30.4
Medium (4.6–5.9%)	2801	32.3
High (over 6.0%)	3239	37.3
*Congressional control:**		
President's party	4395	49.5
Opposition party	4491	50.5
*Congressional initiative:**		
Low (less than 200 bills)	2531	34.3
Medium (201–300 bills)	2822	38.2
High (over 300 bills)	2030	27.5
*Congressional success:**		
Low (0–69% passed)	2042	27.7
Medium (70–79% passed)	3460	46.9
High (over 80% passed)	1881	25.5
*Newspaper coverage:**		
Low (0–200 stories)	2483	42.2
Medium (201–250 stories)	2852	48.4
High (over 250 stories)	3553	9.4
*Magazine coverage:**		
Low (0–100 stories)	4068	69.1
High (over 100 stories)	1820	30.9

Table A.1   (*continued*)

	N Speeches	% All Presidential Speeches
Ceremonial type:		
Initiating ceremony	934	25.0
Honorific ceremony	1126	30.1
Celebratory ceremony	939	25.1
Greeting ceremony	739	19.8
Regional location:		
Northeast	725	23.9
Midwest	898	29.7
South	810	26.8
West	588	19.6
*State's population:**		
Most populous states (1–12)	1580	57.5
Large states (13–24)	586	21.3
Small states (25–36)	358	13.0
Least populous states (37–48)	222	8.1
*State's politics:**		
Partisan democratic	738	27.2
Partisan republican	438	16.1
Neutral	1542	56.7
*State's significance:**		
Densely populated/neutral	1174	43.0
Medium populated/neutral	297	10.9
Densely populated/partisan	730	26.7
Sparsely populated/neutral	71	2.6
Sparsely populated/partisan	460	16.8

*Data not complete through 1985. See "Coding Procedures" in Appendix for relevant dates.

Table A.2   *General Topical Variations in Presidential Speechmaking (1945–1985) (Reported in Percentages)*

	Systemic Topics (N = 2728)	Humanistic Topics (N = 2020)
President:		
Truman	15.4	11.3
Eisenhower	6.3	8.7
Kennedy	6.4	7.9
Johnson	15.0	23.3
Nixon	8.0	9.8
Ford	12.0	10.2
Carter	15.4	12.3
Reagan	21.5	16.4
Party:		
Democratic	52.2	54.9
Republican	47.8	45.1

Table A.2   (*continued*)

	Systemic Topics (*N* = 2728)	Humanistic Topics (*N* = 2020)
Timing:		
First half of administration	45.8	47.8
Second half of administration	54.2	52.2
Type of year:		
Nonelection	36.3	47.2
Election	63.7	52.8
General location:		
Washington, D.C.	58.4	72.9
Domestic city	41.3	24.6
International city	0.3	2.5
Regional location:		
Northeast	25.2	31.0
Midwest	31.1	24.8
South	22.2	31.8
West	21.4	12.4
Occasion:		
Ceremony	26.4	55.6
Briefing	22.7	11.4
Organizational meeting	13.4	15.5
Political rally	28.3	3.2
Miscellaneous	9.1	14.3
Audience:		
Government employees	1.8	1.1
Local and/or press	50.1	40.1
National	8.1	8.2
Invited guests	10.8	18.8
Special interest group	29.2	31.8
Era:		
Early presidency	22.7	19.0
Later presidency	30.7	41.3
Recent presidency	46.7	39.7
Season:		
Winter	16.3	21.0
Spring	22.3	28.1
Summer	19.8	23.7
Fall	41.6	27.1
*Unemployment rate:**		
Low (0–4.5%)	32.3	32.7
Medium (4.6–5.9%)	26.4	32.7
High (over 6.0%)	41.3	34.6

*Data not complete through 1985. See "Coding Procedures" in Appendix for relevant dates.

Table A.3 *Chronological Development of Presidential Speechmaking (Reported in Percentages)*

	Early Presidency* (N = 1914)	Later Presidency† (N = 3154)	Recent Presidency‡ (N = 3819)
General location:			
Washington, D.C.	55.7	68.3	59.2
Domestic city	43.2	20.6	33.4
International city	1.1	11.1	7.4
Audience:			
Government employees	1.2	0.9	2.2
Local and/or press	67.2	50.8	45.6
National	7.3	4.3	8.3
Invited guests	6.0	17.5	17.4
Special interest group	18.3	26.5	27.1
Setting:			
Ceremony	19.3	51.6	38.3
Briefing	27.1	14.5	25.4
Organizational meeting	11.5	10.6	12.2
Political rally	29.7	7.8	15.9
Miscellaneous	12.5	15.5	8.2
Regional location:			
Northeast	27.4	30.7	19.9
Midwest	35.8	20.4	30.4
South	12.8	34.0	31.8
West	24.0	14.9	18.0
Topic:			
Science	5.9	8.5	7.4
Economics	5.4	6.4	9.3
Governance	16.4	7.8	11.9
Human services	4.5	10.5	7.7
Human values	13.4	13.2	11.1
International cooperation	6.9	26.7	19.2
International conflict	4.6	6.1	5.6
Multiple	35.5	13.9	22.5
Other	7.3	6.9	5.3
Type of year:			
Nonelection	36.8	43.6	40.0
Election	63.2	56.4	60.0
Season:			
Winter	13.5	20.1	18.6
Spring	21.2	26.1	27.9
Summer	21.0	25.1	22.2
Fall	44.4	28.7	31.4

Table A.3   (*continued*)

	Early Presidency* (N = 1914)	Later Presidency† (N = 3154)	Recent Presidency‡ (N = 3819)
Timing:			
First half of administration	52.7	46.5	35.9
Second half of administration	47.3	53.5	64.1
Speech activity:			
Single speech	61.0	59.7	55.9
2–3 speeches	19.9	34.5	33.4
4–6 speeches	9.8	5.4	8.4
7 or more speeches	9.4	0.4	2.4
State's population:§			
Most populous states (1–12)	46.9	66.5	60.0
Large states (13–24)	22.6	19.4	21.5
Small states (25–36)	18.2	7.4	12.4
Least populous states (37–48)	12.3	6.7	6.0
State's politics:§			
Partisan democratic	21.1	36.0	27.2
Partisan republican	23.9	10.4	13.6
Neutral	55.0	53.6	59.2

*Early presidency = April 1945 to December 1957.
†Later presidency = January 1958 to June 1970.
‡Recent presidency = July 1970 to December 1982.
§Data not complete through 1985. See "Coding Procedures" in Appendix for relevant dates.

Table A.4   *Individual Speaking Habits of Recent American Presidents (Reported in Percentages)*

	Truman (N = 1407)	Eisenhower (N = 925)	Kennedy (N = 771)	Johnson (N = 1636)	Nixon (N = 1035)	Ford (N = 1236)	Carter (N = 1322)	Reagan (N = 1637)
General location:								
Washington, D.C.	49.7	64.8	70.4	73.3	61.8	46.0	63.8	69.9
Domestic city	49.6	21.4	18.9	21.9	24.2	48.5	28.0	23.7
International city	0.7	13.8	10.6	4.8	14.0	5.5	8.2	6.4
Topic:								
Science	5.8	5.1	10.9	9.0	7.0	6.9	9.5	5.5
Economics	5.8	3.4	5.4	8.1	5.9	8.5	6.4	16.8
Governance	18.2	10.2	6.2	8.0	8.2	11.2	15.7	13.6
Human services	4.4	3.8	10.5	13.4	5.9	7.5	9.2	6.9
Human values	11.9	15.2	10.1	15.4	13.1	9.2	9.7	13.4
International cooperation	5.8	24.2	32.2	18.7	29.1	13.9	18.5	20.8
International conflict	4.0	5.1	5.3	6.7	7.7	3.8	6.0	9.6
Multiple	37.0	26.4	10.8	14.9	13.6	32.0	22.6	8.8
Other	7.2	6.7	8.6	5.9	9.5	7.0	2.3	4.4
Audience:								
Government employees	0.7	2.1	1.7	0.7	0.0	2.8	2.2	1.6
Local and/or press	73.7	48.5	52.0	49.8	49.5	49.8	43.8	43.3
National	6.0	8.3	4.2	4.0	10.9	4.4	7.0	16.1
Invited guests	5.1	11.8	12.7	18.6	19.9	10.5	23.2	20.2
Special interest group	14.4	29.3	29.4	26.9	19.7	32.6	23.8	18.8
Timing:								
First half of administration	42.2	44.8	41.5	45.4	61.7	27.4	45.8	47.2
Second half of administration	57.8	55.2	58.5	54.6	38.3	72.6	54.2	52.8
Type of year:								
Nonelection	30.4	46.7	61.3	34.2	52.9	32.1	42.6	53.3
Election	69.6	53.3	38.7	65.8	47.1	67.9	57.4	46.7

Season:							
Winter	12.9	21.5	14.7	19.5	22.9	16.2	18.6	20.9
Spring	19.1	27.1	25.9	27.1	26.5	30.4	26.2	26.8
Summer	19.8	22.4	27.5	25.4	22.9	21.1	23.4	22.1
Fall	48.2	29.0	31.9	27.9	27.7	32.3	31.8	30.2
Speech activity:							
Single speech	54.5	73.4	60.6	57.6	68.7	42.6	55.5	64.4
2–3 speeches	19.8	23.6	35.0	36.6	26.7	36.2	36.2	32.9
4–6 speeches	13.1	2.9	4.2	5.4	4.4	15.0	7.5	2.4
7 or more speeches	12.7	0.1	0.3	0.4	0.2	6.2	0.8	0.2
Setting:							
Ceremony	16.1	34.8	47.1	54.4	49.4	35.6	39.0	28.8
Briefing	25.2	27.0	13.9	13.7	17.6	18.7	31.1	53.9
Organizational Meeting	8.9	17.9	10.1	10.0	9.5	11.7	10.4	6.8
Political Rally	36.0	10.6	5.6	8.2	8.4	27.4	12.1	7.9
Miscellaneous	13.7	9.6	23.3	13.7	15.2	6.6	7.4	2.6
Regional location:							
Northeast	25.8	42.7	38.5	26.2	18.0	15.9	28.2	17.8
Midwest	32.8	24.1	15.5	20.7	28.8	32.9	26.6	29.6
South	11.5	16.1	26.4	42.3	28.4	33.4	33.1	27.6
West	33.1	17.1	19.6	10.8	24.8	17.9	12.2	25.0
*State's significance:**							
Densely populated/neutral	35.8	49.5	46.6	38.3	51.2	44.6	45.9	49.6
Medium populated/neutral	14.2	7.6	6.2	5.0	8.8	13.9	10.5	10.6
Densely populated/partisan	21.2	21.2	28.8	44.4	20.8	26.9	27.8	20.4
Sparsely populated/neutral	5.6	1.5	4.8	2.0	1.6	0.2	1.4	4.4
Sparsely populated/partisan	23.2	20.2	13.7	10.3	17.6	14.5	14.3	15.0

Table A.5   *Individual Comparisons of Election-Year vs. Nonelection Year Presidential Speaking (Reported in Percentages)*

	Truman		Eisenhower		Kennedy		Johnson	
	Nonelection Year (N = 428)	Election Year (N = 979)	Nonelection Year (N = 432)	Election Year (N = 493)	Nonelection Year (N = 473)	Election Year (N = 298)	Nonelection Year (N = 560)	Election Year (N = 1076)
General location:								
Washington, D.C.	86.7	33.5	70.1	60.0	67.0	75.8	84.1	67.7
Domestic city	11.9	66.1	15.3	26.8	17.1	21.8	12.0	27.0
International city	1.4	0.4	14.6	13.2	15.9	2.3	3.9	5.3
Topic:								
Science	4.2	6.5	4.2	5.9	11.0	10.7	9.3	8.8
Economics	4.7	6.3	3.9	2.8	4.7	6.7	7.9	8.3
Governance	3.5	24.6	3.9	15.6	2.5	12.1	7.7	8.1
Human services	4.7	4.3	4.9	2.8	12.3	7.7	15.2	12.5
Human values	17.5	9.4	17.6	13.2	10.1	10.1	17.9	14.1
International cooperation	14.0	2.1	25.0	23.5	37.6	23.5	20.2	17.8
International conflict	4.0	4.0	5.3	4.9	4.9	6.0	6.6	6.8
Multiple	37.4	36.8	26.2	26.6	9.9	12.1	10.2	17.3
Other	10.0	5.9	9.0	4.7	7.0	11.1	5.0	6.3
Audience:								
Government employees	1.4	0.4	2.3	1.8	1.1	2.7	1.8	0.1
Local and/or press	55.8	81.5	50.5	46.9	50.1	55.0	44.6	52.5
National	9.6	4.5	8.1	8.5	4.7	3.4	4.5	3.8
Invited guests	10.7	2.7	11.3	12.2	14.2	10.4	21.2	17.2
Special interest group	22.4	10.9	27.8	30.6	30.0	28.5	27.9	26.4
Setting:								
Ceremony	26.6	11.5	37.5	32.5	48.2	45.3	59.8	51.6
Briefing	42.5	17.7	29.9	24.5	14.2	13.4	15.2	12.9
Organizational meeting	15.9	5.8	18.8	17.2	12.1	7.0	10.9	9.6
Political rally	1.4	51.2	3.9	16.4	1.7	11.7	1.8	11.5
Miscellaneous	13.6	13.8	10.0	9.3	23.9	22.5	12.3	14.4

	Nixon		Ford		Carter		Reagan	
	Nonelection Year (N = 547)	Election Year (N = 488)	Nonelection Year (N = 396)	Election Year (N = 839)	Nonelection Year (N = 554)	Election Year (N = 759)	Nonelection Year (N = 872)	Election Year (N = 762)
Regional location:								
Northeast	21.1	25.2	56.1	36.1	38.8	38.2	21.1	27.5
Midwest	28.8	39.0	18.2	27.1	7.5	25.0	12.7	22.7
South	40.3	9.7	18.2	15.0	27.5	25.0	57.7	38.5
West	13.5	26.1	7.6	21.8	26.3	11.8	8.5	11.3
Speech activity:								
Single speech	83.4	41.9	77.1	70.2	61.3	59.4	65.0	53.8
2–3 speeches	16.6	21.1	21.5	25.4	33.4	37.6	33.2	38.3
4–6 speeches	0.0	18.8	1.4	4.3	4.9	3.0	1.8	7.2
7 or more speeches	0.0	18.2	0.0	0.2	0.4	0.0	0.0	0.7
*State's politics:**								
Partisan democratic	32.7	19.8	24.2	21.8	35.0	27.9	59.2	39.5
Partisan republican	1.9	25.3	31.8	12.0	11.2	8.8	2.8	12.7
Neutral	65.4	54.9	43.9	66.2	53.7	63.2	38.0	47.8
*State's population:**								
Most populous states (1–12)	53.8	46.3	40.9	62.4	61.2	64.7	71.8	66.3
Large states (13–24)	32.7	21.8	22.7	21.1	17.5	19.1	26.8	18.6
Small states (25–36)	13.5	19.3	10.6	12.0	10.0	5.9	1.4	7.6
Least populous states (37–48)	0.0	12.7	25.8	4.5	11.2	10.3	0.0	7.6
General location:								
Washington, D.C.	68.4	54.5	55.1	41.7	72.6	57.3	77.5	61.2
Domestic city	19.9	28.9	33.1	55.8	19.4	34.4	18.3	29.8
International city	11.7	16.6	11.9	2.5	8.0	8.3	4.1	9.1

Table A.5 *(continued)*

	Nixon		Ford		Carter		Reagan	
	Nonelection Year (N = 547)	Election Year (N = 488)	Nonelection Year (N = 396)	Election Year (N = 839)	Nonelection Year (N = 554)	Election Year (N = 759)	Nonelection Year (N = 872)	Election Year (N = 762)
Topic:								
Science	7.7	6.1	12.3	7.5	10.4	5.2	4.8	6.3
Economics	6.8	4.9	4.3	8.0	11.4	7.2	18.8	14.4
Governance	8.2	8.2	6.4	22.7	9.3	12.0	8.9	18.8
Human services	5.7	6.1	10.7	8.0	11.9	5.5	7.0	6.8
Human values	14.3	11.9	7.6	11.2	3.3	12.0	15.8	10.6
International cooperation	29.4	28.7	22.7	15.4	21.2	10.5	20.9	20.8
International conflict	7.3	8.2	5.5	6.3	5.3	3.1	10.4	8.6
Multiple	9.7	18.0	27.7	18.7	19.2	38.0	8.6	9.0
Other	11.0	7.8	2.8	2.0	8.1	6.4	4.7	4.6
Audience:								
Government employees	0.0	0.0	8.6	0.0	1.4	2.8	2.0	1.2
Local and/or press	43.3	56.4	36.6	55.9	47.1	41.4	40.0	47.3
National	8.2	13.9	6.1	3.6	8.7	5.7	17.6	14.5
Invited guests	23.0	16.4	14.6	8.6	14.4	29.8	23.2	16.6
Special interest group	25.4	13.3	34.1	31.9	28.4	20.3	17.3	20.4
Setting:								
Ceremony	54.1	44.1	47.5	30.0	41.7	37.0	27.3	30.5
Briefing	16.6	18.6	18.2	19.0	34.8	28.3	61.2	45.4
Organizational meeting	11.7	7.0	17.9	8.7	9.6	10.9	6.0	7.7
Political rally	2.2	15.4	7.6	36.7	4.8	17.5	3.4	13.1
Miscellaneous	15.4	15.0	8.8	5.6	9.1	6.2	2.1	3.3

Regional location:								
Northeast	18.3	17.7	22.9	10.9	28.2	28.2	18.1	17.5
Midwest	21.1	34.8	28.2	26.8	32.8	23.9	18.8	37.3
South	33.9	24.1	27.5	27.4	25.5	36.3	36.2	21.5
West	26.6	23.4	21.4	13.2	13.6	11.6	26.9	23.7
Speech activity:								
Single speech	69.7	67.6	62.5	50.3	55.8	36.5	67.7	60.7
2–3 speeches	27.2	26.0	35.3	36.9	36.6	36.0	31.4	34.7
4–6 speeches	3.1	5.9	2.1	11.5	7.6	18.5	0.9	4.2
7 or more speeches	0.0	0.4	0.0	1.3	0.0	9.1	0.0	0.4
State's politics: *								
Partisan democratic	21.1	23.4	34.4	24.9	30.0	32.4	19.4	18.3
Partisan republican	16.5	14.9	18.3	13.5	20.0	5.8	9.7	19.5
Neutral	62.4	61.7	47.3	61.6	50.0	61.8	71.0	62.2
State's population: *								
Most populous states (1–12)	53.2	66.0	48.9	66.2	41.8	64.1	61.3	54.9
Large states (13–24)	22.0	17.7	26.0	17.3	31.8	22.4	32.3	20.7
Small states (25–36)	16.5	9.9	14.5	11.8	19.1	10.4	6.5	13.4
Least populous states (37–48)	8.3	6.4	10.7	4.6	7.3	3.1	0.0	11.0

*Data not complete through 1985. See "Coding Procedures" in Appendix for relevant dates.

Table A.6 *Party-related Variations in Presidential Speechmaking (1945–1985)*
(Reported in Percentages)

	Democratic Speeches (N = 5136)	Republican Speeches (N = 4831)
General location:		
Washington, D.C.	64.0	61.1
Domestic city	30.6	29.7
International city	5.4	9.2
Setting:		
Ceremony	38.9	36.1
Briefing	21.4	32.0
Organizational meeting	9.8	10.7
Political rally	16.4	13.5
Miscellaneous	13.5	7.7
Audience:		
Government employees	1.2	1.6
Local and/or press	55.1	47.3
National	5.4	10.5
Invited guests	15.2	16.0
Special interest group	23.1	24.5
Topic:		
Science	8.6	6.1
Economics	6.7	9.8
Governance	12.5	11.2
Human services	9.4	6.2
Human values	12.2	12.6
International cooperation	17.1	21.5
International conflict	5.6	6.8
Multiple	22.3	19.1
Other	5.7	6.7
Congressional control:		
President's party	78.0	5.6
Opposition party	22.0	94.4
Speech activity:		
Single speech	56.7	61.5
2–3 speeches	31.6	30.6
4–6 speeches	7.8	6.2
7 or more speeches	3.8	1.7
Type of year:		
Nonelection	39.4	46.5
Election	60.6	53.5
*Presidential popularity:**		
Low (0%–50%)	29.8	39.0
Medium (51%–64%)	30.5	47.8
High (over 65%)	39.7	13.2

240

Table A.6   (*continued*)

	Democratic Speeches ($N = 5136$)	Republican Speeches ($N = 4831$)
*Unemployment rate:**		
Low (0%–4.5%)	41.0	16.5
Medium (4.6%–5.9%)	28.4	37.4
High (over 6.0%)	30.6	46.1
*State's politics:**		
Partisan democratic	29.5	24.4
Partisan republican	16.2	15.7
Neutral	54.3	59.9
*Magazine coverage:**		
Low (0–100 stories)	82.5	57.8
High (over 100 stories)	17.5	42.2
*Newspaper coverage:**		
Low (0–200 stories)	32.9	50.0
Medium (200–249 stories)	67.1	32.7
High (over 250 stories)	0.0	17.3
*Regional location:**		
Northeast	27.2	21.0
Midwest	29.4	30.2
South	25.2	28.4
West	18.2	20.4

*Data not complete through 1985. See "Coding Procedures" in Appendix for relevant dates.

Table A.7   *Rank Order Differences between State Population and Frequency of Presidential Speaking (1945–1982)*

	Speech Frequency Rank	Population Rank	Difference in Ranks*
Alabama	39	21	− 18
Arizona	45	33	− 12
Arkansas	43.5	32	− 11.5
California	3	1	− 2
Colorado	15.5	30	+ 14.5
Connecticut	14	24	+ 10
Delaware	46	45	− 1
Florida	7	9	+ 2
Georgia	17	15	− 2
Idaho	37	41	+ 4
Illinois	4	3	− 1
Indiana	10	11	+ 1
Iowa	15.5	25	+ 9.5
Kansas	32.5	28	− 4.5
Kentucky	21	23	+ 2
Louisiana	31	20	− 11
Maine	43.5	38	− 5.5
Maryland	28	18	− 10
Massachusetts	24	10	− 14
Michigan	8	7	− 1
Minnesota	20	19	− 1
Mississippi	40.5	29	− 11.5
Missouri	9	13	+ 4
Montana	24	42	+ 18
Nebraska	29	35	+ 6
Nevada	42	46	+ 4
New Hampshire	24	40	+ 16
New Jersey	11	8	− 3
New Mexico	35.5	37	+ 1.5
New York	1	2	+ 1
North Carolina	18	12	− 6
North Dakota	35.5	44	+ 8.5
Ohio	5.5	6	+ 0.5
Oklahoma	27	27	0
Oregon	24	31	+ 7
Pennsylvania	5.5	4	− 1.5
Rhode Island	32.5	39	+ 6.5
South Carolina	38	26	− 12
South Dakota	47	43	− 4
Tennessee	24	17	− 7
Texas	2	5	+ 3
Utah	34	35	+ 1
Vermont	48	47	− 1
Virginia	13	14	+ 1
Washington	12	27	+ 15
West Virginia	30	34	+ 4
Wisconsin	19	16	− 3
Wyoming	40.5	48	+ 7.5

*+ = high per capita speaking rate, − = low per capita speaking rate.

Table A.8   *Use of Specialized Speaking Situations by American Presidents*
(1945–1985) (Reported in Percentages)

	Traditional Press Conference (National) (N = 165)	Traditional Press Conference (D.C.) (N = 785)	Traditional Press Conference (Local) (N = 169)	Traditional Ceremony (D.C.) (N = 494)
President:				
Truman	4.2	35.2	5.9	9.7
Eisenhower	7.3	23.3	4.1	8.4
Kennedy	3.6	7.6	1.8	6.3
Johnson	5.5	12.2	16.6	26.6
Nixon	6.1	5.0	0.6	9.3
Ford	12.1	2.0	32.5	9.5
Carter	35.8	7.9	32.5	11.8
Reagan	25.5	6.8	5.9	18.4
Party:				
Democratic	49.1	62.9	56.8	54.4
Republican	50.9	37.1	43.2	45.6
Type of year:				
Nonelection	60.0	47.6	34.9	50.2
Election	40.0	52.4	65.1	49.8
Year in Office:				
First	19.4	12.2	7.1	14.3
Second	29.1	21.8	18.9	18.1
Third	23.0	15.2	35.5	23.4
Timing (in Admin.):				
First half	58.8	50.3	33.1	42.8
Second half	41.2	49.7	66.9	57.2
*Presidential Popularity:**				
Low (0%–50%)	29.5	21.3	44.9	41.1
Medium (51%–64%)	53.7	41.5	43.9	32.4
High (over 65%)	16.8	37.2	11.2	26.4
*Newspaper coverage:**				
Low (0–200 stories)	27.5	55.5	62.4	44.6
Medium (200–249 stories)	67.5	38.9	36.6	46.1
High (over 250 stories)	5.0	5.6	1.0	9.3
*Magazine coverage:**				
Low (0–100 stories)	37.5	75.6	74.3	78.6
High (over 100 stories)	62.5	24.4	25.7	21.4
*Congressional control:**				
President's party	59.7	56.8	56.4	56.2
Opposition party	40.3	43.2	43.6	43.8
*Congressional initiative:**				
Low (less than 200 bills)	44.6	21.4	44.4	23.8
Medium (201–300 bills)	35.4	53.6	29.4	40.5
High (over 300 bills)	20.0	25.0	26.1	35.6

Table A.8   (*continued*)

	Traditional Press Conference (National) (N = 165)	Traditional Press Conference (D.C.) (N = 785)	Traditional Press Conference (Local) (N = 169)	Traditional Ceremony (D.C.) (N = 494)
*Congressional success:**				
Low (0–69% passed)	20.0	21.7	37.9	19.9
Medium (70–79% passed)	65.4	50.7	53.6	50.0
High (over 80% passed)	14.6	27.6	8.5	30.1
*Unemployment rate:**				
Low (0–4.5%)	12.3	35.1	18.8	32.8
Medium (4.6–5.9%)	15.9	36.1	8.8	31.3
High (over 6.0%)	71.7	28.8	72.5	35.9

	Traditional Ceremony (Local) (N = 169)	Open Rallies (N = 954)	Partisan Rallies (N = 2354)	Local Foreign Policy Speeches (N = 260)
President:				
Truman	13.0	50.0	8.4	12.3
Eisenhower	15.4	2.9	11.3	7.3
Kennedy	5.9	2.1	9.3	10.4
Johnson	18.3	9.1	18.2	21.5
Nixon	14.8	5.8	8.2	15.4
Ford	10.7	17.3	16.6	8.1
Carter	8.3	3.7	15.3	10.8
Reagan	13.6	9.1	12.7	14.2
Party:				
Democratic	45.6	64.9	51.3	55.0
Republican	54.4	35.1	48.7	45.0
Type of year:				
Nonelection	40.2	2.6	45.0	45.4
Election	59.8	97.4	55.0	54.6
Year in office:				
First	10.7	2.2	14.4	16.5
Second	22.5	13.5	25.6	24.2
Third	29.0	16.6	25.7	18.8
Timing (in administration):				
First half	50.3	45.8	50.0	50.0
Second half	49.7	54.2	50.0	50.0
*Presidential popularity:**				
Low (0%–50%)	40.2	48.2	54.5	30.2
Medium (51%–64%)	28.7	23.0	24.5	44.5
High (over 65%)	31.1	28.9	21.1	25.3

Table A.8   (*continued*)

	Traditional Ceremony (Local) (*N* = 169)	Open Rallies (*N* = 954)	Partisan Rallies (*N* = 2354)	Local Foreign Policy Speeches (*N* = 260)
*Newspaper coverage:**				
Low (0–200 stories)	52.5	55.6	60.4	36.8
Medium (200–249 stories)	41.0	35.1	31.4	52.3
High (over 250 stories)	6.6	9.3	8.2	10.9
*Magazine coverage:**				
Low (0–100 stories)	75.4	81.5	75.4	67.2
High (over 100 stories)	24.6	18.5	24.6	32.8
*Congressional Control:**				
President's party	43.8	16.9	35.1	57.6
Opposition party	56.3	83.1	64.9	42.4
*Congressional initiative:**				
Low (less than 200 bills)	28.8	54.2	55.1	30.9
Medium (201–300 bills)	50.7	40.3	34.1	34.0
High (over 300 bills)	20.5	5.5	10.8	35.1
*Congressional success:**				
Low (0%–69% passed)	24.7	48.1	51.0	21.1
Medium (70%–79% passed)	45.9	28.5	34.3	49.0
High (over 80% passed)	29.5	23.4	14.7	29.9
*Unemployment rate:**				
Low (0%–4.5%)	24.6	58.7	13.3	32.3
Medium (4.6%–5.9%)	42.1	18.8	22.1	41.6
High (over 6.0%)	33.3	22.5	64.5	26.1

*Data not complete through 1985. See "Coding Procedures" in Appendix for relevant dates.

Notes

Introduction

    1. R. P. Hart, *Verbal Style and the Presidency: A Computer-based Analysis* (New York: Academic Press, 1984).

    2. L. Rose, "The Art of Conversation," *Atlantic* (November, 1985), p. 126.

    3. The Appendix of this book presents a more precise, and detailed, description of the data-collection methods used in this study. Readers might wish to familiarize themselves with this material before continuing.

    4. The kind of discernment being discussed here is "rhetorical" discernment, a mind-set that presumes that most human action has a suasory dimension to it. This perspective has been discussed widely in academic and popular circles since classical times. A brief version of this perspective, as it pertains to the modern presidency, can be found in Hart, *Verbal Style and the Presidency,* pp. 4–8.

Chapter One

    1. J. Ceaser et al., "The Rise of the Rhetorical Presidency," *Presidential Studies Quarterly* 11 (1981), pp. 158–171.

    2. B. D. Nash et al., *Organizing and Staffing the Presidency* (New York: Center for the Study of the Presidency, 1980).

    3. "Time Out of Town: JFK vs. Eisenhower," *U.S. News and World Report,* October 22, 1962, p. 47.

    4. Ibid.

    5. "Overexposure as a Presidential Policy," *America,* May 30, 1964, p. 756.

    6. H. Sidey, "The Presidency," *Time,* January 5, 1981, p. 37.

    7. Ibid.

    8. These are the findings of Yale University's Edmund S. Crelin, Jr., as reported in an Associated Press story published in the *Lafayette Journal Courier* in April 1972.

9. For more on this line of thought see A. Montagu, *The Human Revolution* (Cleveland: World, 1965), pp. 108–113.

10. See W. M. O'Barr, *Linguistic Evidence: Language, Power, and Strategy in the Courtroom* (New York: Academic Press, 1982).

11. C. F. Hockett, "The Origins of Speech," *Scientific American* (September 1960), pp. 89–96.

12. "Remarks to the International Labor Press Association," August 18, 1978, *Public Papers of the Presidents, 1978: 2,* p. 1496. *Public Papers* (hereafter cited as *PPP*) are published by the Government Printing Office in Washington, D.C. For the sake of efficiency, these facts of publication will not be repeated in subsequent citations.

13. "Address at the Annual Convention of the National Young Republicans Organization," June 11, 1953, *PPP, 1953,* p. 399.

14. "Address at the Dedication of the Karl E. Mundt Library," June 3, 1969, *PPP, 1969,* pp. 425–426.

15. For more detail on these findings see, respectively, tables A.5 and A.3.

16. One is reminded here of the oft-quoted remarks of the former state Democratic leader in California, Jesse Unruh, who declared that, in politics, there is no such thing as bad publicity.

17. "Remarks at a Reception for Members of the Republican National Committee," September 8, 1975, *PPP, 1975:2,* p. 1350.

18. Ibid., p. 1351.

19. See table A.3.

20. "Remarks at the Portland Youth Bicentennial Rally," September 4, 1975, *PPP, 1975:1,* pp. 1327 ff.

21. See table A.5.

22. For additional information on party differences/similarities, see table A.6. Also, a recent study by C. A. Smith largely corroborates the institutionalized aspects of the presidency noted in this section. See his "The Audiences of the 'Rhetorical Presidency': An Analysis of President-Constituent Interactions, 1963–81," *Presidential Studies Quarterly* 13 (1983), pp. 613–622.

23. W. E. Leuchtenburg, *In the Shadow of F.D.R.: From Harry Truman to Ronald Reagan* (Ithaca, N.Y.: Cornell University Press, 1983).

24. J. W. Prothro, "Verbal Shifts in the American Presidency: A Content Analysis," *American Political Science Review* 50 (1956), pp. 726–739.

25. For an insightful discussion of the durability of America's root political symbols, see C. D. Elder and R. W. Cobb, *The Political Uses of Symbols* (New York: Longman, 1983).

26. L. W. Rosenfield, "The Terms of Commonwealth: A Response to Arnold," *Central States Speech Journal* 18 (1977), p. 89.

27. See table A.4.

28. See table A.5.

29. "Remarks in Seattle at the Silver Anniversary Dinner Honoring Senator Magnuson," November 16, 1961, *PPP, 1961,* p. 729.

30. A technical characterization of Eisenhower's linguistic style is included in my *Verbal Style and the Presidency: A Computer-based Analysis* (New York: Academic Press, 1984), pp. 67–93.

31. "Toast to President Alessandri at a Dinner Given in His Honor by the President," March 1, 1960, *PPP, 1960–1961,* pp. 262–263.

32. "Address at a Dinner at the San Carlos Palace in Bogota," December 17, 1961, *PPP, 1961,* pp. 811–814.

33. "Remarks at the Swearing in of Associate Justice Tom Clark," August 24, 1949, *PPP, 1949,* p. 439.

34. "Remarks at the Swearing in of Homer Thornberry," July 3, 1965, *PPP, 1965:2,* pp. 720–721.

35. "Remarks to the University of Michigan Football Team in Ann Arbor, Michigan," September 15, 1976, *PPP, 1976,* p. 716.

36. This controversy has proceeded at a disconcertingly academic level, but its implications are not unimportant. For an essay that crystallizes the opposing positions see R. E. Vatz, "The Myth of the Rhetorical Situation," *Philosophy and Rhetoric* 6 (1973), pp. 154–161.

37. "Remarks of Welcome at the White House Concert by Pablo Casals," November 13, 1961, *PPP, 1961,* p. 716.

38. Compare, e.g., the data presented in tables A.1 and A.4.

39. See table A.4 for more general information on this matter.

40. Obviously, I have extrapolated a good deal in suggesting a linkage between survey questions pertaining to "the government" and the behavior of individual *presidents.* Given what we know about American politics, however, the extrapolation seems justified. As numerous scholars have reported, Americans are socialized from childhood into seeing the president as the primary embodiment of "government." Thus, while figure 1.4 does not focus directly on chief executives, it is ana-logically related to them. For additional speculation on these matters see D. Easton and R. D. Hess, "The Child's Political World," *Midwest Journal of Political Science* 6 (1962), pp. 229–246.

41. See table A.1.

42. The speeches used in constructing table 1.8 were those that related most logically to legislative activities. Excluded from this analysis were highly generalized speeches (e.g., press conferences) as well as those on "miscellaneous" topics.

43. D. M. West, "Press Coverage in the 1980 Presidential Campaign," *Social Science Quarterly* 64 (1983), pp. 624–633.

44. "Remarks on Signing H.R. 39 into Law," December 2, 1980, *PPP, 1980:3,* pp. 2757–2758.

45. Hart (1984), pp. 46–49. "Certainty" refers to political language indicating resoluteness, inflexibility, and completeness. Included in this semantic measure are such things as leveling terms (all, everyone), rigid verbs (will, shall), and collective terms (bureau, department), among other elements. "Self-reference" indicates a speaker's willingness to invest himself or herself directly in the message and includes all first-person pronouns.

46. "Remarks at a Campaign Rally for Democratic Candidates for State Office," September 24, 1977, *PPP, 1977,* pp. 1653–1656.

47. "Remarks Upon Presenting Medals of Honor," January 29, 1952, *PPP, 1952,* p. 129. The data contained in table 1.10 and figure 1.6 actually understate presidential dependence on the topic of human values since a good many of the

"multiple topic" speeches were primarily concerned with matters of value and since the "other topic" speeches were more closely related to "human values" than to any other speech topics. Thus, table 1.10 and figure 1.6 probably represent only the tip of the iceberg on these matters.

48. "Remarks at a Mount Vernon, Virginia Ceremony," February 22, 1982, *PPP, 1982,* p. 199.

49. An important point to note in connection with this expansion of rhetorical roles is that they constitute an *addition to* the already broadened repertoire of what might be termed psychogovernmental roles making up the presidency. These are neatly captured by Clinton Rossiter in his *The American Presidency* (New York: Harcourt, 1960).

50. These matters will be discussed in greater depth in Chapters Three and Four.

51. J. Ellul, *The Political Illusion,* trans. K. Kellen (New York: Knopf, 1967).

52. Ibid., p. 4.

53. Ibid., p. 6.

54. Ibid., p. 205.

55. Ibid., p. 94.

Chapter Two

1. "Rear Platform Remarks in Austin, Texas," September 27, 1948, *PPP, 1948,* pp. 581–582.

2. W. H. Lawrence, "Truman Says G.O.P. Wants Surrender of Public's Rights," *New York Times,* September 28, 1948, p. 20.

3. R. Brooks, "Thousands of Austin Folk Expected to Hear Address," *Austin American,* September 27, 1948, p. 1; "Solid Democratic Support Asked" (editorial), in ibid.; "Austin Joins Tribute to President" (editorial), in ibid., September 28, 1948, pp. 1 ff.

4. A most useful exposition of the distinctive features of oral communication can be found in C. C. Arnold, "Oral Rhetoric, Rhetoric, and Literature," *Philosophy and Rhetoric* 1 (1968), pp. 191–210.

5. J. L. Austin, *How to Do Things with Words* (New York: Oxford University Press, 1962). A helpful extrapolation of this construct is provided by J. Benjamin in "Performatives as a Rhetorical Construct," *Philosophy and Rhetoric* 9 (1976), pp. 84–95.

6. A. Salmond, "Mana Makes the Man: A Look at Maori Oratory and Politics," in M. Bloch (ed.), *Political Language and Oratory in Traditional Society.* (London: Academic Press, 1975).

7. P. Goldman et al. "Jimmy in Camelot," *Newsweek,* October 29, 1979, pp. 32–34.

8. "Remarks Upon Arrival at the Washington National Airport," November 11, 1955, *PPP, 1955:2,* p. 841.

9. "Remarks to Fellow Patients in the Naval Hospital, Bethesda, Maryland," October 21, 1965, *PPP, 1965:2,* p. 1070.

10. "Remarks by Telephone at the Annual Dinner of the White House Correspondents Association," April 25, 1981, *PPP, 1981,* pp. 384–385.

11. "The President's News Conference at Key West, Florida," January 8, 1956, *PPP, 1956,* p. 32.

12. A review of these data can be found in table A.3.

13. For a helpful review of presidential success in Congress, see R. J. Spitzer, "The Presidency and Public Policy: A Preliminary Inquiry," *Presidential Studies Quarterly* 9 (1979), pp. 441–457.

14. "Remarks at the Signing of the Immigration Bill, Liberty Island, New York," October 3, 1965, *PPP, 1965:2,* pp. 811–815.

15. "Remarks with President Truman at the Signing in Independence of the Medicare Bill," July 30, 1965, *PPP, 1965:2,* pp. 811–815.

16. "Remarks at Southwest Texas State College Upon Signing the Higher Education Act of 1965," November 8, 1965, *PPP, 1965:2,* pp. 1102–1106.

17. Greater detail on this facet of Johnson's speaking can be found in my *Verbal Style and the Presidency: A Computer-based Analysis* (New York: Academic Press, 1984), pp. 113–116.

18. A vivid example of how even a Republican president can be hamstrung by the New Deal/Great Society's emphases is a remarkably cordial and supportive speech Richard Nixon delivered early in his presidency: "Remarks to Employees at the Department of Health, Education, and Welfare," February 14, 1969, *PPP, 1969,* pp. 97–101.

19. "Remarks at the First Annual Commemoration of the Days of Remembrances of Victims of the Holocaust," April 30, 1981, *PPP, 1981,* p. 396.

20. "Address at Commencement Exercises at the University of Notre Dame," May 17, 1981, *PPP, 1981,* p. 431.

21. "Radio and Television Address to the American People Prior to Departure for the Big Four Conference at Geneva," July 15, 1955, *PPP, 1955,* p. 795.

22. "Address to the American People before Leaving on Good Will Trip to Europe, Asia, and Africa," December 3, 1959, *PPP, 1959,* p. 795.

23. An extension of these remarks, albeit a pedagogical one, is provided in my *Public Communication* (New York: Harper, 1983), pp. 13–15.

24. "Address in Lock Haven, Pennsylvania," October 23, 1948, *PPP, 1948,* p. 835.

25. "Remarks at the signing of the Coinage Act," July 23, 1965, *PPP, 1965:2,* p. 782.

26. "Remarks Upon Signing the Government Employee Pay Raise Bill," August 14, 1964, *PPP, 1963–1964:2,* p. 962.

27. "Remarks Upon Signing Bill Amending Securities and Exchange Act," August 20, 1964, *PPP, 1964,* p. 992.

28. These themes are treated in greater depth in my essay, "The Functions of Human Communication in the Maintenance of Public Values," in C. C. Arnold and J. W. Bowers (eds.), *Handbook of Rhetorical and Communication Theory* (Boston: Allyn and Bacon, 1984).

29. "The President's Christmas Message to the Nation Following His Return from His Trip around the World," December 24, 1967, *Weekly Compilations of Presidential Documents* 3 (1967), pp. 1774–1775.

30. These stylistic measures are computer based. Complexity is a measure of characters per word; Realism includes words referring to tangible, immediate, and

practical issues; Certainty involves resolute and inflexible words; and Symbolism is a list of the nation's "sacred" terms. For further detail see Hart, *Verbal Style,* pp. 14–22.

31. "Remarks Upon Accepting Norway's Bicentennial Gift to the United States," July 2, 1976, *PPP, 1976:2,* p. 1951.

32. "Remarks Upon Completing an Inspection of S.A.C. Headquarters," September 29, 1964, *PPP, 1963–1964:2,* p. 1172.

33. "Remarks at the Dedication of the Morgantown, W. Va., Airport," September 20, 1964, *PPP, 1963–1964:2,* p. 1095.

34. "Remarks in Providence at the 200th Anniversary Convocation of Brown University," September 28, 1964, *PPP, 1963–1964:2,* p. 1139.

35. See my "A Commentary on Popular Assumptions about Political Communication," *Human Communication Research* 8 (1982), pp. 366–379.

36. "Toast of the President . . . in Peking," February 21, 1972, *PPP, 1972,* p. 362.

37. As quoted in A. Schlesinger, Jr., *A Thousand Days: John F. Kennedy in the White House* (Greenwich, Conn.: Fawcett, 1965), pp. 632–633.

38. C. Krauthammer, "Lights, Camera . . . Politics," *New Republic,* November 22, 1982, p. 22.

39. S. Hess, *Organizing the Presidency* (Washington, D.C.: Brookings Institute, 1976), pp. 155–156.

40. These and other interesting data about the ceremonial life of the president is reported in M. Gustafson, "Our Part-Time Chief of State," *Presidential Studies Quarterly* 9 (1979), pp. 163–171.

41. H. McPherson, "Beyond Words: Writing for the President," *Atlantic* (April 1972), p. 45.

Chapter Three

1. A. Hitler, *Mein Kampf,* trans. R. Manheim (Boston: Houghton Mifflin, 1943, 1962), p. 469.

2. Ibid., pp. 469–470.

3. Ibid., p. 471.

4. Ibid.

5. Ibid., p. 475.

6. Ibid., pp. 472–473.

7. Mr. Nixon's recollections of these events are recorded in some detail in a "Memorandum for Ray Price" reprinted in full in R. Price, *With Nixon* (New York: Viking, 1977). The remark about surfing occurs on p. 172.

8. Ibid., p. 173.

9. Ibid., p. 174.

10. No doubt the Kennedy ratio is unnaturally high because he had not yet faced reelection when he died. Although it is hard to determine what 1964 would have brought for him, it seems unlikely that his ratio of ceremonies to rallies would have dipped below that of, say, Richard Nixon.

11. A. Montagu, *The Human Revolution* (Cleveland: World, 1965), p. 112.

12. "Address to the Nation about the Watergate Investigations," April 30, 1973, *PPP, 1973:2*, p. 329.

13. Ibid.

14. The terms used here are, of course, largely Max Weber's, whose early investigations of social influence patterns are still informative. For a useful extension of Weber's constructs see S. M. Eisenstadt (ed.), *Max Weber: On Charisma and Institution Building* (Chicago: University of Chicago Press, 1968).

15. "Remarks Upon Arrival at the Airport, Knoxville, Tennessee," May 7, 1964, *PPP, 1964–1965:2*, pp. 633, 634.

16. "Address in Wilkes-Barre, Pennsylvania," October 23, 1948, *PPP, 1948:2*, p. 833.

17. A useful summary of presidential popularity can be found in H. G. Zeidenstein, "Presidential Popularity and Presidential Support in Congress: Eisenhower to Carter," *Presidential Studies Quarterly* 10 (1980), pp. 224–233.

18. One of the more perceptive psychopolitical profiles of Carter is that by Betty Glad, *Jimmy Carter: In Search of the Great White House* (New York: Norton, 1980).

19. "Remarks on Arrival at the Asheville Municipal Airport," September 22, 1978, *Weekly Compilations of Presidential Documents* 14 (1978), p. 1685.

20. "Remarks at the Congressional Medal of Honor Awards Ceremony," October 1, 1978, *Weekly Compilations of Presidential Documents* 14 (1978), p. 1575.

21. "Remarks at the Greater Buffalo International Airport," October 28, 1978, *Weekly Compilation of Presidential Documents* 14 (1978), p. 1887.

22. A useful summary of this and related research is provided in W. J. McGuire, "Persuasion, Resistance, and Attitude Change," in I. de Sola Pool et al. (eds.), *Handbook of Communications* (Chicago: Rand McNally, 1973).

23. For a recent perspective on these matters see K. K. Reardon, *Persuasion: Theory and Context* (Beverly Hills, Calif.: Sage, 1981), pp. 61–90.

24. "Remarks at Syracuse University on the Communist Challenge in Southeast Asia," August 5, 1964, *PPP, 1963–1964:2*, pp. 928–929, 930.

25. "Remarks in Indianapolis at a Ceremony Marking the 150th Anniversary of the State of Indiana," July 23, 1966, *PPP, 1966:2*, p. 760.

26. "Remarks at a Groundbreaking Ceremony for an Industrial Site in Pryor, Oklahoma," August 26, 1966, *PPP, 1966:2*, p. 919.

27. "Remarks at the National Reactor Testing Station, Arco, Idaho," August 26, 1966, *PPP, 1966:2*, p. 919.

28. "Remarks at Franklin D. Roosevelt's Summer Cottage, Campobello Island, New Brunswick," August 21, 1966, *PPP, 1966:2*, p. 876.

29. There are countless descriptions of this aspect of Johnson's personality. Among the most interesting is that by Doris Kearns, *Lyndon Johnson and the American Dream* (New York: New American Library, 1976).

30. "Remarks of Welcome to Chancellor Erhard at Bergstrom Air Force Base, Austin, Texas," December 28, 1963, *PPP, 1963:1*, pp. 91–92. This was Johnson's first speech in Texas, although he had given a press conference the day earlier as well.

31. "Remarks in Texas to the Graduating Class of the Johnson City High School," May 29, 1964, *PPP, 1963–1964:1*, p. 727.

32. "Remarks at the Dedication of the Eisenhower Museum, Abilene, Kansas," November 11, 1954, *PPP, 1954,* p. 1044.

33. "Address at the Boston College Centennial Ceremonies," April 20, 1963, *PPP, 1963,* p. 335.

34. See, e.g., Johnson's "Remarks at a Testimonial Dinner in Beaumont, Texas," March 1, 1968, *PPP, 1968:1,* pp. 316–317.

35. "The President's News Conference of October 26, 1973," *PPP, 1973,* pp. 898, 899, 900, 901.

36. Although Johnson was certainly willing to mislead reporters on occasion, his press conferences were normally much more blunt than Nixon's. An example from Johnson's news conference of November 1, 1967 (*PPP, 1967,* p. 975) illustrates:

Question: Mr. President, again, pressure is building up in the country and round the world to have another bombing pause. Will you discuss with us the pros and cons of that situation?

The President: No. I don't think there is anything that I can contribute that would be helpful. We are doing what we believe and what we know to the best of our knowledge to be the right and proper thing to do. And we are going to continue to do what we believe is right.

I would admonish and caution all of you to avoid irresponsibility and quit grabbing out of the air these speculative future ventures about which we know very little and about which the folks that apparently are guessing for you know nothing.

37. "Remarks at a Luncheon of the National Citizens' Committee for Fairness to the Presidency," June 9, 1974, *PPP, 1974,* pp. 476–477.

38. See, e.g., his "Radio Address on the Philosophy of Government," October 21, 1972, *PPP, 1972,* p. 999.

39. "Radio Address on the American Farmer," October 27, 1972, *PPP, 1972,* pp. 1045–1049.

40. "Address to the Nation on Labor Day," September 6, 1971, *PPP, 1971,* pp. 934, 935.

41. A somewhat dated but, in another sense, timeless essay on the multiple functions of human speech is the delightful book by C. T. Brown and C. Van Riper, *Speech and Man* (Englewood Cliffs, N.J.: Prentice-Hall, 1966).

42. These speeches were given between March 16, 1981, and April 25, 1981.

43. "Remarks at the National Conference of the Building and Construction Trades Department, AFL-CIO," March 30, 1981, *PPP, 1981,* p. 310. It may be a sign of the presidential times that by delivering this speech at a Washington hotel Reagan exposed himself to John Hinkley's assassination attempt. Mr. Reagan had, in retrospect, risked his life in behalf of both public speech and an important special interest group.

44. "Remarks at the Grand Ole Opry House, Nashville, Tennessee," March 16, 1974, *PPP, 1974,* pp. 281–282.

45. "Remarks on Arrival at Des Moines International Airport," October 21, 1977, *PPP, 1977:2,* p. 1853.

46. Ibid. pp. 1853, 1854.

47. Additional detail on geographical patterns can be found in table A.7.

48. "Remarks in Boston at Post Office Square," October 27, 1964, *PPP, 1964,* p. 1466.

Chapter Four

1. M. B. Grossman and M. J. Kumar, *Portraying the President: The White House and the News Media* (Baltimore: Johns Hopkins University Press, 1981), p. 259.

2. "The President's News Conference of June 29, 1972," *PPP, 1972,* pp. 716–717.

3. A major portion of this section represents a revision of an article published by me (along with Patrick Jerome and Karen McComb) entitled "Rhetorical Features of Newscasts about the President," *Critical Studies in Mass Communication* 1 (1984), pp. 260–286.

4. W. Cronkite, "The State of the Press," in M. C. Emery and R. C. Smythe (eds.), *Readings in Mass Communication: Concepts and Issues in the Mass Media* (Dubuque, Iowa: Brown, 1974), p. 483.

5. See S. Agnew, "Television's Coverage of the News," in K. Campbell (ed.), *Critiques of Contemporary Rhetoric* (Belmont, Calif.: Wadsworth, 1972); and E. Efron, *The News Twisters* (Los Angeles: Nash, 1971).

6. R. Cirino, *Don't Blame the People: How the News Media Use Bias, Distortion and Censorship to Manipulate Public Opinion* (New York: Random House, 1971).

7. G. Tuchman, *Making News: A Study in the Construction of Reality* (New York: Free Press, 1978), p. 205.

8. D. S. Rutkus, "Presidential Television," *Journal of Communication* 26 (1976), pp. 73–78.

9. T. J. Buss and C. R. Hofstetter, "The President and the News Media," in S. A. Shull and L. T. LeLoup (eds.), *The Presidency: Studies in Policy-making.* (Brunswick, Ohio: King's Court, 1979).

10. M. Grossman and J. Rourke, "The Media and the Presidency: An Exchange Analysis," *Political Science Quarterly* 91 (1976), p. 469.

11. J. C. Merrill, "How *Time* Stereotyped Three U.S. Presidents," *Journalism Quarterly* 42 (1965), pp. 563–570.

12. E. J. Epstein, *News from Nowhere: Television and the News* (New York: Vintage, 1973).

13. P. Arnston, and C. R. Smith, "News Distortion as a Function of Organizational Communication," *Communication Monographs* 45 (1978), pp. 371–381.

14. S. Gilberg, C. Eyal, M. McCombs, and D. Nicholas, "The State of the Union Address and the Press Agenda," *Journalism Quarterly* 57 (1980), pp. 584–588.

15. R. P. Hart, K. J. Turner, and R. E. Knupp, "A Rhetorical Profile of Religious News: *Time,* 1947–1976," *Journal of Communication* 31 (1981), p. 67.

16. For a sampling of such research see C. R. Bantz, "The Critic and the Computer: A Multiple Technique Analysis of the ABC Evening News," *Communication Monographs* 46 (1979), pp. 27–39; D. L. Swanson, "And That's the Way It

Was? Television Covers the 1976 Presidential Campaign," *Quarterly Journal of Speech* 63 (1977), pp. 239–248; and R. L. Barton and R. B. Gregg, "Middle East Conflict as a T.V. News Scenario: A Formal Analysis," *Journal of Communication* 32 (1982), pp. 172–185.

17. Each of the stories was subdivided into major thematic units (MTUs) which were operationally defined as news sequences uninterrupted by (1) a commercial break or (2) the studio-bound anchor correspondent. The average newscast in the sample contained 3.8 MTUs, each of which lasted for roughly two minutes. Coding was completed using these thematic units as the units of analysis.

18. For a complete set of operational definitions of the coding categories used see the Appendix as well as Hart et al. (1984).

19. N. Minow, J. Martin, and L. Mitchell. *Presidential Television* (New York: Basic Books, 1973).

20. Quoted in ABC World News Tonight, September 19, 1978.

21. E. Berne, *Games People Play: The Psychology of Human Relationships* (New York: Grove, 1964).

22. Quoted in CBS Evening News, May 1, 1970.

23. T. Benson, "Implicit Communication Theory in Campaign Coverage," in W. C. Adams (ed.), *Television Coverage of the 1980 Presidential Campaign* (Norwood, N.J.: Ablex, 1983), p. 110.

24. Swanson, p. 247.

25. ABC World News Tonight, May 1, 1973.

26. CBS Evening News, November 4, 1969.

27. Ibid., November 9, 1977.

28. Ibid., August 16, 1973.

29. NBC Nightly News, November 4, 1969.

30. ABC World News Tonight, September 21, 1977.

31. CBS Evening News, May 1, 1970.

32. NBC Nightly News, November 4, 1969.

33. ABC World News Tonight, August 16, 1973.

34. CBS Evening News, January 14, 1975.

35. ABC World News Tonight, November 4, 1969.

36. Quoted in D. L. Paletz, and R. M. Entman. *Media Power Politics* (New York: Free Press, 1981), p. 417.

37. In actuality, there was one "mention" of Mr. Ford's activities—a picture of him breaking ground at the hospital dedication. It may be a commentary on modern techniques of reportage that Ford's *actions,* not his words, were highlighted in the popular press that day.

38. M. Greenfield, "Invented Politics," *Washington Post National Weekly Edition,* March 27, 1984, p. 27.

39. Lammers's conclusions generally parallel those presented here. See his "Presidential Attention-focusing Activities," in D. A. Graber (ed.), *The President and the Public* (Philadelphia: Institute for the Study of Human Issues, 1982), pp. 145–171.

40. P. C. Light, *The President's Agenda: Domestic Policy Choice from Kennedy to Carter* (Baltimore: Johns Hopkins Press, 1982), p. 95.

41. "Remarks to Members of the President's Committee on Civil Rights," January 15, 1947, *PPP, 1947,* p. 98.

42. "Remarks at the Annual Hubert H. Humphrey Award Dinner," January 27, 1980, *PPP, 1980:1,* pp. 221, 223, 224.

43. For additional information about these trends see table A.8.

44. "Remarks in Springfield, Ill. at the Sangamon County Courthouse," October 7, 1964, *PPP, 1963–1964:2,* p. 1235.

45. "Remarks at a Voter Registration Rally," October 6, 1980, *PPP, 1980:3,* p. 2091.

46. J. McGinniss, *The Selling of the President 1968* (New York: Trident, 1969). See, especially, pp. 62–76.

47. Data on television coverage of these presidential events were obtained from the *Television News Index and Abstracts* (Nashville: Vanderbilt University, 1977, 1979).

48. R. A. Meyers, T. L. Newhouse, and D. E. Garrett, "Political Momentum: Television News Treatment," *Communication Monographs* 45 (1978), pp. 382–388.

49. "Remarks at a Reception for the National Federation of Republican Women," September 17, 1976, *PPP, 1976:3,* p. 2268.

50. "Remarks at a President Ford Committee Reception in Philadelphia," September 23, 1976, *PPP, 1976:3,* p. 2312.

51. "Remarks at a President Ford Committee Reception in Los Angeles," October 8, 1976, *PPP, 1976:3,* p. 2460.

52. "Remarks at a Golden Circle Reception in Pasadena, California," October 24, 1976, *PPP, 1976:3,* p. 2662.

53. "The President's News Conference of October 24, 1946," *PPP, 1946:3,* p. 2662.

54. "The President's News Conference of January 19, 1982," *PPP, 1982:1,* p. 43.

55. Coverage in the *Times* (London) was determined by calculating the square centimeters of textual indexing subsumed under each president's name in the annual indices to that newspaper. Appropriate mathematical corrections were made for alterations over the years in font style and page layout.

56. "Remarks during Ceremonies at the Battle Site at Corregidor, the Philipines," October 26, 1966, *PPP, 1966:2,* p. 1268.

57. "The President's News Conference of January 18, 1961." *PPP, 1960–1961,* pp. 1044–1045.

58. "The President's News Conference of November 14, 1963," *PPP, 1963,* pp. 848, 850, 852.

59. "Remarks at the National Corn Picking Contest, Cedar Rapids, Iowa," October 17, 1958, *PPP, 1958,* p. 752.

60. Ibid, pp. 753, 754.

61. Ibid, pp. 755, 756.

62. See "The President's News Conference of November 17, 1973," *PPP, 1973,* pp. 946–964.

63. "Presidents Always Win," *Newsweek,* September 3, 1973, p. 66.

64. Ibid.

65. "The President's News Conference of August 22, 1973, *PPP, 1973,* p. 719.

66. The reader is reminded that, as we saw in Chapter Two (figure 2.7), ceremonies also peaked roughly during these same months. Clearly, during elections, presidents pull out all the stops.

67. "Remarks and a Question-and-Answer Session at a Town Meeting,"October 31, 1980, *PPP, 1980:3,* pp. 2587, 2589, 2591.

68. "Remarks and a Question-and-Answer Session at Southern Methodist University in Dallas, April 9, 1976, *PPP, 1976:2,* pp. 1044, 1046, 1053.

69. P. Corcoran, *Political Language and Rhetoric* (Austin: University of Texas Press, 1979), p. 171.

70. Ibid., p. 199.

71. Ibid., p. 139.

72. Quoted in M. Schram, "The Medium Isn't the Message," *Washington Post National Weekly Edition,* April 16, 1984, p. 12.

73. Quoted in Schram, p. 12.

Chapter Five

1. *Time,*April 23, 1984, pp. 37–39.

2. Ibid., p. 37.

3. Ibid., p. 39.

4. Ibid.

5. M. G. Krukones, "Predicting Presidential Performance through Political Campaigns," *Presidential Studies Quarterly* 10 (1980), pp. 527–543.

6. "The President's News Conference of September 18, 1980," *PPP, 1980:2,* p. 1829.

7. "The President's News Conference of September 27, 1956," *PPP, 1956,* p. 806.

8. Ibid., pp. 806–807.

9. "The President's News Conference of October 14, 1976, *PPP, 1976:3,* p. 256.

10. "Campaign Stop at Providence, Rhode Island," October 28, 1948, *PPP, 1948,* p. 892.

11. "Campaign Stop at Vinita, Oklahoma," September 29, 1948, *PPP, 1948,* p. 627.

12. "Address at the Stadium in Butte, Montana," June 8, 1948, *PPP, 1948,* p. 358.

13. "Campaign Stop at Las Vegas, New Mexico," June 15, 1948, *PPP, 1948,* p. 358.

14. "Remarks to the Veterans of Foreign Wars Annual Convention, Chicago, Illinois," August 19, 1974, *PPP, 1974,* p. 23.

15. Ibid., p. 24.

16. "Remarks on the Eve of the Presidential Election," November 1, 1976, *PPP, 1976:3,* pp. 2839, 2840.

17. "Radio Remarks in Independence on Election Eve," November 1, 1948, *PPP, 1948,* p. 939.

18. "Remarks at Providence, Rhode Island," November 3, 1972, *PPP, 1972,* p. 1107.

19. "Remarks in Mount Prospect, Illinois," October 29, 1970, *PPP, 1970,* p. 993.

20. "Remarks at Rockford, Illinois," October 29, 1970, *PPP, 1970,* p. 999.

21. "Remarks in San Jose, California," October 29, 1970, *PPP, 1970,* p. 1020.

22. "Remarks in Las Vegas, Nevada," October 31, 1970, *PPP, 1970,* p. 1047.

23. "Remarks at Inauguration Services for the Department of Health and Human Services," May 14, 1980, *PPP, 1980:1,* pp. 908, 910.

24. Ibid., p. 909.

25. Ibid., p. 910.

26. "Address at a Rally in the Public Square, Cleveland, Ohio," October 1, 1956, *PPP, 1956,* pp. 835–836.

27. "Remarks at an Airport Rally in Wichita," October 29, 1964, *PPP, 1963–1964:2,* p. 1521.

28. R. P. Hart, *The Political Pulpit* (Lafayette, Ind.: Purdue University Press, 1977).

29. "Remarks at an Airport Rally in Wilmington, Delaware," October 31, 1964, *PPP, 1963–1964:2,* pp. 1553–1554.

30. "Remarks to White House Conference on Families," June 5, 1980, *Weekly Compilations of Presidential Documents* 16 (1980), p. 1034. "Realism" refers here to "expressions referring to tangible, immediate, and practical issues," i.e., to people, concrete events, and present-day activities. "Activity" refers to "motion, change, or the implementation of ideas." Active language tends to be aggressive and to focus on tangible accomplishments. Finally, "Complexity" is a language measure that calculates the number of characters per word in a given verbal passage. For further information on such matters, see Hart, *Verbal Style,* pp. 14–22.

31. "Remarks to White House Conference on Families," June 5, 1980, *Weekly Compilations of Presidential Documents* 16 (1980), p. 1035.

32. The alterations over the years in Jimmy Carter's speaking on economic matters were pronounced. In his first year in office, Mr. Carter devoted eleven full speeches to this topic; during 1980 he gave forty-one such speeches.

33. "The President's News Conference of October 14, 1976," *PPP, 1976:3,* p. 2531.

34. "The President's News Conference of September 18, 1980," *PPP, 1980:2,* p. 1828.

35. The single exception to these patterns is the state of Massachusetts which, as we saw in Chapter Three, has not (for a variety of reasons) garnered the presidential attention its numbers suggest. Some of these reasons may have been personal in nature and others, as we shall see later in this chapter, probably relate to the political partisanship found in the Bay State.

36. "Remarks at a Campaign Reception for Southern Supporters in Atlanta, Georgia," October 12, 1972, *PPP, 1972,* p. 976.

37. Ibid., p. 976.

38. Ibid., pp. 976, 979, 980.

39. "Remarks at a Campaign Reception for Northeastern Supporters in New York State," October 23, 1972, *PPP, 1972,* p. 1013.

40. "Remarks at Tulsa, Oklahoma," November 3, 1972, *PPP, 1972*, p. 1104.

41. "Remarks at Albuquerque, New Mexico," November 4, 1972, *PPP, 1972*, p. 1122.

42. D. M. West, "Constituencies and Travel Allocations in the 1980 Presidential Campaign," *American Journal of Political Science* 27 (1983), pp. 515, 529.

43. R. Tatalovich, "Electoral Votes and Presidential Campaign Trails, 1932–1976," *American Politics Quarterly* 7 (1979), pp. 489–497.

44. "Remarks at a Fundraising Luncheon for Governor Richard L. Thornburgh in Philadelphia, Pennsylvania," May 14, 1982, *PPP, 1982:1*, p. 637.

45. "Remarks at a Fundraising Dinner for Governor William P. Clements, Jr., in Houston, Texas," June 15, 1982, *PPP, 1982:1*, p. 783.

46. "Address at a Rally in the Public Square, Cleveland, Ohio," October 1, 1956, *PPP, 1956*, p. 830.

47. "Campaign Remarks in Ohio," October 8, 1964, *PPP, 1963–1964:2*, p. 1259.

48. "Remarks at a Fundraising Reception for Senator Robert Taft, Jr., in Cleveland," October 28, 1976, *PPP, 1976:3*, p. 2757.

49. "Remarks at a Rally on Arrival at Grand Rapids, Michigan," November 1, 1976, *PPP, 1976:3*, pp. 2835–2836.

50. J. C. Archer and P. J. Taylor, *Section and Party: A Political Geography of American Presidential Elections, from Andrew Jackson to Ronald Reagan* (New York: Wiley, 1981), p. 205.

51. R. Wolfinger and R. Arseneau, "Partisan Change in the South, 1952–1976," in L. Maisel and J. Cooper (eds.), *Political Parties: Development and Decay* (Beverly Hills, Calif.: Sage, 1976), p. 207.

52. "Remarks in Biloxi, Mississippi," September 26, 1976, *PPP, 1976:3*, p. 2336.

53. Ibid., pp. 2336–2337.

Chapter Six

1. "The President's Remarks with Reporters at Chairlift 6, Vail, Colorado," December 31, 1976, *Weekly Compilations of Presidential Documents* 13, no. 2 (1977), p. 3.

2. Ibid.

3. "Remarks at a Reception for . . . the Conference on Physical Fitness and Sports," February 19, 1971, *PPP, 1971*, pp. 193–194.

4. "Remarks to the International Platform Association," August 3, 1965, *PPP, 1965:2*, p. 820.

5. "Remarks to the Biennial Convocation of the National Federation of Republican Women," September 18, 1981, *PPP, 1981*, p. 811.

6. "Remarks at a White House Luncheon for the Governors' Representatives to the Fifty States Project for Women," October 7, 1981, *PPP, 1981*, p. 901.

7. "Remarks at the Republican Women's Leadership Forum," August 26, 1983, *Weekly Compilations of Presidential Documents* 19, no. 35 (1983), p. 1175.

8. "Remarks to Members of the International Federation of Business and Professional Women's Clubs," August 3, 1983, *Weekly Compilations of Presidential Documents* 19, no. 31 (1983), p. 1088.

9. "Informal Remarks to a Group of Senior Citizens from Whittier, California," October 2, 1973, *PPP, 1973,* p. 837.

10. As quoted in J. Ceaser et al. "The Rise of the Rhetorical Presidency," *Presidential Studies Quarterly* 11 (1981), p. 165. The Ceaser et al. article is an excellent one. Although their comments on the presidency are more impressionistic than data based, their conclusions often parallel those being drawn here.

11. "Address before a Joint Session of the New Hampshire General Court," April 18, 1975, *PPP, 1975:1,* p. 517.

12. M. Schram and P. Taylor, "Of First Five Would-Be Presidents, Only Mondale Wows the Convention," *Washington Post,* June 26, 1982, p. A4.

13. Ibid.

14. Ibid.

15. Ibid.

16. Ibid.

17. Ibid.

18. Ibid.

19. "Remarks to the Student Body of Rio Grande High School, Rio Grande City, Texas," September 22, 1972, *PPP, 1972,* p. 892.

20. Ibid., pp. 892–893.

21. M. Novak, *Choosing Our King* (New York: Macmillan, 1974), p. 127.

22. For additional detail on these momentous matters see P. Strumm, *Presidential Power and American Democracy* (Santa Monica, Calif.: Goodyear, 1979), pp. 137ff.

23. B. Buchanan, *The Presidential Experience: What the Office Does to the Man* (Englewood Cliffs, N.J.: Prentice-Hall, 1978), p. 67.

24. S. M. Lipset and W. Schneider, "The Decline of Confidence in American Institutions," *Political Science Quarterly* 98 (1983), pp. 379–402. I am certainly not arguing here that presidential ceremonies serve no important social end. Indeed, as I have argued elsewhere, the quasi-institutional system of church-state relations in the United States is largely the product of a carefully orchestrated rhetoric of God and country, a rhetoric so well worked out over 200 years by American presidents that it has effected a kind of theological détente in the United States, keeping rival religious factions separated, if not cordial. All presidents, Jimmy Carter and Ronald Reagan notably included, have reaffirmed this rhetorically based contract over the years and therefore exercised an important function of leadership. Still, given the possibilities afforded by human communication, rhetorical/presidential successes like these, while important, have not predominated in the history of the recent American presidency. For additional information on this perspective, see my book, *The Political Pulpit* (Lafayette, Ind.: Purdue University Press, 1977).

25. M. Greenfield, "The 'Mondale' Issue," *Washington Post Weekly Edition,* October 8, 1984, p. 29.

26. H. Fairlie, "The Decline of Oratory," *New Republic,* May 28, 1984, p. 19.

27. "The Right to Vote," March 15, 1965, Reprinted in H. R. Ryan (ed.), *American Rhetoric from Roosevelt to Reagan* (Prospects Heights, Ill.: Waveland, 1983), pp. 176–177.

28. H. McPherson, "Beyond Words: Writing for the President," *Atlantic* (April 1972), p. 43.

Index